Praise fo̶

THE FALL

D0287377

"Exhaustively well-reported and colorfully told. . . . Through it all, you hear Vinton's heart beating, pounding actually. He loves ski-racing people, the places, the blinding magic of that elite snowy world. And, with that, you swim easily with his story as if carried on a current."

—Biddle Duke, *The Stowe Reporter*

"[*The Fall Line*] tracks the stars of the U.S. team up to their conquest of the Vancouver Olympics. Worth reading for his portrayal of Bode Miller alone—as nuanced as Miller is complicated—it's richly detailed and vivid throughout, informed by Vinton's unrivaled behind-the-scenes access to the sport's athletes, coaches and peripheral players."

—Joe Cutts, *Skiing Magazine*

"Superbly crafted." —Kelley McMillan, *Outside Online*

"Insightful. . . . [S]hould be considered mandatory for anyone with an inkling of interest in ski racing."

—Madeleine Osberger, *Aspen Daily News*

"Mr. Vinton has stamped his cold feet by many a finish corral; he knows his racing history. . . . *The Fall Line* is a well-researched, measured, respectful account." —Christopher Solomon, *Wall Street Journal*

"Most of the world tunes into ski racing only every four years, and Vinton capitalizes on the opportunity to detail what happens in between, with so much more involved in the sport than just preparing for the Olympics." —Kurt Kragthorpe, *The Salt Lake Tribune*

"His stars are U.S. skiers Bode Miller and Lindsey Vonn, but Vinton wisely avoids making this book a celebration. Instead, he focuses on the inherent tension that is the mark of all sports, and how the very best at it must come to terms with regulatory bodies, parents, lovers, spouses, sponsors, coaches, doctors, trainers—and, mostly, themselves." —James Hill, *The Washington Post*

"[A] well-paced tale of U.S. ski success, with an insider's look at the '10 season, including Bode Miller, Lindsey Vonn and gang."
—*Sports Illustrated*

"This is a ripping, compulsively readable, deeply reported journey into the sporting world's least-known subcultures. Nathaniel Vinton delivers the danger, the surprises, and the high-octane personalities that will take readers to the edge, and then past it."
—Daniel Coyle, *New York Times* best-selling author of *The Secret Race* and *The Talent Code*

"*The Fall Line* unfolds like an exhilarating downhill race. Chronicling the lead-up to the 2010 Winter Olympics, Nathaniel Vinton weaves deftly between technical descriptions of the art of skiing and intimate portraits of the sport's motley band of luminaries. This is as inside as an account can be of one of the most exciting seasons in American sports history." —David Epstein, author of *The Sports Gene: Inside the Science of Extraordinary Athletic Performance*

"Nathaniel Vinton's reporting skill and skiing expertise underpin this thrill ride with the U.S. Ski Team. All the politics and drama around the making of a U.S. dynasty are delivered with new insights and details on its daring—and sometimes rebellious—stars. You don't know Bode Miller or Lindsey Vonn until you read *The Fall Line*."
—Selena Roberts, filmmaker, best-selling author, and former sports writer for the *New York Times* and *Sports Illustrated*

"*The Fall Line* is a riveting, richly informed ride down the world's most renowned ski slopes, chronicling the ascendance of American skiing and the outsized stars, Bode Miller and Lindsey Vonn, who epitomize it."
—Wayne Coffey, author of *The Boys of Winter*

THE
FALL LINE

America's Rise to Ski Racing's Summit

Nathaniel Vinton

W. W. NORTON & COMPANY

INDEPENDENT PUBLISHERS SINCE 1923

NEW YORK   LONDON

Copyright © 2015 by Nathaniel Vinton

For information about permission to reproduce selections from this book,
write to Permissions, W. W. Norton & Company, Inc.,
500 Fifth Avenue, New York, NY 10110

For information about special discounts for bulk purchases, please contact
W. W. Norton Special Sales at specialsales@wwnorton.com or 800-233-4830

Manufacturing by RR Donnelley, Harrisonburg
Book design by Daniel Lagin
Production manager: Anna Oler

The Library of Congress has cataloged the hardcover edition as follows:

Vinton, Nathaniel.
The fall line : how American ski racers conquered
a sport on the edge / Nathaniel Vinton.
        pages cm
Includes index.
ISBN 978-0-393-24477-9 (hardcover)
1. Downhill skiing—United States—History.
2. Skiers—United States. I. Title.
GV854.4.V56 2015
796.93'5—dc23

                    2014033594

ISBN 978-0-393-35269-6 pbk.

W. W. Norton & Company, Inc.
500 Fifth Avenue, New York, N.Y. 10110
www.wwnorton.com

W. W. Norton & Company Ltd.
Castle House, 75/76 Wells Street, London W1T 3QT

1 2 3 4 5 6 7 8 9 0

For my Liz

"I discovered quickly enough that none of them, no matter how talkative otherwise, was about to answer the question or even linger for more than a few seconds on the subject at the heart of it, which is to say, courage."

—Tom Wolfe, 1983

CONTENTS

FOREWORD

By the time the photographers noticed Bode Miller walking unaccompanied down Lafayette Street, he had almost reached the courthouse doors of the New York County family court. As they ran frantically toward him, Miller needed only a few calm strides to slip inside the lobby, where cameras weren't allowed. Casting a gimlet eye at the commotion behind him, he headed for the metal detector and, beyond that, the elevators.

It was Monday, December 9, 2013. The previous day, Miller had finished second in a giant slalom race in Beaver Creek, Colorado, his seventy-sixth career podium finish on the World Cup tour. I had seen him there, talked to him briefly about his rancorous dispute with Sara McKenna. Now he was here in lower Manhattan for a status conference at the family court. He was seeking joint custody of their nine-month-old son. Miller was aiming to race in the Olympics in Sochi in two months.

I found him on a bench in a public area on the eighth floor. For three years, I'd been working on this book about downhillers, and Miller had given me fair access. Miller's career coincided with one of the book's central subjects, the golden age of US alpine ski racing, and his cooperation was essential. I'd interviewed Miller in swank hotels and on car rides, by telephone and while standing in the snow on mountains big and small, where it was not uncommon to see him outrun the media like he had done outside the courthouse on this day. I got about ten minutes alone with him before one of his attorneys walked up. When I introduced myself as a reporter, he answered her alarm with a quick word that I "knew" him.

This was news to me. I find Miller mostly unpredictable. Though I have been writing about him for more than a decade, have witnessed hundreds of his races, and watched him thrash his way through some dense thickets of personal turmoil, I could never claim to know him. Some of this is the obligatory detachment of journalism, but mainly it's Miller's enigmatic personality. Even the people closest to Miller tell me they are often mystified by his choices and actions. While doing research for this book, I discovered that the impulse to explain Miller seems to grow weaker the closer one gets to him. He disavows almost all portrayals. His inner circle associates are content to shrug a lot. Not even his mother claims to fully understand him.

What's clear is that Miller is the anti-Lance; unlike Armstrong, Miller is capable of sporting dominance but not greedy for it. In his late thirties, he can still do things on snow that no one else even attempts. His greatest performances don't always coincide with victories, but often they do. A little over two months after our courthouse chat, he won bronze in the Olympic men's super G event at the Sochi Games, becoming the oldest Alpine skiing medalist in Olympic history. That race was a capstone to one of the most extraordinary careers in the history of alpine ski racing—not just statistically, but in terms of the dramatic twists, false endings, and the stubborn demonstrations of will and vision that are the hallmark of an artistic temperament.

Lindsey Vonn is more straightforward, her motivations more firmly fixed and less contradictory than Miller's: Vonn wants to win ski races and be famous, and by age thirty her success on both fronts is unprecedented for an American. Marketing people sometimes called her the next Maria Sharapova, but the real model was Roger Federer: steady, multilingual, diplomatic, and often unbeatable.

Like Miller, Vonn's natural habitat is the World Cup circuit, the annual race series staged primarily in the Alps, where racers encounter the sport's most formidable fields and most demanding courses. Since the World Cup began in 1967, only a tiny number have collected as many wins and titles as Lindsey Vonn.

As the 2014 Olympic Games approached, Vonn was the global face of the sport, a jet-setting swirl of marketing commerce, the blonde savior of NBC Sports, and the girlfriend of golf star Tiger Woods. But a series of painful setbacks kept Vonn from racing at Sochi. First came the ferocious emergence of a challenger to her World Cup throne, Tina Maze of Slovenia. Then, after a mysterious illness, came a nasty crash at the February 2013 world championships in Austria, where she tore ligaments and fractured bones in her right knee. After an accelerated rehabilitation program, Vonn reinjured the knee in a November training accident, requiring more reconstructive surgery. Vonn missed the Sochi Games but the next winter returned to the World Cup circuit, smashing a thirty-five-year-old record for most victories among women racers, and capturing bronze at the 2015 alpine skiing world championships at Beaver Creek, near her hometown of Vail.

I interviewed Vonn for this book, but a more revealing resource was the archive of notebooks, transcripts, and recordings I'd accumulated covering the sport. My notes from my first interview with her in the fall of 2002 were for a profile in *Ski Racing*, the magazine that had just given me my first journalism job; back then she was Lindsey Kildow, a promising seventeen-year-old who already exhibited a certain deceptive toughness.

Six months before that, I had watched Lindsey's first Olympic race at close range, while working on the women's downhill venue at the Salt Lake City Games. I was a ski coach that winter, and a group of local racers I worked with had volunteered to help prepare the snow; I was their chaperone at Snowbasin. Between Lindsey's sixth-place finish in the Olympic combined that February and my interview with her in September, she had begun her relationship with Thomas Vonn, the older teammate she would later marry. She had also navigated the first dislocations of her parents' brutal divorce.

Over the next five years, I interviewed Lindsey dozens of times as she became a full-fledged skiing star and I moved to Europe and reported on the sport for the *New York Times* and the *International Herald Tribune.* I continued to follow her progress in teleconferences and press huddles at the bottom of various mountains. In 2007 I moved to New York and started working at the *Daily News,* where my regular beat—performance-enhancing drugs in sports—frequently entailed following athletes into courthouses.

In this era of false sports idols, the US downhillers seemed real. I started writing long on them, trying to bring some context to the success that the US Ski Team had begun to enjoy—in particular, the parallel careers that took Miller and Vonn, two radically different people, to the most rarefied heights. But most of all I wanted to let the sport be the star, to shed light on the inner world of an underappreciated sport that is presently engaged in a struggle for its own survival.

For better or worse, victory at the Winter Olympics can define a ski racer's entire career, especially in America. History judges a downhiller based on one ninety-second performance, maybe within the context of one or two statements that skier made publicly within a slightly wider time frame. But most people understand that in any field even the most flawless two-minute performance is meaningless if not considered alongside the groundwork, aspiration, and crazy strokes of good and bad fortune that precede it.

An intention of this story is to finally give readers a chance to appreciate how much goes into a single ski race—the mental preparation, the physical effort, the travel and equipment involved. That is why the narrative of this book arcs through a twelve-month period—in my view, one of the most suspenseful and revealing episodes in the history of alpine skiing.

In the first decade of the century, as every hardcore skiing fan knew, the US Ski Team had transformed itself from a band of outsiders on the World Cup circuit to one of the tour's powerhouse teams. How the US finally found the sport's elusive summit was one of the great untold American sports stories, and it involved a broader cast of characters than Miller and Vonn.

I chose to start my twelve-month story in 2009 not just because it was a pivotal moment for both Miller and Vonn, but because the events of that year brought into relief some of the existential challenges alpine skiing faces: climate change, the proliferation of the X Games and similar adrenaline spectacles produced by the likes of Red Bull, and the inextricable danger that inheres in downhill racing itself. Most of all, I wanted to unpack the drama that accompanied the 2010 Winter Games in Vancouver.

In 2009, the US Ski Team set out to consummate its decade-long World Cup revival with a plan to capture unprecedented success at Vancouver, to complete a historic turnaround and avenge the humiliating defeat at the 2006 Games. At stake was the creativity and devotion of a whole community of coaches, parents, administrators, and others invested in realizing the team's lofty ambitions.

The story opens in the first months of 2009, as one winter season begins to wind down and the next year's Olympics appear on the horizon (the alpine skiing events for the 2010 Games would be contested at Whistler Mountain, a place known for its difficult race courses and meteorological uncertainty).

When the reader meets them in February 2009, Vonn and Miller are both approaching a crossroads in their respective careers. Vonn, twenty-four, stands poised to validate a lifetime of sacrifice by grasping the one prize that has eluded her: Olympic gold. Miller, on the other hand, is hesitant; at age thirty-one, he is injured and distracted, ambivalent not about the Olympics but about the forces around it that he fears will compromise his values and his sanity.

These two brilliant athletes are in search of a definitive athletic performance. They have come farther than any previous American ski racer has, but history will not properly recognize their achievements unless they distinguish themselves on the biggest stage. No matter how well they have done elsewhere, Olympic gold at Whistler remains the only way for them to get the recognition they believe they deserve.

Theirs was the first fully professional generation of Olympic skiers, and also the first to fully assimilate to European Alpine culture. They were the last generation of American skiers who in their early childhood hadn't been enticed away from the race hill by a novel array of snowy pursuits. Today there is snowboarding. Today there are sponsored expeditions to wild mountain ranges. Today there are spectacular halfpipes and terrain parks at every ski area and beyond. The flourishing varieties of American snow sports since the 1990s have raided racing's talent pool.

But downhill racing remains foundational. Many of the best new-school professional skiers in films and ski magazines are former racers. The ones who stuck with it in the 1990s and survived the brutal winnowing of World Cup racing in the decade that followed took their sport to heights that no previous Americans had ever had the opportunity to investigate.

THE FALL LINE

INTRODUCTION

The Fall Line

The most celebrated downhiller of all time is probably Franz Klammer, the Austrian farm boy who, on a sunny afternoon in February 1976, launched himself down a mountain on the edge of Innsbruck to win Olympic gold in front of his adoring countrymen.

Klammer was twenty-two years old that day, the best of the four Austrians entered in the men's downhill. With fifteenth place in the running order, he was the last man on his team in the start house, high up on Patscherkofel. As he stood at the gate, all of the top-ranked skiers had already navigated the course, a complicated descent that followed a jagged forest trail for nearly two miles and dropped 2,854 feet in elevation along the way. The previous racers had left grooves and divots in the snow which, along with the mountain's naturally rough terrain, promised a dangerous ride.

Downhillers like Klammer move between extremes of isolation and community. The most celebrated races usually begin someplace uninhabitable—a glacier, a treeless peak, or a howling mountain pass. Organizers erect tents or crude huts there, and on race days an intense loneliness prevails. A support staff may hover, but the racers must do this thing alone. As they silently wait their turn, they can often look out and see the medieval town where they slept the night before.

Meanwhile, large and festive crowds gather at the finish line, where oompah bands and hot drinks offset the cold weather. The race typically ends right at the edge of town, and local schoolchildren often take a field trip. A high-energy announcer might warm up the crowd by interviewing former champions, and then the first racers finally appear high on the horizon, perhaps soaring off some jump, then streaking down the final pitch and across the finish line. After they come to a stop, they speak into the announcer's microphone while they are still out of breath, describing their journey, the fears or hopes that preceded it, and the surprises that arose. Their voices commonly carry the distinctive dialect of a remote mountain frontier.

Every alpine ski race involves returning home, a solitary crossing of the wilderness with tests of courage along the way. This primordial narrative gives downhill its epic character, and it applies at each level of the sport, from the eight-year-old girl in the start gate of a thirty-second slalom course on a tiny hill in Minnesota to the grizzled national hero standing atop the terrifying Streif downhill in Kitzbühel, Austria. Each racer leaves the gate with the single goal of getting back to the settled world as quickly as possible. The more urgently a downhiller moves along, the more treacherous the odyssey.

Ski racing is religion in Austria, and the men's downhill race on February 5, 1976, was a national holiday. When the countdown for Klammer's start began, the streets and autobahns of Salzburg and Vienna were nearly deserted, as motorists pulled over to find a television set. In hundreds of high mountain villages like Mooswald, where Klammer grew up, families huddled around the radio to hear the live call on ORF, the national radio broadcaster, featuring the excited nasal voice of announcer Edi Finger. Nearly forty years later, Austrians can tell you where they were when they watched or listened to that race.

As Klammer exploded frantically from the start, Switzerland's Bernhard Russi waited near a stack of hay bales to find out if his medal would be gold or silver. The reigning Olympic champion, Russi had taken mortal risks to finish the course in 1 minute, 46.06 seconds, a time that gave him almost a full second advantage in a sport where a tenth of a second often separates the podium finishers from their peers. Klammer, now hurtling down the mountain in his yellow speed suit, was Russi's only remaining threat.

There are no judges in ski racing, only the merciless ticking of the clock, and from the instant Klammer lunged onto the course it was clear that he intended to trade grace for velocity—to ski in a way that would deposit him on the top step of the podium or else in an Innsbruck hospital. Maintaining his aerodynamic tuck cost Klammer the ability to use the joints of his coiled body to absorb the terrain. He was repeatedly jolted upright, off the ground, where he windmilled his arms, fought to get back on two feet, and dropped back down into his tuck.

In the finish, Russi would later say, the earth began quaking with the roars of an estimated 60,000 Austrian fans bellowing encouragement for their "Franzi." At the early intervals, where split times were recorded, Klammer trailed Russi, but despite the wild approach, he was clearly carrying speed. His body lurched and twisted as he compensated for the rolling terrain, but the skis beneath him traced smooth arcs through the snow. He went faster and faster.

When Klammer hit the last timing interval trailing Russi by just 0.19 seconds, hunger for victory overcame all instincts for self-preservation. As he entered the Bernegg section, a shady bowl about 15 seconds above the finish line, he chose an unexpected path. Veering left of the line other skiers took, he skied a line that put him only a few feet from the picket fence that bordered the course. It held back a dense crowd of screaming fans.

There Klammer initiated one of the most beautiful turns in the sport's history. Although the run is justly famous for Klammer's reckless abandon on the upper sections of the course, Klammer also treasures this moment—a patiently executed turn that he convincingly claims is the first instance of a downhiller carving, the method of efficient turning that later came to define modern alpine ski racing.

Standing on his left leg and driving his knee forward and inward, Klammer pressured his ski's edge with such precision that it sliced smoothly over the washboarded surface of the shadowy slope. For six full seconds, Klammer traveled along a single, flawless parabola, like a kid riding the world's wildest carousel. When Klammer completed the turn he had accelerated to more than 70 miles per hour and was moving parallel to another picket fence, on the other side of which was a teeming, ecstatic mass of people. Bursting into sunlight, Klammer shot over a bump into the final straightaway, dropped into his tuck, withstood a few more hard jolts, and rocketed across the finish line. The clock read 1 minute, 43.73 seconds—33 hundredths of a second faster than Russi.

Few human pursuits take a more complete and exacting measurement of a person's sense of balance than ski racing, a sport where participants move across a slick surface and uneven topography at speeds that can outpace the ability to compute one's surroundings. Most downhills involve going well over 100 feet per second.

Even beginner skiers know the intoxication Franz Klammer felt each time he clicked into the spring-loaded bindings that fixed his boots to his skis. Standing with each foot locked into a heavy, elongated base enhances stability, and with a little speed and some interesting terrain, a skier very quickly feels a powerful connection to the earth. Many skiers spend a lifetime chasing this sensation; great skiers follow it to the edge of their physical limits and beyond. Sometimes the cost of these snowy thrills is never standing up again.

Klammer says he honed his sense of balance, a vital component of his skiing prowess, following his father into the woods above Mooswald to harvest lumber to supplement the modest income from the family's farm and guesthouse. Klammer was only fourteen years old when he joined in the work. Where the slopes became too steep and slippery for their horses, Klammer and the other men from the village climbed in studded boots, cutting small trenches that ran vertically down the mountain. In a rainstorm, when the mud soft-ened, they sent the logs down these slick, muddy chutes. Often Franz's job was to stand at a turn in the trench and swing a long hook to redirect the sliding logs.

In the winters of his childhood Klammer, like so many great racers, skied by necessity, strapping his leather boots to wooden skis to get to school. After winning some village races, he soon found opportunities to join the training camps and regional competitions recognized by Austria's national ski team. Though he came from a relative backwater, the teenaged Klammer arrived on the racing scene amid a democra-tizing evolution in skiing equipment. Throughout the 1960s, as metal and plastic skis became common, a corresponding shift in technique created an opening for brave and creative racers who knew how to manage the increased speeds.

Klammer's victory at the 1976 Games was no fluke. Klammer con-tinued to bounce and stagger down the world's most perilous slopes, usually landing on his feet, well into the 1980s. No ski races are less forgiving than those on the alpine skiing World Cup, the annual tour that comprises the most elite level of the sport. Klammer won twenty-five World Cup downhills, including four victories at Kitzbühel, the scary Wimbledon of downhill.

Throughout the late 1980s and 1990s, alpine ski racing continued to evolve. In order to make firmer guarantees to buyers of broadcast television rights, the sport's overseers hardened the snow, making it icier and slicker. The surface held up better during bad weather and heavy use, which had the effect of making races more fair for those going late in the start order, but mainly the snow—injected with water, sometimes treated with chemicals—got faster.

As average speeds on the World Cup tour rose, ski companies began manufacturing skis that harnessed natural forces as never before. The dimensions and internal construction of these new skis gave racers an unprecedented ability to carve clean turns. But the increased control came at a cost; now the smallest mistakes, the inev-itable limitations of a skier's balance, could lead to ghastly crashes.

Equipment rules were created, and endlessly adjusted, their efficacy always unclear.

Today, racers regularly travel as fast as 90 miles per hour down the same icy forest trails where their predecessors topped out at half that speed nearly a century ago. (In 2013, Johan Clarey of France exceeded 100 mph at Wengen's Lauberhorn downhill). They hit jumps, and struggle to minimize and control their flight. In the event of a crash there are nets and airbags, and helmets and armor, but the racers' only real protection is their brutally honed ability to maintain their footing.

One of the pioneers of the new technology was Bode Miller, whom Klammer calls "the most exciting racer to watch of this modern time, by far." Like Klammer, Miller often pushes the envelope, where nearly every movement he makes is an improvised response to a disruption of his equilibrium. By 2002, when the twenty-four-year-old Miller won two silver medals at the Winter Games in Salt Lake City, his signature move was the miraculous recovery.

Whatever the origin of his uncanny balance, Miller's ability to find his footing in moments of duress earned him the adoration of the sport's most ardent fans, even when he crashed. While many of his competitors endured catastrophic injuries—comas, paralysis, amputation—Miller somehow survived, despite skiing at or beyond the commonly accepted risk limits. At the midpoint of Miller's career, when the Internet had become a repository of video highlights, many of the most popular ski racing clips showed Miller slipping like a man who stepped on a banana peel, somehow arresting his fall and often ending up right where he wanted to be in the first place.

Of course, there is more to ski racing than near-crash reels. There are, for instance, Olympic medals to be won. And in 2006, at the Winter Games in Torino, Italy, Miller, then in his prime at twenty-eight, famously came up short in all five of the alpine skiing events, despite his being a credible contender in all of them and a favorite in some. This spectacular defeat, along with an apparent nonchalance that infuriated some observers, immediately defined an exceptional human as a monumental disappointment before a worldwide audience. Back in the

United States, the very name of the country's greatest ski racer became a punchline.

Loser. Goat. Flop. Bust. Fool. Embarrassment. Douche bag. Ugly American. All these labels, and worse ones, were attached to Miller as he wobbled out of Torino without a medal. He was the US Olympic Team's first Facebook flameout. Hate mail arrived at his mother's house.

The surreal perception gap that opened was evident in the reactions to Miller's faltering in the Torino super G event, a race he was certainly qualified to win. Miller was nearing the finish when a small misjudgment, bred of aggression and fatigue, threw him off the course in a most dramatic, Milleresque way. He was moving about 60 miles per hour when the edge of his left ski caught a ripple in the snow and shot off on a separate trajectory. As his left leg jerked violently out from under him, Miller tottered onto his right ski and balanced there as he hurtled toward the fences.

Photographs of this vulnerable moment adorned hundreds of sports pages the next day. In the pictures, an airborne Miller leans forward down the mountain as if making an elaborate bow to the crowd. His left leg, with the seven-foot ski still attached to it, appears to shoot out behind him in a donkey kick. In many newspapers, these photos stood adjacent to critical and sometimes belittling stories. Here is a reckless clown, they said.

But the photos were deceptive. By happenstance, the on-hill broadcast team had installed a special slow-motion video camera on the very turn where Miller made his mistake. That camera had a high enough shutter rate to capture the preternatural composure that belies Miller's supposed recklessness. Footage of the mishap became an instant classic among hardcore skiing fans, who to this day rewatch it endlessly online.

In the clip, as Miller veers off course, his trailing ski catches in the snow at least seven times—first the tip, then the tail, alternatingly. Throughout all this yanking and jolting, Miller flails his arms and twists his torso, trying to get back on two feet. He is far enough off course now that the snow is no longer the smooth, hard surface of the main track, but the piled-up ridges of loose snow that course workers have pushed to the side of the slope. As his left ski shudders and vibrates with each bouncing impact, Miller grows still. He leans forward, his eyes focused on the undulations of the hillside that are rushing up to meet him, and somehow, in this moment of sensory overload, he summons the talent and serenity to quiet that whiplashing leg and pull it back under his body. The errant ski comes around to point downhill, and at the very moment Miller plants his foot back underneath him, the clip abruptly ends. The darkened screen offers two options: replay or share.

The single most important element in alpine skiing is the skier's relationship with the fall line, the path an object would travel if it were free to move on a slope under only the power of gravity. It is the slippery ideal at the heart of alpine ski racing, the organizing principle that unifies skiers of all levels and eras. Every racer learns this term early in his or her career, but the best racers have an instinctive feel for it, an infatuation and respect. The fall line is the fastest way down a mountain, but because race courses require athletes to move sideways across the hill between gates, they repeatedly pass in and out of it.

Much of the art and technique of ski racing involves channeling the power of the fall line while diverging from it, maneuvering body and skis in a way that transfers gravity into an energized traverse. With a coordinated set of movements, and an intimate relationship with their equipment, the best downhillers can almost tame gravity through the fifty or more turns that make up a run. Swinging back and forth, leaving smooth grooves in the snow, they can move with such precision through the gates that their paths align and a channel begins to form in the surface along the most strategic line. Only the best racers have the strength and self-control to cut inside these ruts and go even straighter, even faster, and even closer to the fall line and all its promise of glory and destruction.

Lindsey Vonn has mastered this art like few before her. Throughout a long career (she joined the US Ski Team in 1998, when she was fourteen), she has exceled in every discipline. In the seasons following Miller's Torino debacle, Vonn overtook him as the most decorated American ski racer. Vonn seems to possess an internal gyroscope that allows her to find the fall line and embrace gravity whenever possible. Despite a catastrophic knee injury in February 2013, she has continued breaking the sport's most hallowed records, and had even begun exploring a bid to compete on the men's World Cup tour, a separate circuit that includes some of the classic downhills that women never get to test.

Someone completely unfamiliar with skiing can quickly begin to appreciate what makes Vonn much faster than her peers by watching for snow spray. To a casual observer, the jets of snow shooting out from underneath a racer's skis might seem beautiful, suggestive of mastery, but in fact that displaced snow indicates friction, which, after fear, is a racer's greatest enemy. As Vonn descends a course, her skis usually cut in smooth arcs across the surface. Only rarely does she pressure her skis so abruptly that she skids and wastes momentum.

Clean skiing is the carved turn: one where the skis bend and their edges slice into the mountain to track along sharply defined channels of their own making. Carved turns leave behind curving grooves in the snow, as fine and shapely as those a figure skater etches onto an ice rink. Good racers must manage their skis in this fashion around every gate, and they must do it repeatedly, linking together an unbroken series of carved turns across changing terrain and varying snow conditions.

Push a lawnmower or a baby carriage and you can understand some of the forces at play. Turning such an object takes both hands pulling and pushing in concert. At issue is the momentum that would continue forward if not for the pilot's execution of a combination of moves with each hand to redirect it. Ski racing is similar, except that a racer's body is both the object being steered and the steering mechanism. Vonn uses her hips, knees, ankles, and (not least) her trunk muscles to redirect herself, flirting and fighting with forces that pull her in several directions.

For Vonn, the fall line is both enemy and ally. In every run she is working out an athletic compromise with gravity, alternately resisting it and surrendering to it. Making it down the mountain quickly and making it down the mountain safely are often irreconcilable goals, and few know this better than Vonn, who throughout her career has endured hideous crashes that left her with broken bones and torn ligaments. In dozens of rag-doll tumbles, she has injured her hips, knees, hands, and brain. The smallest miscalculations have knocked her silly, bloodied her face, and sent her spinning off into the Red Room, the mordant euphemism racers use for crashes serious enough to fling them into a course's red-orange safety netting so hard that it wraps around them as they plow to a stop. This is the cost of doing business if the business is winning ski races. If Vonn did not suppress her desire for comfort, she would have to settle for seeing other people win.

"I never think about what if I crash," Vonn says. "While I'm skiing, I try to make the next gate. I'll still try to not crash while I'm crashing into the net. I try to save myself until the last second. There's no time for me to change my mind-set. I'm still fighting."

Although her Torino travails were somewhat obscured by Bode Miller's, the 2006 Games felt like a Waterloo for Vonn as well. It was in a training run there, on the women's downhill course at San Sicario, that Vonn—then Lindsey Kildow—crashed so violently that her rescuers immediately strapped her to a spine-immobilizing backboard and flew her via helicopter to a hospital in Torino. Doctors at the Centro Traumatologico Ortopedico found no damage to her skeletal structure but discovered a deep bruise extending over her backside and lower back. She had no chance in her events, though she did participate.

The calamities of Torino shaped Vonn's career in one way, and Miller's in another, particularly in the three years that followed the 2006 Winter Games.

Unburdened by the public spotlight, Miller happily resumed winning and found new ways to achieve the underdog status that motivated him, chiefly by leaving the US Ski Team to race independently. Vonn, meanwhile, redoubled her training commitments and established herself as the most dominant female racer in the world. Newly married to her coach and making millions from her primary sponsor, Red Bull energy drinks, like Miller she built a personal team around herself.

In 2008, Miller and Vonn both won the sport's most prestigious trophy, the overall World Cup title. Though each preserved a dogged, uncompromised self-confidence, the Torino disappointments haunted them both and limited their reputations at home. In the eyes of mainstream America, an Olympic gold medal is the only credential that really matters. This unfortunate circumstance bewildered their European peers and the sport's most dedicated fans, who knew that Miller and Vonn were the engines propelling American ski racing to new heights in the first decade of the twenty-first century. This historic burst of success included other racers like Julia Mancuso, Daron Rahlves, Ted Ligety, and more, but its undisputed leaders were Miller and Vonn.

The story of the renaissance in American skiing coincides with another. In the three years after Torino, existential threats to the sport itself became apparent. First among these was climate change. The winter of 2006–07 was at that point the warmest ever recorded in the Alps, and possibly the warmest in the last five hundred years. Hundreds of races were canceled, including Kitzbühel, underscoring the reality that the mountains where alpine skiing thrives are thawing, with winters getting wetter and shorter on average. The glaciers where ski racing was born are shrinking at an accelerating pace, and with them the available training space for elite skiers at key moments in the season. If average temperatures continue to rise, ski areas will be forced to raise prices or go out of business, limiting the number of young people with access to the sport, particularly in the lower-elevation hotbeds of American ski culture like New England and the upper Midwest, which gave rise to Miller and Vonn.

Snowy winters returned to the Alps in 2008, but by then there was another troubling trend: a spate of gruesome injuries to prominent racers including Aksel Lund Svindal, Dane Spencer, Scott Macartney, Matthias Lanzinger and Daniel Albrecht. Though none of these skiers died, the severity of their injuries—and the morbid viral appeal of the accident footage online—spurred organizers and administrators of alpine skiing to address the inherent danger of the sport in dramatic ways.

The link between global warming and downhill racing's carnage issues was evident in the increased speeds, and their consequences. Warm air softens the snow, eventually making a course unraceable, so to protect race organizers and television broadcast-rights holders from cancellation, organizers have perfected various snow-hardening techniques. Where rain or warm winds could once have made racing impossible, today's World Cup hosts manufacture a deep base of ice weeks before the event to insure their sponsors and partners against millions in losses.

Dexterity on ice had always been part of ski racing, but by 2009 a World Cup skier was expected to race on a surface that would be unrecognizable to a previous generation. Organizers injected water into the snow with special nozzles fitted onto fire hoses. The shallow cuts the skis make in a World Cup slope mean reduced drag, and contributed to the rise in downhill speeds. The trend is alarming to the sport's governing body, the Fédération Internationale de Ski (FIS), where top officials would like to see speeds reduced as much as possible.

"We are convinced that speed is not spectacular," says FIS president Gian Franco Kasper, who argues that a racer hitting 120 kilometers per hour is dull viewing if he or she is sitting in a tuck. "The normal television viewer does not realize if you have 110 or 120. It's rather the fight of the man against the mountain. That, you see, that's spectacular, but if they just sit down like this, like in speed skiing, that doesn't bring anything. That's why we always said let's keep the speed down as much as we can. It's not easy to do."

In the years after Torino the FIS redoubled its efforts. Hard, fast snow was here to stay, but the FIS instituted a new set of equipment regulations and course redesigns. These prompted a bitter backlash from many racers, including Bode Miller, who felt that the new restrictions were robbing the sport of its anarchist soul. But neither the athletes nor the officials could see an easy way to reconcile the sometimes conflicting desire to preserve the formats and liberties of a sport that reveres tradition while minimizing the danger that had the potential to turn it into something inhumane.

Like climate change, the new safety measures posed a philosophical question to the next generation of downhillers. Would they get a chance to test their skills and courage against the same mountains their predecessors had raced on? Or would this be the last generation of real downhillers? It is a conundrum that mystifies the sport's leaders, like Bernhard Russi, now a top course designer and FIS race official, who argues that the feared homogenization of ski racing will not extinguish the omnipresent danger that gives the sport its power and, to great athletes, its allure.

"We try to control more and more and more and more," says Russi. "In downhill, we even try to control danger, and then it becomes more dangerous. Because if danger is not obvious anymore, it's getting dangerous."

PART 1

One Year Out

March–April 2009

CHAPTER 1

Crossroads

Among the eccentricities of Bode Miller's approach to the sport was his stony demeanor in the start house, which at any high-level ski race can be a frightening, tense place. As his rivals lined up for the competition, many would stamp their feet, snorting and spasming like bulls at a rodeo. But not Miller: his routine was to stand still and expressionless, often gazing blankly at the mountains across the valley. As if in a trance, he often maintained this inscrutable calmness until the last second.

So it was on February 4, 2009, one year before the 2010 Winter Olympics were set to begin, when Miller stood on deck at the start of the world championship super G race at Val d'Isère, France. The best ski racers on the planet had gathered there for the two-week series—the World Cup tour had taken a customary intermission—and this was the first men's event on the schedule. There were seventy racers from twenty-seven countries on the start list, and Miller was to run twelfth. When he stepped into the starting gate, he wore on his face the thousand-yard stare that often served as prelude to an unmissable performance by the sport's most original showman.

Thirty-one years old, with aching joints and a broken relationship with his own national ski team, Miller was also the most decorated American ski racer of all time, with two Olympic silver medals, five world championship gold medals, and victories at some of the world's most prestigious annual races, like the Lauberhorn downhill at Wengen, Switzerland, and the Hahnenkamm combined in Kitzbühel, Austria. He had won thirty-one World Cup races; only six men were above him on the career victory list, none of them American.

But defeat defined Miller's career just as clearly. Since qualifying for the US Ski Team in 1996, Miller had suffered punishing losses that would have driven most people from the sport. Some of these were well-known failures committed on a global stage, but others were statistical disasters that revealed themselves only after a dive into the record books: healthy leads in the World Cup standings that evaporated before season's end, or races he dominated until a mistake in the final section. Once, early in his career, Miller went two World Cup seasons without finishing a slalom race—a combined total of seventeen races where he either crashed or screwed up so badly he didn't qualify for the second run.

This season, Miller was in the midst of one of his deep lows. Winless in twenty-six races, he was mired in eighth place in the World Cup standings (having finished each of the previous seven seasons in the top four). Two months earlier, in Colorado, in a nasty crash on the difficult World Cup downhill slope at Beaver Creek, Miller had injured his left ankle. To accommodate the swelling, he had gone up a size in ski boots, which compromised his ability to finesse his line.

But the world championships, which took place every two years, were a fresh start, and Miller was highly motivated. Along with the gold, silver, and bronze medals came a big cash prize, as well as the right to carry around the title *Weltmeister* for two years (German is the sport's unofficial first language, and world championship wins are noted in the record book with the letters "WM"). Miller was making his sixth world championships appearance, but his first since breaking free of the US Ski Team. He was independently funding a small support staff to help him on the mountain, and a victory would win him a hefty bonus from his sponsors and vindicate his break with the national team.

At the championships—as at the Olympics—there were races for men and women in each of the four types of competition that comprise alpine ski racing: slalom, giant slalom, downhill, and super G. These four disciplines vary along a spectrum of curviness and speed, but there are other variations that make each as distinct from the next as a 100-meter-dash is from a marathon.

Together, slalom and giant slalom are the technical disciplines, and they are often paired for a weekend of racing on the World Cup circuit. Even smaller ski areas are capable of hosting such races. The same cannot be said of the downhill and super G, which are known as the speed disciplines or speed events, and require a much bigger mountain and expensive safety precautions.

Miller was one of the rare all-rounders in the sport, but it hadn't always been so. Like most New Englanders, he grew up restricted almost totally to the tech events, learning to ski near his family's off-the-grid home near Franconia, New Hampshire. When he landed a precarious place on the US Ski Team in 1996, people called him a remedial case in speed events. He was simply undeveloped compared to teammates who had grown up in the American West, linking 60 mph carved turns at Sun Valley or Crystal Mountain. He had to fight to catch up, a process obstructed by his penchant for crashing as well as by the bifurcated structure of the US team, which fielded a speed team and a tech team and tended to force racers into one or the other.

Only after Miller won his first World Cup GS and slalom—back-to-back races in December 2001—did he really begin exploring the big-boy downhills, the giant European runways with big jumps and gory legends. One of them, St. Anton, spat him out, shredding his knee enough to cause him chronic pain for the rest of his career. But he came back even more determined to be a downhiller and in 2004, at age twenty-seven, won his first World Cup race in that exalted discipline.

The cult of downhill is the lifeblood of ski racing, the wild heart beating amid the sport's regimentation. The fastest discipline, with peak speeds regularly cresting 80 and even 90 miles per hour, downhill's inherent danger gives ski racing an allure that attracts some of the greatest athletes alive. The old race courses like the Saslong and the Lauberhorn, where challenging sections remain virtually unchanged for decades, are pilgrimage sites for racers and fans alike. So while Miller never lost his love for rat-a-tat slalom, it was downhill glory he began stalking in his late-twentysomething prime.

Along the way he found super G, which was the next best thing. The newest of the four alpine disciplines, super G is a hybrid that appeared on the World Cup calendar in 1983 and was incorporated into the Olympic program in 1988. Super G courses are shorter and turnier than downhills, but longer and faster than GS runs. Like a downhill, each super G race consists of one run (tech races involve two runs, times added together). But while a downhill is a perennial thing, with numerous training runs leading up to each race, each super G sees a coach selected to arrange the gates, which are different every time. Success depends on a careful inspection on race morning—a window of time in which racers and their coaches can make a reconnaissance of the course and conditions (they may not ski, but rather must descend the course sideslipping, their skis perpendicular to the fall line).

On this sunny morning in Val d'Isère, Miller stood in the super G start, the beeping of an electronic timing system signaling the final countdown to his run, his mental engines revving behind a still expression. Miller, a former world champion in the event, charged onto the course, making four big pushes with his poles like a man swinging an axe, and then folding his six-foot-two frame into his tuck.

As was customary during Miller's runs, everyone stopped to watch. His fellow racers suspended their post-race interviews mid-sentence to see what line Miller would take through the gates. Young kids in the crowd, many of them junior racers, looked up to see the way he leaned back on the tails of his skis and allowed his arms to swing wildly, making a virtue out of the very habits that their coaches inveighed against. Mainly, everyone on hand waited to see if Miller would stay upright, crash violently, or execute one of the acrobatic recoveries that were his signature.

"Everybody is waiting," Franz Klammer would say with a smile, "saying, 'I have to watch, Bode is still to come. What will he do?'"

Miller took his typical all-out approach that day, diving in on the tight line and smashing gates out of his way with his body armor. Grinding through the bony pain in his sore ankle, he carved tight arcs, even throwing in a few quick skids when the speed got too great. Things were just getting interesting when, about 27 seconds into the course, he fell down on his side, sliding on the hard snow. Miller regained his footing almost instantly, but he was off line, and as he continued down the mountain, he had no hope of winning a medal.

At the end of the day, the fastest racer by nearly a full second was Didier Cuche of Switzerland, who finished in 1 minute, 19.41 seconds. Miller was 2.43 seconds slower than that, and ended up in twelfth place. He immediately turned his attention to the next race on the program, the downhill scheduled for February 7.

———

The alpine world ski championships, an event dating back to 1931, is a property of the FIS, a Switzerland-based organization that has about 10,000 registered athletes in more than one hundred member national ski associations. The FIS sanctions nearly 6,800 competitions, including nearly every snow sport at the Olympics: alpine, cross-country, snowboarding, freestyle, Nordic combined and jumping. (Biathlon, which combines cross-country skiing with rifle marksmanship, has a separate federation.)

In addition to all that, the FIS also oversees the annual alpine skiing World Cup, the engine of the sport's progression and its most competitive racing since the tour began in the winter of 1966–67. The World Cup lasts all winter. Every fourth year, it takes a one-month hiatus for the Olympics. And every other year (the odd-numbered ones), the February break accommodates the world championships, the biggest stand-alone event, in which racers aren't sharing the stage with sports like figure skating and hockey.

The FIS, ever mindful of tradition, enforces a set of international competition rules that apply to everything from the Olympics down to junior races around the world. And one of the ironclad FIS rules dictates that all competitors in downhill races must have first been given an opportunity to test out the course's straightaways and jumps. Racers must start one training run—though they are not required to finish it.

Typically, World Cup race organizers schedule two or three training runs in the days leading up to a downhill race, which makes each stop a weeklong affair. Saturday downhill and Sunday super G is a common program. Some of the deeper teams use the training runs as qualifying heats for the team's limited number of start positions in the race itself. Most of the top racers use the training runs to test out equipment.

There is also a lot of experimenting with "line"—the choice of path the skier takes down the course. In downhill, the gates may be spaced hundreds of feet apart and might not even mark turns, but instead align neatly in a corridor, so that a racer passes directly between three or four paired gate panels while following the gentle curve of a ski trail. Courses can send the racer down a mountain over jumps, plateaus, ravines, ridges, and steep pitches. A straight shot down a steep pitch is called a schuss, and a big jump might be called a sprung—named for someone, like a Russi-sprung. Two or more sudden turns meant to slow a racer down are called a chicane. The strip of snow most of the racers follow during the run is called the track. It is carefully prepared and kept free of obstacles of any kind. When one side of the track is higher than the other, that is a sidehill—the fall line runs off into the woods on one side while the course itself goes in another direction.

Veteran racers have the advantage of experience on difficult and intimidating courses, certain sections of which gain a notoriety of their own. The Tofane Schuss at Cortina and the Zielsprung at Kitzbühel are World Cup rites of passage. Rookies almost never win on these courses, or on the Lauberhorn downhill, which has taken place on virtually the exact same track since 1930. The Olympics and world championships, on the other hand, are often staged on courses that are relatively unfamiliar even to the most experienced skiers.

Such was the case in Val d'Isère, where the downhills took place on La Face de Bellevarde. It was a steep and icy descent that had been the venue for some of the races at the 1992 Winter Olympics, but had not been used since. Seventeen years later, the Val d'Isère organizers, led by French skiing legend Jean-Claude Killy, had revived it, and were dismayed to find that not all the racers were grateful. Because of the steep gradient, the course had to be extra turny, with gates set widely across the hill to control the racers' speed. With so little time in the fall line, the top racers said, it felt more like a super G than a real downhill.

But the Bellevarde course was a treat for spectators; standing in the finish area, they could view about 90 percent of the men's downhill course. From that vantage point, they might see one racer starting his run while another crossed the finish line. This feature turned out not to matter on race day, however, as thick fog settled over the mountain. The race jury—a small group of FIS officials and the local organizing committee—deliberated and concluded that, although the fog's thickness varied, visibility was good enough for the race to be run. The race referee, Günter Hujara of the FIS, would stand in his skis near the top of the course and use his radio to call for racers to be held at the start if the fog got too thick.

The first racers had a window of blue sky to race in, but then the fog returned. Close to half of the first thirty skiers emerged from the start house into a soupy gray mist that prevented them from seeing the course well enough to ski with the necessary aggression. When the eighteenth racer, Klaus Kröll of Austria, kicked out of the start, there was good visibility at the top but a band of fog across the middle of the course. Bode Miller was running nineteenth, and he slid into the start blocks to watch Kröll disappear into the fog, going highway speeds with no protection into near-zero visibility. If Kröll made it to the finish in one piece, Miller knew, it would only be because he stood up out of his tuck and peered over his ski tips for geographic features that might tell him where he was going—not the proper mind-set for a downhiller, who should be thinking always of finding a faster route to the bottom.

When the start official told him to get ready, Miller was stunned. He didn't stand a chance in these conditions. All morning long, he had been steeling himself for two minutes of suicidal risk, and the start holds hadn't made it any easier. Unsure whether his turn would arrive in twenty minutes or two hours, Miller had drained himself mentally just staying focused, and now suddenly they couldn't spare a minute to see if the clouds would blow out.

"There's a huge fog bank down there—stop the race," Miller said, but the start official, wearing a radio headset, did not respond. He was taking orders from the jury members, who were stationed at various points below Miller on the course, and there was no directive to stop sending racers. Miller turned to a nearby coach from Austria, whose radio he knew was set to the same frequency as Hujara's, but the coach would not transmit Miller's request.

"Ten seconds!" the starter warned. Hujara was not calling for a hold. Miller knew that if he didn't start the race when he was told, he would be disqualified. The countdown began, and Miller had no choice but to go or to forfeit his turn.

Frustrated, distracted, and not without fear, Miller pushed onto the Face de Bellevarde, edged up to 60 miles per hour or so, and skied straight into a blinding wall of fog. Instantly, he experienced vertigo. In his feet, Miller felt jolts from ruts he couldn't see. From the corner of his eye, he saw the exact locations where he had wanted to be. Slipping down the course on a different trajectory than the one he'd planned, he managed to finish in eighth place, just ahead of Kröll but a full 1.60 seconds behind John Kucera of Canada, who had started second and eventually won the gold medal.

Miller's friend Aksel Lund Svindal, a big twenty-six-year-old all-rounder from Norway, was running just behind him, and encountered fog equally as bad. Like Miller, Svindal thought the whole thing was scandalously unfair. He and Miller were two of the best downhillers in the world and they had zero chance at a medal. Both men were outraged at the finish when racer twenty-one, Michael Walchhofer of Austria, was given a rerun because of the fog.

That's the way of it in an outdoor sport. The weather is an active participant in any ski race. This is why alpine skiing resists medal predictions. Only a few variables come under the racer's control. And control, as Klammer had demonstrated in 1976, is overrated.

In the weeks leading up to the championships at Val d'Isère, Miller had mentioned publicly that he was considering retirement. To fans who followed his career closely, the approach of the 2010 Winter Olympics made Miller's departure from the sport seem even more likely; given the savage criticism heaped upon him at the previous Olympics, it was hard to imagine his suiting up for Vancouver, and all the hoopla that would surround it.

Now he appeared poised to reprise the zero-for-five medal strikeout of Torino at the 2009 world championships. With the super G and downhill behind him, his best opportunities for a medal were gone. His once-awesome giant slalom abilities had diminished, and although he could sometimes be fast in slalom, his finishes in that discipline were so infrequent that he had slipped abysmally low in the standings. This meant he usually started late in the order, sometimes in the thirties, waiting at the start of a rutted course with kids ten years younger than he was.

But looking at the Val d'Isère competition calendar, there did seem to be one chance for Miller to win a medal, and for all-rounders like him it held a special appeal. In addition to alpine skiing's four core disciplines, there is a fifth event, the combined, that comes with its own medals and ranking systems. Often overlooked and occasionally maligned as a clunky anchronism, it is the most historic of all of alpine skiing's five medal events, and arguably the most meaningful.

The modern combined event usually consists of one run of downhill and one run of slalom, both staged on the same day. The racer with the lowest combined time wins. The format and scoring of the combined event has evolved dramatically since its invention in the 1920s, but the current iteration as designed by the FIS is probably the simplest to follow. It is known as the super combined, and Miller was one of its most masterful participants—when he could finish. Only a very small number of racers have the versatility to contend in the super combined, and they are the best all-around ski racers in the world. While they aren't always masters of the alpine racing universe, they at least control its perimeters.

Miller was a competent slalom skier in 2009, though a shadow of the agile twenty-four-year-old who had won by huge margins on tricky slalom hills like Schladming and Adelboden. Mastery of the speed events had come at the expense of time spent on training slalom and testing equipment. By now, Miller was heavier than he was in those 2002 races, the skis and course setting had evolved, and a wave of younger skiers had adopted moves Bode himself had pioneered to depose an earlier generation of aging slalom aces.

Miller was by no means a safe bet on February 9, when the Bellevarde course played host to the men's world championship super combined—this time, without any fog. Forty-nine competitors from nineteen countries took part in the event, which began with the shortened downhill portion at 10 a.m. Consisting of thirty gates that guided racers on a mile-and-a-half-long path, the course started 8,366 feet above sea level and dropped 2,303 feet in elevation, the equivalent of one and a half Empire State Buildings.

When the downhill run was complete, the fastest racer through the course was Svindal, who had started eighteenth and completed the course in 1 minute, 30.99 seconds. The next best time belonged to Miller, who had started two positions behind Svindal and finished with a time that was four hundredths of a second slower.

Afterward, Miller retreated to his usual off-snow refuge, a motor home he kept among the television trucks parked near the base of the mountain. The slalom portion of the race wasn't scheduled to begin until 5 p.m., giving the athletes a chance to eat lunch, change their equipment, ski through some training courses, and inspect the slalom.

At one in the afternoon, many of the racers watched Lindsey Vonn win the women's downhill, which took place on a slope across the valley from the men's venue. With two world championship gold medals—she had also won the super G earlier in the week—to go with her leading position in the World Cup standings, Vonn looked poised to be one of the small handful of athletes the American broadcaster NBC would anoint as medal hopefuls at the Olympics a year later, a benediction that would mean a prominent place in its programming, with intimate biographical profiles and in-depth coverage of her races. She would have guest appearances on *Today* and the *Tonight Show*, and her image would be used in NBC's promotional spots.

At five, as night fell on Val d'Isère, the men's slalom course was illuminated by powerful floodlights, and a large crowd gathered at the finish line for the conclusion of the men's super combined. The spectators could look up the slope and see the last section of the Face de Bellevarde now forested with blue and red plastic poles. There were 114 of them, arranged in pairs to form fifty-seven gates between the start and the finish line.

In slalom especially, racing on a fresh surface gives the early racers an advantage over those starting behind them. To offset this benefit in a combined race, the starting order for the slalom portion of the event is typically a reversal of the top thirty finishers from the downhill portion. This means that the racers who are slower in the downhill (many of them slalom specialists) get to ski the slalom leg on smooth snow.

This arrangement benefited Julien Lizeroux of France, a twenty-nine-year-old racer from the town of Moûtiers, an hour's drive down the valley. Never a great downhiller, Lizeroux had managed to finish the morning's run in twenty-second place, finishing 2.89 seconds behind Miller and 2.93 behind Svindal.

Starting on a mostly fresh surface in the slalom, Lizeroux thrilled the partisan crowd with a beautiful run, springing nimbly back and forth across the ice as he wove his way through the gates and stopped the clock at 49.98 seconds—more than a full second faster than any of the six racers who went before him. Lizeroux's total time of 2 minutes, 23.90 seconds was the fastest so far, and it stayed that way for a long while; the next nineteen skiers all failed to put up a better combined score. With only two racers to come—Miller and Svindal—Lizeroux was guaranteed a medal on home soil.

As Miller slid into the start, a video cameraman sidled up to him and trained his lens on the American's stubbled face. The images were broadcast live to millions of people—it was prime time in Europe—and the commentators reminded viewers that although Miller hadn't won a World Cup slalom in more than four years, he had finished second at a slalom race in Finland in November. But that was before the ankle injury; today, no one knew what Miller would summon.

Miller had maintained his skills for exactly this kind of moment. Though rusty, he remained good enough that a specialist like Lizeroux could rarely get more than a second over him on a minute-long course. Now, with a cushion of nearly three seconds from the downhill, all Miller had to do was survive the slalom course on his feet to guarantee a medal.

Or, as television commentators were telling their audiences in perhaps a dozen different languages at that exact moment, Miller could go for gold. He could take chances, go straight, try to erase his tiny deficit from the morning's downhill and steal the prize from Svindal. When the countdown began, Miller was looking out at the horizon with his familiar stoniness, then he tipped forward, pushed hard with his poles, and started onto the course.

The gates were offset from one another, requiring fifty-six direction changes, but Miller went as straight as possible at the inside poles. He steered his feet around the base of each pole as he knocked each of them down with his hands, his shins, even the tops of his boots. This kept most of Miller's body on a more direct path toward the finish than his skis were taking.

For the first seven turns of the course, Miller shifted his weight from leg to leg, making his skis bend and carve into the snow in smooth arcs, harnessing the centrifugal forces to send his bulky frame back and forth across the slope. But on the eighth turn, his left ski slipped into a deep groove left by the previous racers and he lost his footing, causing him to go down on his side. Miller dropped his right hand to the snow to hold himself up. His sense of balance helped him recover his footing, but a more conservative approach would have had him steering his skis into the same groove from the beginning of the turn, rather than colliding with it.

It took Miller 15.66 seconds to reach the first interval, where he passed through a beam of light hooked into the timing system. It had taken Lizeroux 15.53 seconds to get there, so Miller was on his way to a silver medal at least. Unaware of his time, but aware that the mistake had cost him, Miller pushed on.

On the thirty-first gate, Miller shaved the line too close again. Aiming his skis just to the left-hand side of the gate, he applied pressure to them too soon. His left ski gripped the ice and started tracking on an arc that curled too tightly. This time, his ski tip went on the wrong side of the gate, followed by his foot. Miller had straddled the pole. The impact of hooking his ski on the gate jolted him, but he managed to stay upright. His race was over—if he continued after straddling he'd be disqualified—so he pulled to a stop, unbuckled his ski boots, and turned his gaze up the hill, studying the gate that had tripped him. Up at the start, Svindal knew Miller had gone out when he heard a rapturous explosion of cheers rumble up from the finish area, where the crowd knew that their Lizeroux had captured a silver medal.

A minute later, Miller stood to the side of the course and watched Svindal steer carefully through the same turns where Miller had been aggressive. Rather than slicing clean arcs, Svindal often smeared his skis on the snow, creating friction that slowed his time but increased the chance he would stay on his feet.

Svindal worked his way down the hill, making a few mistakes even with his conservative approach, and the cushion of his lead shrank at each interval, but didn't disappear. In the end, his slalom run was more than two seconds slower than Lizeroux's, but his cumulative time was 0.90 seconds faster, winning him the gold medal.

The American sports media that had savaged Bode Miller in 2006 had mostly ignored him since then, but as the Val d'Isère races wound down, a few commentators veered away from celebrations of Lindsey Vonn's ascendancy to take note of Miller's struggles and deliver him a few fresh whacks from across the ocean.

The *Chicago Tribune* charted Miller's losing streak, dismissed his stoic comments about it as "mumbo jumbo," and labeled him a "tedious bore." The *Denver Post* called Miller "irrelevant" in the headline of an article asserting that the only people who cared about him now, in the twilight of his career, were those who "mindlessly celebrate rebels simply for their rebellion, however misplaced it might be. The rest of us just don't care anymore."

On February 13, Miller's disastrous championships continued when he failed to finish the men's giant slalom, won by a powerful young Swiss racer named Carlo Janka. And no one was surprised on February 15, at the men's slalom, when the letters "DNF" flashed across the scoreboard next to Miller's name, indicating for the crowd that he did not finish.

There was something unusual about the way Miller reacted after blowing out of the second run in that slalom, the final medal event of the championships. Rather than coming down to the finish area, or finding a gap in the fence so he could bypass the finish altogether, Miller stayed where he was on the side of the course, waiting for someone to come down from the start with the jacket he'd left up there. When it arrived, Miller put it on and then sat down on the snow. With his skis still attached to his feet, he spent the better part of an hour quietly watching the other racers go whizzing by. Almost all of them were younger than he was, some by a decade or more. As the podium settled itself out (Pranger AUT, Lizeroux FRA, Janyk CAN), Miller loitered on the side of the course, alone. Given his recent musings on retirement, and given his abysmal results in the current season— fifteen DNFs so far—it seemed unlikely that the ski world would be seeing much more of him.

Soon the action photographers on the side of the course had walked over to Miller, the crampons on their boots feet squeaking in the icy snow, and raised their long telephoto lenses. This was one constituency that didn't think Miller was irrelevant. The photographers loved him. No skier had delivered them more photographic gifts over the previous decade than this unpredictable American. The ski photographers swarmed, thinking these might be the last images of him on an elite racecourse.

The pictures they shot of Miller show him sitting on the snow in the white coat of his private team, looking at his phone, and then staring out across the mountain, lost in some unknowable sequence of thought, perhaps calculating the price of gold.

CHAPTER 2

The Showcase Athlete

There was a predatory beauty to Lindsey Vonn's tuck, the commitment to speed it conveyed, a hunger for the finish line that surpassed any fear. With her arms extended in front of her, hands piercing the cold air, she plummeted down the slope, her legs crowding up against her chest, where she subtly shifted them to adjust the trajectory of her descent.

It was February 22, 2009, and Vonn, the star of the US Ski Team, was racing in a World Cup super G race at Tarvisio, an Italian town near the converging borders of Austria and Slovenia. The World Cup tour had resumed as soon as the world championships were over, and there would be another three weeks of racing before the season ended and Vonn would get a break.

At the championships, Vonn had won both the super G and the downhill, and might have extended her gold medal streak if not for a freak accident that occurred during her downhill victory celebration. At a post-race party she had grabbed a bottle of champagne, intending to spray it toward some photographers, but instead she felt the jagged edge of the bottle's broken neck slice into the flesh of her thumb. That necessitated a flight to Austria for emergency surgery to repair a damaged tendon.

Now here she was, closing out the World Cup season with a bandage and post-surgical brace on her right hand, which prevented her from pushing hard out of the start. The Tarvisio race was the fifth super G of the season, and the twenty-fifth women's World Cup race of the season. She hadn't quite locked up the title yet, but she was on her way.

At the age of twenty-four, Vonn was what the Austrians called a *Vorzeigeathletin*—a showcase athlete. She had amassed trophies and records and earned millions of dollars in endorsement fees and prize money. But with every scorching turn down this course she reasserted her ownership of the most precious and nontransferable thing in her possession: the ability to carve beautiful and efficient turns down a vertiginous, frozen slope.

To a naked eye, Vonn's turns seemed somehow to increase her speed. That was because the fall line is equivalent to the boat in water-skiing, and Vonn's control over the shape of her turns was so complete that whenever she was in the fall line she was applying forward-driving pressure to her skis, and whenever she was out of it—necessarily cutting across the hill—she was lightly shifting her weight from one leg to the other, starting a new turn. The perfect efficiency of this transition, after a lifetime of practice, involved letting her upper body tip into the fall line first, leading her legs into the new turn, pressuring the newly-weighted ski and bending it. At the apex of the turn—usually just as she rounded a gate—she might be crouched over curling skis, but a snapshot would show that her hips and chest were pointing straight down the fall line, and a speed measurement device would register a burst of acceleration. At these moments Vonn was often angulated—both legs extending out to one side, her hip just inches from the snow, while she braced against the centrifugal forces at work as she turned.

It was textbook form, a feat of counterbalancing and fluid movement that Vonn had started to perfect in Colorado as a teenager. People called Vail her home mountain, and while that wasn't wrong, she had first cultivated these abilities somewhere less glamorous: Buck Hill, Minnesota, a 310-foot bump just minutes from her family home in the suburbs of the Twin Cities.

A reliable factory of American ski racers, Buck Hill sits beside Interstate 35, lit up at night by bright floodlights and often covered with slalom training courses. As a little girl in the early 1990s, Lindsey had spent night after night skiing laps there, weaving through the icy slalom training course and letting her momentum carry her past the last gate, all the way back to the motorized rope tow. She would grip the rope in her mittened hands and let it drag her back up to the top to go again, but faster.

In Tarvisio, Vonn stood up out of her tuck position only when obliged to do so by one of the forty-one turns marking the course. She rounded them in smooth, swooping arcs, the energy of each turn concentrating itself in her coiled legs and in her flexing, razor-sharp skis. Just when it seemed that the pressure was too great for the human frame, Vonn made a subtle realignment of her hips and knees that redirected that energy back across the hill. This was her life's work, the mastery of millimetric moves that allowed her to shoot herself across the mountain as if richocheting between two invisible, elastic walls.

It was in Colorado that she first really experimented with those forces and those moves. She'd moved there at age twelve, turning her back on the conventional rites of passage for an American teenager so that she could race at Vail. There, she'd given every hour of her days to perfecting her turns, not just on ice but on the wide, rolling trails where Ski Club Vail trained downhill and super G.

By 2009, Vonn had long since surpassed the records of her childhood idol, American downhiller Picabo Street. If Vonn won this super G at Tarvisio, it would be the nineteenth of her career, moving her beyond Tamara McKinney to become the winningest American woman in World Cup history.

At the start of the run, the brace had forced Vonn to favor her left hand while she pushed with her poles to get up to speed. About nine and a half seconds into the course was a timing interval, and twenty-three of the sixty-four women in the race reached it faster than Vonn did. But after that, in the challenging part of the race course, where the only thing Vonn needed to do with her hands was drive them forward, she quickly made up for the handicap, carving expert turns through the forty-one gates and crossing the finish line with a time of 1 minute, 21.72 seconds. That was a full 0.51 seconds faster than the runner-up, Fabienne Suter of Switzerland. The twenty-nine racers who followed Suter all finished within a second of one another.

Only two Americans had more career World Cup victories than Vonn: Phil Mahre had won twenty-seven races when he retired in 1984, and Bode Miller had so far racked up thirty-one victories. No one doubted that Vonn had the talent and drive to surpass those records, but nothing was certain in ski racing, where one wrong move could tear a person's body apart.

Ski racing was part of Lindsey Vonn's family heritage, a passion she inherited from her father, Alan Kildow. As a teenager in the late 1960s, Kildow skied at Mount Telemark, a small ski area in Wisconsin where an Austrian immigrant named Erich Sailer was teaching the latest racing doctrines. Sailer's methodology was rote repetition and disciplined mastery of fundamental skiing technique; Kildow thrived in the program. At age seventeen, he won the overall title at the 1970 national junior championships.

After a string of successful performances the following year, the US Ski Team named him to its "talent squad," its third-tier team for up and coming racers, and a sponsor helped send him to Europe to train with the Austrians, who included a young prospect named Franz Klammer. That winter, Kildow got exposure to some of the world's most sophisticated coaches and biggest mountains, and even trained alongside the best ski racer in the world, Karl Schranz. It was heady stuff for a kid from Milton Junction, Wisconsin. While skiing on a glacier one day, Kildow crossed over a bare spot and tore ligaments in his knee.

The injury ended Alan Kildow's racing career, but he stayed in the sport; in 1969, Erich Sailer had moved his coaching enterprise to Buck Hill, and he hired Alan to be one of his assistant coaches while he studied economics at the University of Minnesota. After college Alan married Linda Krohn, a fellow student at William Mitchell College of Law in St. Paul, and their first child, Lindsey Caroline Kildow, was born on October 18, 1984. A stroke Linda suffered that day kept her hospitalized for more than a month.

Alan introduced Lindsey to skiing when she was two and a half years old. Lindsey would follow her father down the slopes, or would stand at the top and wait for him to prepare a bulky video camera and capture images of her as she came down the hill. Lindsey enjoyed the whole experience—the colorful ski gear, the breaks for hot chocolate. She begged for more, so her father started taking her on longer trips to mountains in Colorado.

Meanwhile, Buck Hill was a ready outlet for Lindsey's growing skiing passion, living as they did almost within sight of it. The very smallness of Buck Hill was part of its charm. The great Jean-Claude Killy remarked on it in *Comeback*, his 1974 memoir. "Nothing I had seen in the ski world prepared me for Buck Hill," Killy wrote, describing a race he'd done there. "We almost didn't see it!"

The longest runs sloped gently for about 1,000 feet from top to bottom, dropping a little more than 300 feet in elevation. The mountain had snowmaking equipment, and its runs were lined with floodlights so people could ski in the early evenings of the Minnesota winter. It also had a ski racing program that Sailer had turned into something of a powerhouse. Skiers from Buck Hill had gone on to the US Ski Team, and others had gone on to race for the top college teams.

Lindsey's parents signed her up for the racing program when she was seven, and for the next three years, several evenings a week and all day on Saturday, she would make laps on a cluster of runs reserved for race training. Soon Lindsey's skiing became the focal point of the busy Kildow household. Alan, by then making a name for himself in banking and insurance litigation, could go straight from work to Buck Hill to supervise his daughter's training. There he would find his wife waiting in the lodge with Lindsey's four younger siblings—among them, a set of triplets born when Lindsey was five.

Repetition was the key to it all. On a weeknight Lindsey would ski for two hours, and with each circuit taking little more than five minutes she could easily make twenty laps or more in a single night. On a twenty-gate course that meant four hundred turns a night, every one of them on rock-hard, icy snow. You needed sharp edges, but more than that you needed to be disciplined, to arrange your limbs in such a way that you could dig those edges into the ice and carve through it. Carving a ski was like swinging a golf club or pitching a baseball, a long, fluid movement, precise and habitual.

At Buck Hill, the clearly marked path to the US Ski Team revealed itself to Lindsey from the outset. In 1992, when she was eight, she could look to a group of Buck Hill alumni on the US Ski Team, including Kristina Koznick, who at sixteen years of age was ranked thirty-sixth in the world in slalom. Lindsey Kildow saw Koznick and the others getting to travel the world on skis, then coming back to Buck Hill to train in their cool uniforms and special equipment. They skied with grace and strength, and Lindsey set out to be just like them, climbing the rankings step by step, night after night, turn after turn.

She was nine when she made her first ski trip to Europe, attending a two-week training camp that Erich Sailer organized in Austria in the summer of 1994. It was overseen by the esteemed Austrian coach Mathias Berthold, and took place on the Hintertux Glacier. Lindsey had seen big mountains before, during the summer ski camps Sailer ran on the year-round snowfields atop Mount Hood in Oregon and at Red Lodge, Montana. But the Alps were big on a different scale.

Among the participants was a vivacious fifteen-year-old blonde from Vail named Sarah Schleper, an expert powder skier said to be one of the most promising young racers in America. Schleper, whose father ran a ski shop in Vail, was about as cool as a teenager could get. She dominated the regional competitions in Colorado, winning races at the Junior Olympics and getting invitations to US Ski Team camps.

When she returned from Austria, Lindsey asked her father what it would take to reach Schleper's level. Alan Kildow took out a piece of paper and began mapping the entire pyramid for her—all the echelons and branches of the sport. The US Ski Team was part of the United States Ski Association, the nonprofit that governed competition in all the skiing sectors recognized by FIS: cross-country, jumping, snowboarding, Nordic combined, and freestyle. In alpine skiing, USSA oversaw regional youth races like those Lindsey was familiar with. But when she turned fifteen she would be eligible for FIS races, which were more competitive and would give her an international ranking. The US Ski Team filled its ranks with young racers around the country who stood out in FIS rankings in each discipline.

Alan Kildow's sketch pointed to a problem for Lindsey: the speed events. Ideally, Lindsey would start racing super G sometime around age twelve, and not long after that she'd be ready for downhill. But races in those disciplines weren't staged in the Midwest in any serious way. If Lindsey were going to get on track to be the next Picabo Street, she was going to need a bigger mountain than Buck Hill.

Vail was the first and only choice. Lindsey already knew the Colorado resort from several trips she'd made there with her father. They'd skied all over the vast mountain, and stayed with local legend Pepi Gramshammer, an Austrian former racer who ran a popular inn and restaurant at the base of the mountain. But those were just vacations. Now Lindsey was going to train with the local ski team, one of the best junior race programs in the country. Ski Club Vail had more than two hundred athletes, top-notch training facilities, and a large coaching staff led by former US Ski Team head coach Chip Woods, who had worked with Tamara McKinney, Tommy Moe, and many other racers.

By fifth grade, Lindsey was using every winter break from school to train in Vail, her parents making the 1,000-mile drive again and again. They'd pile all her ski gear into the back of the family's SUV and hit the interstate for the sixteen-hour journey. Lindsey often crawled into a sleeping bag early in the drive, waking up somewhere in Nebraska. It was grueling, and in the winter of 1995–96 a decision was made that Lindsey and her mother would move to Vail for a few months so that Lindsey could train full time. Erich Sailer's feelings were hurt, but Lindsey had made up her mind.

That winter, eleven-year-old Lindsey and her mother lived in a two-room unit at a modest condominium complex just across the interstate from the ski area. Lindsey's four siblings stayed at home in Minnesota with their father, and Lindsey was home-schooled. Her nagging suspicion that she was missing out on the normal rites and routines of childhood couldn't extinguish the exhilaration she felt being in Vail. The mountain wasn't the steepest but it sprawled—the country's biggest ski resort, with more than 5,000 skiable acres compared to roughly 45 at Buck Hill.

Racing had been built into the resort's image since its founding, and Ski Club Vail had special privileges at the mountain. Several runs would be closed off for training, and the mountain even opened chairlifts to the club at dawn so that racers could train downhill before the public arrived. Vail was one of the only mountains in the US to regularly host World Cup events. When the tour came through, SCV kids and coaches provided the manpower to maintain the courses.

As impressed as Lindsey was with the program, it was impressed with her too. Woods knew right away that he had inherited a talent. Lindsey had extraordinarily sound technique, a discipline honed by solid coaching on a good mountain where every turn counted. Woods put one of his best coaches, Reid Phillips, in charge of introducing her to speed events. Lindsey could spend a few sessions making big turns on downhill skis that were much longer than anything she'd used before, then return to slalom training and her technical skills would come right back.

As at other top programs, SCV made ample use of video analysis. After every training session, the skiers would drop by the clubhouse at the base to watch footage of their efforts played in slow motion as coaches described the consequences of each misarranged body part: the left shoulder that dips and causes the right ski to wash out, the narrow stance that prevents a racer from making the proper angles with her lower body. For the average teenager, it might be torture to have the least graceful moments of your day frozen on a screen while your peers look on. But Lindsey's coaches at Vail would later recall her as absorbing their lessons like dry desert sand, taking their tips from the video sessions and immediately incorporating them into her technique. They would remember an uncomplicated kid with a great temperament, pleasant and funny, with no sense of entitlement.

At Vail, Lindsey finally got to ski the speed events, and she took to them instantly, blazing down closed slopes at speeds that would have taken her from the top of Buck Hill to the bottom in a matter of seconds. It was an intoxicating sensation, skiing upward of 60 miles per hour. Lindsey learned that when you try to change your trajectory at such speeds, mysterious forces present themselves. When you follow a trail around a bend, the forests lining the outside of the bend seem to pull you toward them. Unlike gravity, these forces vanish when you stop moving, but their power is unforgettable. And because of the high-speed lifts and groomed runs up to four miles long at Vail, she could experiment with them.

At the end of her first full winter in Vail, Lindsey skied so fast that she qualified for the 1996 J3 Junior Olympics, the top regional USSA race for the best skiers born in 1981 and 1982. She was born in 1984, but a special dispensation was made for her to participate. Despite falling in the slalom, she got up and still managed to finish second. A few weeks later, her name appeared in *Ski Racing* magazine in an issue with a cover photo of Picabo Street, her new idol.

Lindsey was on the US Ski Team's radar in the fall of 1996, when she turned twelve and hit a growth spurt; the decision was made to relocate the whole Kildow family to a tiny apartment in Vail. At the time of the move, Lindsey believed it was temporary—that they were just "testing it out." But midway through that season, Alan and Linda informed their kids that it was permanent. They'd sold the house in Minnesota. That was when Lindsey discovered how much was being sacrificed for her to realize her aspiration of being the next Picabo. Her mother had left behind a career and her little brothers and sisters had been uprooted. Alan was commuting back to Minneapolis for the work week and returning to Vail for weekends.

By the time cracks started appearing in her parents' marriage, Lindsey had already begun to internalize a conviction that the family had given up so much for her skiing dreams that nothing less than absolute achievement would justify the loss. This mind-set persisted long after the divorce proceedings and custody disputes that would follow—it continues to the present day, feeding her ambition. If Lindsey sometimes seemed high-strung to her teammates, it was at least partly because so much was invested in her career.

Strangers sometimes looked upon her biography and figured Lindsey had made it as a ski racer because her privileged youth had given her every opportunity. She considered it a family debt she was obligated to repay in gold.

Mountains are capricious. In any given race, an uphill gust of wind can cost a racer a tenth of a second or more, knocking her from podium contention. Occasionally, pebbles get churned into the snow and nick a ski's metal edge, leaving a tiny burr that causes a minuscule increase in friction. Compounded over the course of a run, it can slow a skier by a few critical hundredths of a second.

Usually it helps to start early in a race, before the track gets rutted. But sometimes the sun emerges from the clouds midway through an event, offering a high-definition view of the undulating terrain and the marks left by the earliest racers; on days like that, the later racers can choose a smoother line, and so conserve energy and be able to crouch more deeply in their tuck toward the finish.

Every racer quickly learns that the mountain is a living, breathing factor in every ski race—more important than what any of his or her competitors are doing. Whoever masters the most variables and takes the smartest risks can call herself the world's fastest skier that day, but a more authentic claim can be made by the person who in seven races over seven different days—some sunny and some foggy, some on soft snow and some on hard—has the best cumulative performance.

That's why the overall World Cup title has been the sport's standard of excellence since the tour began in 1967. Racers win it by accumulating points over the course of the winter, beginning in October with a single giant slalom on an Austrian glacier and ending in March with the World Cup Finals, where the top racers take part in one last race in each of four core disciplines (but no combined race). In the thirty to forty races that come in between, each winner gets 100 points, the runner-up 80, third place 60, on down to the thirtieth racer, who gets one point. Adding it all up at the end of the year yields a title more meaningful than any single day's race.

People sometimes get lucky at the Olympics, but the World Cup is an almost pure meritocracy. It may have fewer global viewers than the big championship events, but it remains the obsession of the best racers and of the sport's hardcore fans. It also happens that the circuit has the hardest courses, the deepest traditions, and the strongest fields of racers. (At the Olympics, no nation may enter more than four skiers in a race; in the World Cup, the best nations may enter ten or more.)

"You people make me laugh with your Olympic obsession," the great Marc Girardelli told Phil Hersh of the *Chicago Tribune* in 1992. Girardelli, who had won two silver medals at the 1988 Games, was referring to Americans, who typically didn't show much regard for the overall World Cup title. "The World Cup is worth ten times more," he said. "It's much tougher to stay at the top for a whole year than to win one race on a given day." (An Austrian by birth, Girardelli raced for Luxembourg for most of his World Cup career; he didn't obtain Luxembourg citizenship in time for the Olympics in 1984, where he would have been a favorite. He won the overall World Cup five times.)

The trophy itself is a crystal orb, a 26-pound piece of leaded glass shaped like a globe on a pedestal. Made in Bavaria, it has had more or less the same design since the 1970s, when the World Cup's chief sponsor was Evian and the globes were etched with the stylized skier logo central to Evian labels (according to Gian Franco Kasper of FIS it was a 70,000-Swiss-franc-per-year partnership). The pantheon of champions who have won it is alpine skiing's truest honor roll, missing only a few of the greats, notably Franz Klammer, who won twenty-five downhill races before super G was invented, and Michael von Grünigen of Switzerland, who won twenty-three giant slaloms. They were specialists, and the overall usually requires a broader portfolio of skills—the ability to win in three events, or at least dominate two. Picabo Street won six of the nine downhills in the 1994–95 season, but finished only sixth in the overall standings.

As consolation for the specialists the FIS recognizes them, too, awarding a season discipline title to the person topping the standings in each event. They receive a smaller crystal globe. Winning the season downhill title typically earns a racer a bonus from the company supplying their skis. The other discipline titles come with a reward too, but the downhill bonus is often bigger. And the overall title is the biggest.

The win at Tarvisio bumped Vonn's World Cup points for the season up to 1,374, giving her a 299-point lead over rival Maria Riesch (whose seventeenth-place finish gave her 14 points). But there were still nine races left—in Bulgaria, Germany, and Sweden—with plenty of variables, expected and otherwise, for Vonn to bring under control.

A year earlier, when Vonn had won the 2008 overall title, she was the first American woman to win it since Tamara McKinney in 1983. When the moment finally came for the ceremony where she would receive the trophy, she was radiant with pride. She stood beside Bode Miller, who won the men's title that year and stood next to her during a photo session, holding an identical trophy and looking far less enthused by the pomp and circumstance.

Miller, who had also won the title in 2005, was famous on the World Cup circuit for his lack of interest in trophies as physical objects—a disregard that sometimes seemed to border on actual contempt. In one notorious incident, he had used a world championship gold medal to stabilize the lid of the toilet in his motor home. Another time, he used a trophy cup to marinate chicken wings. One of Miller's first little crystal globes survived in his possession for only a few days before shattering to pieces inside a bag that he'd checked for the last leg of his flight home to New Hampshire.

That wasn't Lindsey. She would take good care of her trophies, especially the crystal globes. For now, they were mostly stashed at her various apartments in Utah, Colorado, and Austria. Someday she was going to put all those plaques, engraved plates, and chalices in a massive trophy case, like the one Karl Schranz had at his hotel in St. Anton, or the one that Annemarie Moser-Pröll—winner of a record six overall World Cup titles—had installed in the café she opened in her hometown of Kleinarl. That was what you did if you were a showcase athlete.

Bode was something else. While Lindsey was setting records at Tarvisio, the men's World Cup tour had resumed at Sestriere, a six-hours drive east across the top of Italy, and Miller was not on the start list. He was in California, embarked on a totally different kind of trip.

CHAPTER 3

The Crash Pilot

Just as the photographers at Val d'Isère had suspected the week before, on February 15, when they found Miller ruminating on the side of the world championship slalom course, Miller had been thinking hard about his future. All told, Miller had spent nearly an hour sitting there, alone with his thoughts about pulling the plug on his disastrous 2009 season. When he finally came down, some reporters were waiting for him at the finish, including Andrew Dampf, a sports writer from the Rome bureau of the Associated Press.

Miller said he wanted a break and had decided to skip the World Cup races at Sestriere. It wasn't retirement—just a vacation. He would only miss a week. He wanted some warm temperatures and sun. It was a nice little scoop for Dampf; skipping races was exceedingly rare for Miller, and he was ruling out retirement.

But Miller hadn't told the whole story. The championships ended, everyone went home, and three days later the Austrian Press Agency published a bigger scoop. The February 18 story from APA ran under the headline *"Bode Miller hat eine Tochter; Kindergeburtstag statt Welt-cup"*—"Bode Miller has a daughter; children's birthday instead of World

Cup." That was the first published news story to disclose the existence of Neesyn Dacey—Miller called her Dace—who would be one year old on February 19. Her father, the APA had learned, was going home to celebrate with her in California.

While Bode's entry into fatherhood hadn't been a total secret on the World Cup tour, it wasn't something he'd gone out of his way to advertise. Neesyn Dacey's mother was someone Bode had been seeing in 2007; he and Chanel Johnson had already gone their separate ways before the pregnancy announced itself.

Now Miller, who hadn't been absent from a World Cup venue since 2006, had a new set of priorities. Where the 2010 Olympics fit into them was a difficult story for reporters to explore, in part because Miller had more or less stopped giving interviews several years earlier. Moreover, his independent team didn't have an official spokesperson, and if a reporter spoke to anyone at the US Ski Team—not just press officers, but coaches and administrators as well—there wasn't a single person who could say, a year before the Vancouver Games, whether Miller would be there or not. Questions like that prompted awkward shrugs. Miller had said some venomous things about the national team in the past, and though he remained friends with people there, no one on the team presumed to be the interpreter of his thoughts.

To understand such a divorce, you have to go back to the beginning of the marriage, when Bode Miller needed the US Ski Team a lot more than it needed him.

Back in 1997, in an interview US Ski Team coach Phil McNichol gave to Steve Porino of *Ski Racing* magazine, McNichol described what it was like to work with the team's hottest prospect, a crash-prone nineteen-year-old from backwoods New Hampshire who had arrived on the team with eccentric equipment, radical opinions and philosophies, and a technique that some coaches found hideous.

Watching Bode Miller ski was "like watching *Mission Impossible* when they're trying to disarm the bomb," McNichol said. "Do they clip the yellow wire or the green wire? Sometimes it's the right one, some-times it ain't."

From the start, Miller exhibited an unconventional stance. When his arms weren't spinning wildly he held them out to his sides, not thrust out in front of him. He kept his legs widely spaced so he could tilt his knees sharply inward and outward for quick transitions between turns. He constantly shifted his body forward and backward, sometimes putting all of his weight on the tail of his skis. The moves distinguished him from every other racer. American skiing great Phil Mahre likened Miller's posture to the cartoon character Gumby. Occasionally Miller dragged a hand for better balance—a tripod coming down the hill. He wore mittens, not gloves.

For all of the hurly-burly of everything above his ankles, Miller's skis were tracking cleanly on lines his peers could only dream of skiing. But frequently it didn't work out. He crashed so often that his rankings were a concern and for several years his place on the national team was precarious. But Miller got just enough good results to continue, and even went to the Olympics in 1998, because the US men's tech squad—the slalom and GS skiers—had been dismal for years. (In the 1996–97 season, the American men didn't score a single World Cup point in GS.)

In the next years, Miller took his kamikaze style to the World Cup, and instantly everyone in the ski world was watching America's wild child. Some thought his approach to the sport represented squandered talent. Others saw his wild unpredictability as a virtue—an experiment far more interesting to observe than the continued dominance of the Austrians.

Whether to denounce or endorse Miller, people often used the same word: reckless. His slalom résumé told the story clearly enough. Between 1997 and 2009, Miller raced 105 World Cup slaloms; in seventy-two of them he crashed, got disqualified, or skied so badly in the first run that he didn't qualify for the second. Then there were winters, like the 1999–2000 season, when he entered ten World Cup slalom races and failed to complete a single one of them. Austrian newspapers called him the *ewige sturzpilot*—the eternal crash pilot.

As he started to figure out the World Cup circuit, Miller showed little interest in skiing conservatively, rejecting countless pleas that he dial things back in order to finish. As Miller saw it, skiing right on the edge of crazy was the only way; how else would he train one of his greatest genetic strengths, his naturally keen reflexes? Miller was explicit about this following his first World Cup victory, a giant slalom at Val d'Isère on December 9, 2001—the first GS win by an American man in the World Cup in eighteen years. The Salt Lake City Games were close at hand, and as the pre-Olympic media spotlight shifted toward him, Miller was asked about his recklessness. He said it was inseparable from his ability to ski unlike anyone else.

"It comes from pushing myself in training, pushing myself harder, making mistakes, figuring out how to ski at that level, anticipating mistakes, and learning how to respond in a tough, quick situation," Miller said at the time. "I ski like that all the time and a lot of guys never ski like that. The more you ski like that, the more you get used to it. You learn to adapt."

It was true: when Miller wasn't crashing, he was exceptionally fast. In the thirty-three World Cup slaloms he had managed to complete, he finished on the podium twelve times and won the race five times, often winning runs by huge margins; just weeks before the 2002 Winter Games, when Miller won the tricky slalom at Adelboden, Switzerland, the runner-up was 1.92 seconds slower—a difference greater than the time gap separating second place and twenty-fifth. These numbers reflected what witnesses to those races saw, an athlete with a one-of-a-kind style of skiing—a radical technique, a daring turn shape. Viewed in this light, all the unfinished runs signaled a sort of stubborn patience. Maybe it was the opposite of recklessness. Maybe it took an abundance of self-control to commit to such a costly approach to skiing—to endure the painful crashes and the sneering of naysayers, and not alter the program.

Delayed gratification came to Miller in the 2002 Olympic combined event at Snowbasin, near Ogden, Utah. In the downhill leg, he almost flew off course near the bottom of the Russi-designed Grizzly course;

although his impossibly acrobatic recovery stole the show, Miller finished with a 2.44-second deficit. But Miller nuked the slalom hill, his arms pinwheeling and his torso lurching frantically to keep up with his Fischer skis, which traced a line that no other skier in the world dared approach. Miller took the silver medal. The gold went to Kjetil André Aamodt of Norway, one of the sport's all-time greats, then thirty years old, who promptly anointed the twenty-four-year-old Miller the future of the sport.

"He's revolutionized the way of skiing, as I see it," Aamodt told reporters. "Nobody has ever skied that fast."

Miller, who also won silver in the Olympic giant slalom, left Salt Lake City as skiing's new sensation. Everyone loved the story of the kid from the White Mountains whose flower-power parents, Jo and Woody, had raised their kids in an off-the-grid fantasy camp perched atop a steep and slick mountain path that helped shape their eldest son into such a natural skier.

He signed a million-dollar contract with Rossignol, the venerable French ski equipment manufacturer, and hired New York agent Lowell Taub. Miller published an autobiography written with a family friend, Jack McEnany, that described growing up in a rustic cabin, his parents' divorce, and his early impressions of the World Cup. He was just getting started; over the next two seasons Miller won eight World Cup races, took three medals at the 2003 world championships and narrowly missed the crystal globe twice—the overall title that every top racer most covets. Adoring teenage girls in Slovenia and Austria blogged breathlessly about him on their website, Bodelicious.net. In a profile in *The New Yorker*, Hermann Maier's coach called Maier's new rival *"ein Bewegungstalent"*—a movement prodigy.

Along with the wealth and recognition came endless obligations, which ate up what little time Miller had for reflection and renewal. His contracts with sponsors required him to make appearances at parties and press conferences that separated him from his teammates and opened his life to public scrutiny. The US Ski Team scrambled to learn how to manage the needs of its biggest star in a generation, but Miller was impatient to have a more customized, personal program. He began traveling the tour in a motor home, and arguing more with team administrators. He also lost faith in Rossignol, and switched to Atomic before the 2004–05 season.

From the outside, that was the winter when Miller seemed to finally put all the pieces together. He won seven World Cup races, two world championship golds (downhill and super G), and the overall World Cup title. He had reached the pinnacle of his sport at age twenty-seven. But something was eating at him. In the news conference that followed his clinching the overall title in Lenzerheide, Switzerland, Miller came across as seriously grumpy.

"This might be a springboard to something," he said. "But I don't know where I'd spring to. Maybe just away."

The fact was that Miller felt alienated. His fame and busy schedule had separated him from the things that grounded him: his friends, his solitude. He now had a lifestyle unlike any of his teammates and certainly unlike any of his relatives and friends back in Franconia. But when he explained the realities behind the illusion—the isolation, the energy-draining obligations, favor seekers—he sounded like a whiner. Miller may have been one of the most natural skiers on the planet, but he was also a fish out of water. Raised in a radically anti-consumerist home, he had licensed a video game in his name. Here was a guy who grew up without television but now basically worked in it—television images, after all, were the basic currency underlying the economics of his sport. Miller had grown up around marijuana. But it was on the banned substance list, and now he was frequently required to pee in cups for anti-doping agencies.

A week after winning the 2005 overall World Cup title, Miller came home from Lenzerheide and told Matt Lauer on the *Today* show that he wasn't committed yet to the Torino Olympic Games. When he returned briefly to Franconia, his parents saw a new gloominess around their son. Woody quizzed him about it and learned that Bode felt trapped. Jo was inclined to see it as part of a pattern; it was her observation that her son would grow and expand as a person for a year or so and then hit a plateau, struggle with things, then refocus and succeed. This, however, was not just a plateau, but what his mother later called "a downward type of trip."

Skipping the Olympics would have been a shocking renunciation, and Miller didn't have the wherewithal to do it. In fact, he doubled down for 2006, signing contracts and agreeing to an increasingly complex schedule that all but guaranteed he would not only be racing the next season but also pitching corporate pasta from Barilla and sneakers made in Nike's factories on the other side of the planet. There was plenty to be conflicted about. Bode Miller, the hippie child whose father had once been arrested protesting General Electric's construction of the Seabrook nuclear power plant in New Hampshire, was now earning the majority of his income based on the publicity platform provided by NBC, a subsidiary of General Electric.

That angsty off-season, Miller articulated his personal predicament about the upcoming Torino Games in an interview with *60 Minutes* correspondent Bob Simon for a segment that would air in January.

"If I could put down, you know, unbelievable performances, really inspirational performances that, you know, talk to people's hearts, where people got emotional, and still not come away with any medals, I think that would be the ideal Olympics for me," Miller said.

The 2005–06 season was, for Miller, self-destructive from the very outset. He feuded with his coaches, partied like a wild man, and found ways to insult just about everyone around him. As Torino approached, it seemed like Miller thought being a jerk would make everyone ignore him. First, there was a series of undiplomatic comments he made during interviews in the lead-up to the Games, which included swipes at Lance Armstrong, Republicans, anti-doping agencies, and Austrian skiing great Hermann Maier. Then came his disclosure on *60 Minutes* that he had skied "wasted" at the previous season's World Cup finals. Although Miller uttered most of these remarks months before the Games, during what were otherwise thoughtful sit-down interviews, most of the comments were published in quick succession in the runup to the Olympics, assuring that Miller was the most visible of the 211 athletes named to the US Olympic team that year. In the weeks before Torino, he appeared on the covers of *Time*, *Newsweek*, *Outside*, *Sports Illustrated*, and more.

Then the Games started, with Miller slated to compete in all five alpine skiing medal events at Sestriere. Miller made a risky equipment choice in his first event, the downhill, racing on a pair of skis he had tried only once. He finished fifth, 11 hundredths of a second from the podium. Two days later came the combined, in which Miller won the downhill leg but was disqualified for missing a gate in the slalom. The super G was the real blowout—the race where the slow-motion camera caught him getting so violently twisted around that he averted disaster only because of his catlike recovery instincts.

Along with these costly errors, Miller made mistakes off the slopes: he was seen at night in Sestriere bars with a group that included a former *Playboy* model, and on one of those outings had made an obscene gesture at a photographer, whose picture of it ended up on the AP wire. He had also gone to great lengths to avoid a huge group of American journalists who had waited in the cold at the bottom of the race hill to speak with him after each run, and then chased him through snowbanks and over fences to get his side of the story.

In the giant slalom, Bode hit a pebble in the course and demolished his edge, rendering the ski largely unusable. He managed to finish sixth. In the slalom, five days later, he only made it fifteen seconds down the course before straddling a gate. By then, the pictures of his late-night antics had spread, and there was probably nothing that Miller could have said to avert the deluge of jokes and hate coming his way.

Miller was sincerely unconcerned about the medals, but people in America didn't know what to think of his insouciance. The last shred of good will was exhausted when he found Jim Litke of the Associated Press waiting outside the door of his motor home with a notebook in hand and gave him a remarkable interview. Miller said plenty of sensible things, and Litke quoted him at length in the fine column he wrote, but it included the soundbite, "I got to party and socialize at an Olympic level."

Those ten self-immolating words echoed in a way that they never could have for previous generations of Olympic athletes, instantly generating widespread contempt and becoming a sort of epitaph for Miller's public image. It cemented a perception that Miller hadn't cared about the Olympics at all, and many observers interpreted it as a self-protective copout. People said Miller was lazy, sullen, uninspired, spoiled, and selfish. Alpine skiing couldn't have looked worse.

"Miller has set himself up for much of this," said NBC's Olympic host, Bob Costas, in a rare bit of editorializing during the network's prime-time Torino coverage. "He claims to disdain attention, commercialism, and hype, and Miller will now find out, no matter how he looks at it, if you don't care enough to consistently give your best, and at least sometimes do your best, then pretty soon nobody else will care, either."

The saddest part of all was the fulfillment of Miller's darkest predictions. Over the years, and especially that year, Miller had said repeatedly that he thought the focus on medals was unhealthy and that he wasn't obsessed with them. Now, that longstanding attitude was being interpreted as a deficiency.

"The personification of failure," *USA Today* columnist Christine Brennan called him on national television. "The bottom line is this," said Jon Saraceno of *USA Today*, "Bode Miller is a loser." Sally Jenkins of the *Washington Post* (a friend of Lance Armstrong and a coauthor of two books with him), wrote a withering column that claimed Miller's attitude violated "a basic contract between the Olympic athlete and spectator." *Sports Illustrated*'s Tim Layden, a pressroom beacon of fairness and perspective, wrote that Miller had "disrespected" the Games.

After Torino, Miller took a two-week vacation in Paris and Florida, and then went to the World Cup finals in Sweden where he immediately returned to form, decisively winning the super G and finishing second in the downhill. The rift with his team widened over the year that followed; Miller claimed that the team's strictures held him back, and the team's coaches, particularly Phil McNichol, believed that Bode's customized program conflicted with the needs of the rest of the team, monopolizing the coaches' time and energy.

The situation deteriorated further the following year, when the US Ski Team instituted a series of rules that required all athletes to stay in the team hotel at races, effectively barring Miller from staying in the motor home he had traveled with on the tour since 2003. "The Bode Rules," as they soon became known, rankled Miller's teammates as much as they did Bode himself, and brought the conflict to a head.

One year after Torino, Miller's relationship with the US Ski Team was completely dysfunctional. The final straw came in the spring of 2007, when McNichol asked Miller to "reintegrate" himself with the team and also contribute financially. Miller refused to pay for even a dollar of his own program. With his earning potential and savings, he figured, he might as well start his own team with people he trusted—people who wouldn't place bans on motor homes. After eleven years with the national team, Miller broke away and formed his own independent squad.

"I do not believe I can excel and perform at the level I demand of myself under the guidelines the ski team has presented," Bode said in a statement issued by his agents on May 13, 2007. "I will continue to ski as an American, under the US flag, and am proud to do so."

Miller hired away some of the US team's best people, including downhill coach John McBride and team manager Jenny Holden. His mother's brother came aboard (he was "Uncle Mike" to the entire US team, which he'd been coaching for several years). Miller put his agents, Lowell Taub and Ken Sowles, in charge of rounding up sponsors. Miller funded the staff's travel, outfitted them in uniforms, and set a hyper-personalized strategy for his own success on the World Cup tour. Miller named his project "Team America," in honor of the subversive puppet film by *South Park* creators Matt Stone and Trey Parker.

The gamble was quick to pay off. Miller was electrifying in 2007–08, winning the downhills at Bormio, Wengen, and Kvitfjell, finishing second at the Hahnenkamm and winning the combined there, and taking victories and podiums elsewhere—earning prize money that helped offset the reported half-million-dollar price tag of his solo project. Other national teams were delighted to let him piggyback on their training sessions, or he could go solo. Managing a staff added new responsibilities to Miller's already overburdened winter schedule, but he was exempt from the US team's promotional duties and declined nearly every interview request.

The media blackout was one reason Miller was able to quietly slip away from the World Cup tour for the birth of his daughter. Between starts in two far-flung World Cup races—the first in Croatia on February 17 and the next in British Columbia on February 21—Miller stopped in California to visit the pregnant mother, who promptly went into early labor and delivered the child on February 19, 2008.

Three and a half weeks after that, Miller won the 2008 overall title. A contingent of family members came from Franconia to Europe to celebrate the wildly successful first season of Team America. Throughout the entire season, just to prove that he could do it, Miller had reportedly renounced alcohol, even on his thirtieth birthday. But he partied hard as the season closed out at that year's finals in Bormio, Italy.

The next season, Miller tried to build on the success. He invited some younger US Ski Team castaways to his summer training sessions, and expanded his motor home fleet to include three comfy vehicles that could house his serviceman, coaches, cook, and manager. McBride left for a job with the Canadian team, and Miller elevated a trusted old friend from his ski academy days, Forest Carey, to the lead coaching role.

Then came the unlucky season leading up the demoralizing strikeout at the 2009 world championships in Val d'Isère. Miller was prepared for the 2008–09 season, but things didn't break his way. His fastest downhill skis were used up, debilitated by too many seasons of hard treatment, and the new engineer at the Head factory had trouble replicating them. There were clashes with FIS officials, and then came the ugly crash at Beaver Creek on December 5, when Miller crunched his ankle.

After Val d'Isère, there were plenty of reasons for Miller to take a little vacation someplace warm. Not the least of them was the sensational news that the bad boy of Torino was now somebody's father.

On the weekend of February 28, 2009, Bode Miller skipped another pair of World Cup races, the annual giant slalom and slalom at Kranjska Gora, Slovenia. His absence revived the speculation that his "vacation" was in fact something much more permanent—a sneaky retirement that sidestepped ceremony and explanation. Curious reporters had no one to query but the US Ski Team men's head coach Sasha Rearick, who checked with Team America for an update.

"Bode's enjoying his time at home with his daughter and resting up his ankle," Rearick told the Associated Press. Rearick had extracted that much information from Forest Carey ahead of the Slovenian races, and Carey had told him that Miller's return to snow was now scheduled for March 5, the first training run for a pair of downhills on March 6 and 7 in Kvitfjell, Norway. Rearick relayed that information to the AP: "He will be there for sure," Rearick said.

In San Diego, Miller was in heaven, happily ensconced in a marina that had become his home. He had arrived back from Val d'Isère in time to join Dace and her mother for a trip to Disneyland to celebrate the girl's first birthday. Since then, he'd been spending as much time as possible with his daughter. Now that he had been pulled into Dace's orbit, he realized how tough it had been to stay focused and perform. It had already been a grueling season, with races in eight European countries plus the US and Canada.

It wasn't only Miller's ankle and the poor results at Val d'Isère that had disheartened him, it was the skiing he'd seen from his peers, even from some of the winners. Miller thought it was uninspired and conservative, the work of strategists racing as if they had everything to lose. Miller believed some of his peers were "dumbing down" their skiing to win points, rather than risking it all for the big win or the inspiring effort. Guys were skiing for money, he said, not for the progression of the sport.

"It was a real drag," Miller would say in an interview later. "The top guys, the guys who are winning medals, are winning them by skiing in a way that doesn't touch people at all, that doesn't represent any greater battle, or higher calling or anything like that."

On March 2, 2009, Heinz Hämmerle set out from western Austria for the twenty-hour drive to Kvitfjell, Norway, where three men's World Cup races would be taking place later that week. A taciturn Austrian who had worked for the Head ski company for almost thirty years, Hämmerle was one of the World Cup's most experienced ski servicemen. In the back of his van were the tools of his trade: a table, vises, files, lights, wax, and power drills. There were also two dozen pairs of skis for the two Head skiers assigned to Hämmerle: Bode Miller and Hans Olsson.

Being a World Cup serviceman meant that Hämmerle had mastered the art of tuning skis so that racers could gain an advantage in a sport where victory often came down to a hundredth of a second. It also meant he spent a lot of time behind the wheel, driving from race to race and stopping off at the ski factory in between. This time, the journey would involve a ferry ride across the Baltic Sea to Norway. After the races there he would drive another seven hours north and east into Sweden, for the World Cup finals. Hämmerle wouldn't be back home for three weeks.

Driving straight north on the autobahn, Hämmerle skirted Ulm, Hannover, and Hamburg. He was eager for the Kvitfjell races, knowing that Miller stood a strong chance of winning. A year earlier, he had won one race there and finished second in two others. He assumed Bode was coming to Norway, as did everyone else working for the company.

Support from Head was one of the critical components of Miller's independent team. The company provided Miller with a steady flow of equipment and two servicemen to keep everything properly tuned. The company paid Miller handsomely to use their products, to carry the skis onto podiums, and to rest them on his shoulder during television interviews. An added value was in the research and development input Miller constantly gave when new skis were being built. After his twelve years on the World Cup circuit, on five different ski brands, few people in the world knew more about ski design than Miller.

Even before they'd been paired, Hämmerle had known that equipment was a big part of Miller's career. He skied on the stiffest skis. He made the strangest modifications to his ski boots, and constantly experimented with the placement of the bindings. Yet it was hard for Hämmerle to know Miller—especially this year. Hämmerle hadn't seen him in weeks. Bode had left Val d'Isère claiming he was going to skip a race. Fair enough—the overall title wasn't his priority. But then another week had gone by and Miller had skipped more races. Hämmerle had expected an explanation, but there hadn't been a call. In fact, Miller wasn't telling him anything. It felt a little disrespectful.

Hämmerle was not alone. Nobody seemed to have heard anything from Miller since February 20, when he confirmed the reports that he was a father. He offered no explanation for his absence—no press release, no statement to the cluster of international journalists covering the races. Unlike other top racers, Miller didn't use social media to update fans on his whereabouts and feelings.

Miller's whereabouts were a pressing mystery to many people, including Hämmerle's boss, Rainer Salzgeber, the director of Head skis, who had begun getting so many calls from reporters that he had to turn his phone off. Forest Carey hadn't heard much from Miller either, but he was certain enough that Miller would race in Norway to fly to Europe that week to get Miller's motor home, which since Val d'Isère had been parked near Innsbruck, Austria. It had fallen to Carey to drive the 1,200 miles to Norway.

When Carey arrived, his phone blew up with messages from people wondering where Miller was and when he would arrive in Norway. Carey had even gotten a phone call from Head's owner, Johan Eliasch, the Swedish tycoon who had reinvigorated the company and lured many top racers away from Atomic. Eliasch, a man who advised prime ministers and dated Sharon Stone, had personally called Carey to find out what Miller was thinking. Carey hadn't been able to tell him, because after Bode went AWOL no one was getting through.

Hämmerle, meanwhile, was confident that the quest for the down-hill title—Miller was still very much in the running, only thirty-five points behind the leader, Michael Walchhofer of Austria—would bring Miller back. Hämmerle was ready to do his part. It took him about nine hours in his van to get to Kiel, the north German port town where he would board the ferry to Norway. A few hours on the boat, and he'd have another drive to Kvitfjell. Just before Kiel, Hämmerle stopped for gas, and he saw some World Cup journalists. They told him that Miller wasn't coming to Norway, that his season was over.

That was how the person tuning Miller's skis learned that his services wouldn't be necessary.

Bode Miller's home, in the spring of 2009, was a 1984 Hatteras house-boat he kept docked in the harbor in San Diego, California. It shared qualities with the motor homes he had lived in on the World Cup tour. It seemed that Miller felt most comfortable in accommodations he could use for escape. Perhaps the cozy confines reminded him of the New Hampshire cabin where he'd lived in the paradise of his early childhood.

The fastest American on skis had grown up in an environment of deliberate slowness. In 1974, when Bode Miller's freethinking parents, Woody Miller and Jo Kenney, got married and started their family, they envisioned a simpler, more self-reliant lifestyle, in which they wouldn't rush off in a car to work every day. They decided to build a home off the grid, where they would grow their own food, minimize their consumption and needs, and teach their children to respect the natural world and live in its cycles.

All this might help explain why Miller had always seemed so con-flicted about the success he found at the top of alpine ski racing. By the time he reached the age his parents were when they renounced mate-rialism and went into the woods, Miller could have looked around and seen that he had aligned himself with some of the most extreme man-ifestations of international capitalism.

So while Lindsey Vonn was charging through the end of the World Cup season, Miller was taking a big step back from the ski world, letting his email inbox fill up with people wondering what it all meant for Team America. Deliberate isolation from the sport, Miller felt, was the only way he could assess his motivations and commitment. The new demands and delights of fatherhood had led Miller to pause his career while he considered whether he wanted to return to ski racing at all.

What he knew was that he wanted to spend time with his daughter, Dace. Miller had always been good with children and enjoyed interacting with them, but parenthood was a whole new game. His mother Jo saw him learning what it meant to let a child grow independently, to keep trying things and sometimes fail but to figure them out on their own. Jo's eldest, Bode's older sister Kyla, had three kids, and it thrilled him to be around them, to be reminded that all babies were different, and that their parents were their entire world. For the first time, he was giving serious thought to retirement.

Miller had been a World Cup ski racer for thirteen years—a long career by any standard—and he'd been fully invested in the sport since at least age fourteen. Over time, the pursuit had gotten more and more complex. His career wasn't just about him anymore; for a decade he had been a little corporation, the hub of a circle of agents, equipment technicians, sponsors, and buddies from Franconia in his entourage.

He had been able to customize things for his own comfort and sanity, to surround himself with people he trusted, and, with Team America, to break new ground. But the infrastructure of his racing career made it hard for him to think clearly about retirement—to peel away the considerations of responsibility and sacrifice and focus on the simple question of whether he should ski in 2009–10.

Miller knew better than anyone that the approaching Olympics had the potential to make his life even more complicated if he wasn't careful about his decisions—and even if he was. At the very least, it seemed, he would have to repeatedly address questions about the Olympic medals he hadn't won in Torino.

The Olympics remained inspiring to Miller, a unique chance to narrow his focus and accomplish something special. His two silver-medal performances at the 2002 Games were among his favorite memories. But the 2010 Games also threatened to gobble up all his free time, commoditize his name again, and open his life up to the sports media-sponsor industrial complex.

Miller didn't want his private dramas explored in the way that American Olympic audiences had come to expect. Not that there was a shortage. In the three and a half years since Torino, Miller's brother had suffered profoundly from a traumatic brain injury incurred in a 2005 motorcycle accident. In the spring of 2007, Miller's cousin had died in Franconia in a grisly roadside showdown with a police officer. These painful chapters, along with Miller's turn to fatherhood, might become grist for magazine stories and NBC profiles, and Miller wanted none of that.

It is fair to point out that every American Olympic star faces such sacrifices and finds a way to balance them against the perks that come with representing one's country. This time, three years after Torino, Miller was being extra careful with the emotional calculus, making certain his heart was in it before he signed up for the whole Olympic clusterfuck. If it wasn't, he would just stay in California—maybe sail away on one of the yachts docked along the shore in San Diego.

CHAPTER 4

An American Dynasty

In the end, it took Lindsey Vonn less than an hour to win the 2009 overall World Cup title, the most coveted trophy in ski racing. That was the sum of her finish times in all of her point-scoring runs on the season's long tour: 51 minutes and 39.63 seconds of what could strictly be called ski racing.

The means to that end had been the committment of nearly every waking hour for more than six months, and the non-waking hours too if you counted her careful sleep habits, part of her masterful jetlag management program. By the second week of March, when Vonn got to the World Cup finals in Åre, Sweden, she had been living in hotels and airports almost nonstop since competition began in October. The tour had taken her to thirty-four races in twelve countries. Along the way, Vonn had given hundreds of interviews, tested countless skis and boot configurations, and filled what little free time remained with training and workouts.

The investment paid off. Vonn's 2008–09 winter was arguably the most successful season by any American ever: two world champion-ship golds, the World Cup downhill and super G discipline titles, and nine World Cup wins. The ultimate measure of her achievement were the 1,788 World Cup points she had accumulated by the end of the season's last race on March 14. It was an American record, though the scoring system had been different in the early 1980s, when Phil Mahre and Tamara McKinney won World Cup overall titles. The only other American to win skiing's greatest honor was Bode Miller, and his highest total was 1,648.

Vonn lifted the crystal globe during an awards ceremony that followed the last race. Beforehand, she carefully arranged her uniform and equipment so that all of the sponsor logos were showing. There were wisecracks about being wary of the champagne bottles that were passed around; her hand was healing nicely after the injury a month earlier. Vonn and the winner of the men's title, Aksel Lund Svindal of Norway, clutched their trophies and posed for photographers alongside their coaches and servicemen. The FIS couldn't have picked two better ambassadors, both of them hardworking, articulate, photogenic all-rounders who dispelled the myth that the sport was controlled by the Alpine nations.

Vonn had clinched the title with three races left, but the chase for the men's overall was competitive to the end, with Svindal and Austria's Benjamin Raich going into the last race of the season separated by only two points, 1,009 to 1,007. Svindal was in front, but Raich had an advantage; the final race on March 14 was slalom—Raich's best event and Svindal's worst. Raich failed to finish, and the globe went to Svindal, his second since 2007.

At the close of the 2008–09 season, Austrian skiers had collected 10,740 points to Switzerland's 7,786 (the United States was fifth best, with 4,158, including Miller's contribution). This calculation was for the Nations Cup, and Austria's ownership of it for the previous twenty years was a reflection of the Austrians' having not just a few stars but also a deep bench, with legions of secondary players who cracked the top thirty every week.

Dynasties came and went in Alpine skiing, despite the perception that the Austrians had always dominated. In the 1980s, the Swiss ruled the World Cup, and the French were the team to beat in the tour's early years. Further back in the sport's history, even the British had once been a ski racing powerhouse.

All it took was a few good racers for a national team to rise up the Nation's Cup standings. The Crazy Canucks of the late 1970s and early 1980s, for instance, were a group of Canadian downhillers who fed off each other's triumphs and temporarily unseated Franz Klammer from his throne. And the 1990s saw the advent of the Attacking Vikings, a Norwegian team led by Kjetil André Aamodt and Lasse Kjus, who won big and retired old, leaving a strong legacy in place for their protégé, Aksel Lund Svindal.

Most of these squads made a virtue of being interlopers in the Alps. Outsider status became an empowering force for the teamwork and creativity sometimes missing from the more established central European teams. The trick for all of these programs was to bring a cluster of talented skiers to the top and keep them there long enough to develop the systems and attitudes that bred more success.

The US Ski Team had found this strange alchemy in the years coinciding with Bode Miller and Lindsey Vonn's careers. It wasn't possible to pinpoint how and when it started, but the first glimmer came in 2001, when Daron Rahlves upset the host Austrians by winning the world championship super G. That year's event—the world championships take place every other year—was at St. Anton, hallowed ground for the Austrians, home to their most influential ski school and some of their most beloved racers.

The silence from the vast crowd present that day was widely reported. Rahlves had beaten Hermann Maier and Stephan Eberharter, the two greatest Austrians of that era. A small picture of Rahlves ran the next day on the front page of the *New York Times* recognizing the historic feat. Only four world championship medals had gone to American men in the previous thirty years—four medals in 150 opportunities. The last guy from the States to win a world championship medal had been A. J. Kitt, with a bronze in Japan in 1993.

In the four years after Rahlves's stunner at St. Anton, he and Miller and GS skier Erik Schlopy combined for eight more world championship medals in thirty tries. American women raked in hardware too, confirming the US's reputation among the Alpine skiing nations as a team that rose to big occasions.

In the decade that followed, the United States put forward a golden generation of ski racers. At no time in the team's history had a group of ski racers performed this well for this long. Between 2003 and 2009, the US Ski Team won more world championship medals, more World Cup titles, and more frequent and prestigious World Cup races than at any time in its history. It had taken twenty-eight seasons of World Cup competition for the US Ski Team to earn its one-hundredth victory in 1994. Fifteen years later, the team had nearly doubled that total, ending the 2008–09 season with 198 victories.

The only comparable explosion of victories came in the early 1980s, when brothers Phil and Steve Mahre, the downhillers Bill Johnson and Cindy Nelson, and a powerful women's tech team led by Tamara McKinney, won dozens of World Cup races. In 1981, Phil Mahre became the first American man to win an overall World Cup title, and he repeated in 1982. In 1983, both he and McKinney won overalls, fully legitimizing the Americans on the World Cup circuit. Recognition at home followed with the 1984 Winter Games in Sarajevo, where American skiers won five medals. That record was still standing in 2009.

And that was the rub. The US Ski Team that had flourished in the early 2000s had yet to ratify its success on the Olympic stage, the only category of alpine ski racing that most American sports fans cared about. There was a yawning gap between the US team's stature in the alpine skiing world and the way it was perceived at home, and few people felt that gap as acutely as the team's president and chief executive officer, Bill Marolt.

***

Bill Marolt was six years old when he first encountered the best skiers in the world. It was 1950, and the FIS had finally resumed staging the alpine skiing world championships after the great disruption of World War Two. For the first time, the organization looked beyond Europe for a host resort and settled on Aspen, Colorado, still a rough-and-tumble mining town. When Marolt was born there in 1943, three years before the first chairlift arrived, there were no stop signs on the dirt roads leading out to the ranches like the one his family had just outside town. The Marolt Ranch is now the Aspen Golf Club.

As soon as they were able to walk, the Aspen kids had been hiking up into the mountains around town with wooden skis on their shoulders and racing each other down, taking care not to drop into the open shafts of the defunct silver mines that punctured the hillsides. Marolt, his brothers, and their friends favored Ajax, one of the mountains encircling the little town's gridwork of venerable hotels and saloons. They skied with an enthusiasm that made up for their limited equipment.

When the championships arrived, Marolt was mesmerized by the technique and daring of Zeno Colò of Italy, Stein Eriksen of Norway, Georges Schneider of Switzerland, and Christian Pravda of Austria. Skiing might have been an exotic sport at the time, but for Marolt, these were the great heroes. He was determined to follow in their tracks. The United States didn't win any medals in Aspen, but one American participant who held his own was Gail Spence, a member of the University of Colorado ski team who soon after the championships moved to Aspen, opened a ski shop, and began coaching the Aspen Ski Club, giving a fourth-grade Marolt his first rigorous instruction in ski racing.

The American ski industry was just starting to boom, led by displaced Austrian instructors and entrepreneurial veterans of the Tenth Mountain Division who had learned the sport in preparation for the Allied invasion of Hitler's Alpine strongholds. Ski areas were opening everywhere in America, and Spence's little squad of Aspen racers went farther and farther for competitions, racing in Steamboat Springs, Jackson Hole, Crested Butte—even Terry Peak, South Dakota.

Upon graduating from high school in a class of twenty, Marolt went to the University of Colorado at Boulder, where an eager young coach named Bob Beattie recruited him to ski. It was 1961, and USSA had tapped Beattie to prepare an American team for the 1962 world championships in Chamonix. Beattie was a force of nature who transformed his group into the modern US Ski Team, and Marolt was a member of the original squad—racing in Europe, competing at the 1964 Olympic Games (he finished twelfth in the giant slalom at Innsbruck), and witnessing the birth of the World Cup tour, which Beattie had helped conceive. Years later, Marolt's buddies from those years would form the inner circle that ran US skiing.

Marolt finally put away his race skis to pursue coaching in 1969. That year, he became the head coach of the University of Colorado ski team, a position he held for ten years, leading the Buffaloes to seven national championship titles. In 1979, the US Ski Team named him its director of development, and soon promoted him to alpine director. He led the team through its strong showing at the 1984 Sarajevo Games before returning to the University of Colorado to serve as athletic director. With his wife, Connie, at his side, he coaxed millions from deep-pocketed donors, built a new stadium, expanded women's sports, and got along famously with the fiery, right-wing CU football coach Bill McCartney. In 1990, the Buffs won the national championship.

Meanwhile, the US Ski Team was in a tailspin. After the successful 1984 season, an exodus of veteran racers and coaches, along with some complex administrative restructurings, caused a loss of direction and knowledge. A whole generation of American skiers lost their way on the World Cup. Rock bottom was the 1988 Olympic Games in Calgary, where the US team's best performance was a ninth-place GS finish by Edith Thys.

In the first half of the 1990s, American skiers occasionally won World Cup races, but the team had structural problems. A large and fractious board of directors fell to political infighting, and a dizzying series of chief executives spun in and out of the organization. The turbulence threw the team's finances into disarray and coaches were forced to trim budgets, sometimes in midseason. By 1995, the success of Picabo Street and her teammate, Hilary Lindh, barely masked the rest of the team's struggles. Things were particularly dysfunctional in the men's World Cup technical team; four of its skiers quit midseason, seeing brighter prospects in a small Stateside racing tour unsanctioned by FIS, or in making daredevil descents of huge Alaskan peaks for helicopter-assisted ski movies.

In 1996, a group of USSA's trustees went to Boulder to try to persuade Marolt to leave the University of Colorado and take charge of the organization. There had been previous overtures, offering him a chance to lead the national team, but this time the trustees assured him he'd also have control over the country's entire racing system. As CEO, he could coordinate everything from the World Cup team to youth ski league racing from Maine to Alaska.

After twelve years of transformative work at CU, Marolt decided he was ready for the new challenge. And USSA needed a savior: the team had ended the 1995 season $2.2 million in debt. The job was particularly intriguing because the IOC had just awarded the 2002 Winter Games to Salt Lake City, and most of the skiing events would take place within minutes of the ski team's headquarters in Park City. The new race venues would open up new training opportunities for all the athletes.

When Marolt arrived in the fall of 1996, he put a new goal up on the wall: "Best in the World"—a lofty ambition for a team that had finished behind eight nations, including Slovenia, in the previous year's Nations Cup. At first, it was just an internal motivational tool, but around 2000 the motto started appearing at the bottom of the ski team's press releases and corporate communications. The European teams caught wind of the slogan and laughed, but as the American team steadily improved, that didn't matter. The slogan became a rallying cry for the team's athletes, coaches, and donors.

"It seemed vaguely ridiculous, almost cute, like a doting parent talking about an obviously homely baby," wrote *Ski Racing* editor Tim Etchells in 2003, as the team climbed to third in the Nations Cup. "[Now] it seems more like a masterful psychological ploy."

But the "Best in the World" campaign had its downside. After Torino, the motto had become a problem for the organization, a handy beating stick for critics who saw boastful overconfidence in Marolt's organization. The front page of the *New York Times* had called the team "a flashy, cocky group." The 2006 Olympics, which was supposed to be the consummation of the US Ski Team's extraordinary alpine revival, was a bust.

In addition to Bode Miller's dismal ordeal and Lindsey Vonn's crash, there was Daron Rahlves, who had won at a test event on the Olympic downhill slope at Sestriere two years earlier and led one of the training runs at the Games. On the day of the downhill race, Rahlves fizzled, perhaps in part because of a last-minute decision to run on a pair of untested skis.

The anguish might not have been felt as acutely by the athletes as it was by the coaches, who had invested an enormous amount of energy, imagination, and ego in their jobs, only to be branded as Olympian choke artists at a venue where, truth be told, the race hills weren't even that challenging. After publicly stating a goal of eight medals, the team came away with two. It was, in the words of men's downhill coach John McBride, a "kick in the nuts."

The US team was still wounded a few months later, when Marolt took key members of the staff to the site of the next Winter Olympics for a retreat. In Vancouver, they evaluated what had gone wrong and made plans to fix it—to collect a harvest of medals that would redeem the alpine team in the eyes of a skeptical American public. By the end of the 2008–09 season, the US Ski Team was already three years into a stratagem to make the 2010 Olympics the most successful in the team's history.

The plan didn't include Bode Miller. It was built principally around some of the racers who were heirs to his innovations, but had become stars in their own right on the World Cup tour. Two of them were Ted Ligety and Julia Mancuso, a pair of young skiers who had won gold medals in Torino—Mancuso in the giant slalom, Ligety in combined.

Both these racers had stepped up in the years after the 2006 Games, and both of them experienced a pivot of fortunes in the final week of March 2009, as the competition season wound down in the Chugach Mountains of Alaska.

For the alpine skiers on the US Ski Team, the end of every season is punctuated by the US national championships, a series of races in each discipline for men and women that rotates annually between a small number of resorts including Winter Park, Colorado, Squaw Valley, California, and Lake Placid, New York. The 2009 event was at the Alyeska Resort near Girdwood, Alaska. The event would later be remembered as the Volcano Nationals because of the concurrent eruption of Mount Redoubt, which spewed volcanic ash all over the ski area, dry on wet—just the earth's molten core reminding the ski racing world that geology made this all possible.

A half hour southeast of Anchorage, Girdwood is an unpretentious little cluster of cabins, including one that figured prominently in the criminal trial of the former US senator Ted Stevens (he was accused of underreporting renovations). The skiing is beautiful and similar in one respect to Whistler Mountain, 2,000 miles to the southeast and the site of the alpine skiing events for the Vancouver Olympics: both mountains are extremely close to the ocean. At Alyeska, a tidal inlet is visible from the race hill. Such proximity to the sea means that sudden storms can roll in, lifting moisture from the ocean and depositing it on the mountain as heavy, wet snow. The potential danger for ski racers is great; a racer pressuring his or her edges too hard in these conditions is liable to blow out a knee, or worse.

No sooner had the racers moved into the big hotel at the base of the mountain than a series of storms rolled in and dumped high-moisture snow on the race hill, forcing the cancellation of training runs on March 25 and 26, and of the national championship super G race on Friday, March 27. Sidelined, the racers found opportunities for amusement in the nationals' traditional last-day-of-school atmosphere. Each year, the US Ski Team's A Team, B Team, and C Team are there, along with a hundred or so top young racers who are striving to join them, many missing a chunk of their senior, junior, or even sophomore years of high school in Vermont or California. Historically, the mix includes some NCAA champions, some kids who don't appear to ever go to any school at all, and even some Canadian invitees.

Over the previous decade, American ski racers had rarely promoted themselves as national champion—it was a devalued distinction. Now that an ever-increasing number of US athletes were distinguishing themselves on the World Cup tour, at the world championships, and at the Olympics, they were coming home tired, loaded with prize money, and ready to relax. They came to the national championships because they had to—except for Bode Miller, who for years hadn't bothered to attend. The nationals still mattered hugely to junior racers, as an audition before the US team coaches, who were weeks from making roster selections for the coming season. But the dirty secret was that at nationals, the best US racers sometimes sabotaged their runs, which helped boost the world rankings of the junior racers who stepped up and did well there.

Yet Alyeska was no beginner's slope as Ted Ligety learned on March 28, when the weather cleared and organizers scheduled a training run on a truncated version of the men's downhill course, moving the start down the mountain and mobilizing volunteers to haul as much snow as possible out of the race track.

Just before his run, Ligety was talking trash with twenty-year-old Tommy Biesemeyer from upstate New York, vowing to outrace the young upstart. After Ligety pushed out of the start and built up some speed, he entered the first turn, leaning forward to carve his ski into the super-soft snow. He felt his skis dig in and meet just enough resistance to halt his lower body's movement down the slope as his upper body sailed over the tips of his skis. The momentum carried him into a violent, pinwheeling crash that bloodied his face, and, somewhere amid the tumbling, bent his right knee at an unnatural angle. As ski patrollers arrived and loaded him into a toboggan, Ligety knew something was unstable between his femur and his tibia.

At the hospital, imaging tests on his right knee revealed ruptures of two ligaments, the medial collateral and posterior collateral, as well as bruising of the bone on his tibial plateau, a weight-bearing area on the top of the shinbone. The injury wouldn't require surgery—the more important anterior cruciate ligament was unharmed—but Ligety would be confined to a straight-leg brace for eight weeks. Instead of spending the spring mountain biking in southern Utah and then getting on skis in the early summer, Ligety would be in physical therapy, much of it involving tedious long walks on a treadmill. His injury was an unpleasant surprise to the US Ski Team, given what an important symbol he and his success were for the team heading into the Olympic season.

All told, more than 70 inches of snow fell on Alyeska in seven days at the US nationals, along with an inch or so of volcanic ash. Most of the top skiers, accustomed to World Cup ice, moved tentatively on the untrustworthy surface, while the younger skiers in the back of the pack waged battles with enormous ruts. The racer who most prospered in the poor conditions was the twenty-five-year-old Californian, Julia Mancuso.

Mancuso finished second in the downhill and third in slalom. The final race of the series was the giant slalom; 17 inches of snow fell in the twenty-four hours leading up to the March 30 race, and Mancuso won it. The result was a breakthrough, her first victory of any kind in two years. Since 2007, Mancuso had been mired in an abysmal slump, and she had closed out the most recent World Cup season ranked twenty-seventh in the overall standings, her best result a sixth-place GS finish. It seemed natural that Mancuso finally returned to form in a blizzard, conditions that mirrored those Mancuso had grown up in while learning to ski in Squaw Valley, the rugged Lake Tahoe resort that is home to some of the world's best skiers.

Squaw Valley wasn't a country club mountain, where you got a little fold-up map and decided on a wide-open trail through the forest. At Squaw, you designed your own route through varied topography, taking the legendary KT-22 chairlift up and traversing a long ridgeline from which you could choose any one of a thousand lines down through a wilderness of rocky outcroppings and trees. Much of it was inaccessible to the grooming machines that smoothed the surface of the intermediate runs. It was unmappable.

For Mancuso, who was skiing the whole mountain by age five, devotion to skiing was a byproduct of family trauma; in 1989 her father, a prominent local developer, was jailed for participating in a $140-million marijuana smuggling operation. Ciro Mancuso served two prison terms, one for seventeen months and another for four years. In between, he and Julia's mother, Andrea, were divorced. "When it first happened, I was young and I didn't understand what was going on. Then my dad was home for a long time before he had to finish out the rest of his sentence," Mancuso would recall many years later. "To be honest, being a kid with your parent in jail for a non-violent crime, when you go visit him, you're like, this is the stupidest thing ever."

Julia and her older sister, April, found solace in skiing—a lot of it; Julia was skiing four or five days a week by age eleven, when her father began his second jail term. She would be picked up from school at noon and dropped off at the lifts to ski until four.

There was a rich ski racing culture at Squaw, site of the 1960 Winter Games, but the real focus was on freeskiing—especially when storms rolled into the Sierra Nevada mountains that ringed the town. Powder days were serious at Squaw. Everyone there knew the best skiing happened just after a big overnight snowstorm, when a deep cushion of freshly fallen snow would cast a mysterious hush over everything in town, muffling even the early-morning thumps of the explosives that ski patrollers detonated high up on the mountain to trigger controlled avalanches. When the mountain opened and the hordes of hardcore skiers who congregated at dawn started going up the lifts, everything accelerated. There was only so much mountain; the powder was going to get tracked out—its pillowy softness compressed by the passage of so many skiers and snowboarders. No matter how much fun you were having, you had to hurry.

This was the origin of an old adage that Julia Mancuso had heard often while growing up there: *There are no friends on a powder day.* It was a familiar mantra of the ski bums who came down off the hill after that incomparable first run, their faces frozen in joy, and carried all their momentum into the chairlift line rather than pausing even for a minute to look back up at their tracks. There was still more powder up there on that beautiful mountain, and if their companions had fallen they didn't want to know about it.

"No friends" was both a justification and a warning, and it was hugely beneficial for your skiing. Even if your crew was the most precious thing in the world to you, leaving them aside kept you on your game. It made you a little more prepared for every day on the mountain. It forced you to locate that outer limit of your abilities, to take only calculated risks, constantly evaluating just how fast you could push this powder-day pace and not step into catastrophe. It was a very personal thing, finding the confidence to get aggressive on mountains as intimidating as Squaw Valley's six peaks.

For Julia Mancuso, the axiom might have been amended this way: *There are no big sisters on a powder day.* Some of the world's best skiers were based at Squaw Valley in the mid-1990s—skiers who went all over the world getting filmed from helicopters while they made harrowing first descents, skiers who appeared in magazines like *Powder*, skiers who won Olympic races. But none of them loomed larger in Julia's mind than her big sister, April.

By age fifteen, April Mancuso was regarded as a ski star. She competed internationally and got free equipment from the ski companies. The US Ski Team invited her to summer training camps to ski alongside Picabo Street. But where April really made heads swivel was at home, freeskiing at Squaw, divebombing the mountain with a fearless group of big local boys from the Squaw Valley Ski Team. April was right there with them, unafraid to point her skis downhill and launch herself off cliffs like Adrenaline Rock, a 60-foot drop where you didn't land on the snow below so much as burrow deep into the center of a giant crater.

Trying to keep up with April on powder days did for Julia what gate training under Alan Kildow's supervision did for Lindsey Vonn. Julia chased her sister everywhere. At Squaw, the route to the best snow often went through narrow chutes that dropped like elevator shafts, funneling the snow into wide, open bowls. The only way to get into some of them was to wiggle your way out onto a tiny ledge past a point of no return where the earth fell away. As you plunged in, the granite walls shot by you on both sides, encouraging you to go straight and try to stay upright.

Trying to keep up with April and the boys in such terrain took Julia beyond the comfort of her abilities, forcing her to improvise as she went, using every muscle to stay upright and keep moving. Rather than making the same exact moves turn after turn on a hard-packed trail, Julia was following her sister's tracks down near-vertical headwalls, ducking tree branches and veering around boulders, often in a snow-storm so thick that it was hard to tell where the clouds ended and the earth began. "Cold smoke" they called it. Julia couldn't rely on her eyes; she had to feel her way down the mountain with her feet, learning the different sensations that the varieties of snow produced underfoot—the scrape of the month-old base under six inches of new fluff, the tug of resistance at her shin telling her that an overnight wind had formed a crust on top of yesterday's snowfall.

Even when Julia wasn't trying to hit jumps, covering jagged terrain at such high speeds sent her skyward all the time. Sometimes she'd be floating through the powder when she saw a boulder or a cliff rushing up to meet her. Survival meant jamming in a quick turn, and that meant getting her feet onto something solid to pivot against, and that meant extending her body and feeling with her ski for the ground like a nervous swimmer testing the water with a toe—then finding it, dropping into a crouch, and springing sideways just in time to sail past the obstacle and glimpse April and the guys disappearing around the next bend.

This skiing education was probably the source of the balance that made Julia Mancuso, in the years that followed, one of the best ski rac-ers in the country. Training with the Squaw Valley Ski Team, she skied every discipline, rapidly mastering the technique and tactics of each, but skiing at Squaw added an unteachable element to her moves, the soft touch she'd gained chasing her sister through the chutes. There was a certain looseness to her skiing, even on a race course. By age thirteen, Julia could make nine turns down a face, slicing clean arcs into the ice where other racers skidded, but if the tenth turn called for letting her skis drift, Julia could relax and let her skis float softly over the surface of the snow until she needed to engage the edge again and sail forcefully across the hill.

CHAPTER 5

Live Free or Die

ode Miller wasn't at the 2009 national championships in Alyeska, but just before those races commenced he had made his first public appearance in more than a month, popping up on cable television for the March 17 episode of Bryant Gumbel's monthly newsmagazine show, *HBO Real Sports*. Miller had all but frozen out the media for the two years he'd led Team America, but he had chosen to grant the show a rare glimpse inside his world, with access to his childhood home in New Hampshire and to his motor homes on the World Cup tour. He also sat for a series of interviews with the segment's producer, Jon Frankel, who asked the most important question of all: did Miller intend to race in Vancouver?

"Right now I feel like it would be a terrible decision to race in the 2010 Games," Miller said. "The least that I'll deal with will be the whole thing from '06 again."

Competing in Vancouver, Miller said, would set him up for misery. Meanwhile, the show aired clips of Miller's travails in Torino and the searing media coverage that followed. Miller said it had been costly to manage other people's expectations in 2006.

"I put a huge amount of energy into trying to tell people who I was and how I was and why I didn't feel like I was going to win five medals," Miller said. "And why I didn't really care if I did win five medals or not, so that they wouldn't think I was a dick when I didn't win five medals and said, 'Hey, I'm not that bummed out about not winning five medals.'"

Miller said he was proud of the two silvers that he had won at the 2002 Games in Salt Lake City, and the records that he had set in US skiing. He said he believed that Americans generally liked winners— and forgave them—and stated flatly that no one in the world could beat him when he skied at his best. He acknowledged that he could win more races if he "dumbed down" his skiing, but said that wouldn't be "a pure exhibition" of his skills.

And he said he didn't regret anything about 2006.

"If I'd won medals, would it have been different? Yeah. Would it have been better, I doubt it," Miller said. "I just don't feel like I have anything to prove in that area. I wouldn't change what I did. Of course, does it suck to get criticized and be called the worst things? Yeah, it sucks, but you have to accept that people don't know."

At the end of the segment, Frankel asked if, despite everything Miller had told him about his system for valuing success (which aligned neatly with what Miller had been telling everyone on that subject for many years), it wouldn't be nice to finally win an Olympic gold medal.

"It seems like you haven't heard a single thing I've been saying," Miller said.

Frankel started to respond, but Miller cut him off.

"No," he said. "A gold medal is going to mean nothing to me. Less than nothing, actually. It devalues so much that I've already done and it adds nothing."

Frankel protested that in fact he had been listening to Miller, but was only wondering if Miller, at this late stage in his career, had had an epiphany, a sudden realization that he wouldn't be able to race forever and that there were still things he wanted to accomplish in the sport.

"I had that epiphany when I was eight," Miller said. "And I've lived life the way I have. That's exactly what I've been talking about this whole time. There *are* some things I want to accomplish, and they've been what I've been focused on. They've been what I've been doing the whole time, and it's been awesome. It's been exactly what I wanted."

Skiing runs deep in Bode Miller's family. The woods where he grew up contain the ruins of a failed ski resort that his maternal grandparents tried to start in the late 1940s. Jack and Peg Kenney were an enterprising couple who in 1946 bought an old farmhouse and barn on 450 acres of mostly wooded land on the side of Kinsman Mountain, near Franconia, New Hampshire.

Shortly after they acquired the land, Jack built a rope tow and began charging customers to use it. But the little operation was never able to compete with Cannon Mountain, the rugged ski area about six miles away, with its famed tramway, or Mittersill, an adjacent ski area that boasted famous ski instructors imported from Switzerland and Austria.

Instead, the Kenneys converted their land and its buildings into a summer sports getaway: a residential tennis camp with dormitory cabins, knowledgeable instructors, and, of course, Jack and Peg Kenney, charismatic and adventurous. By the 1960s, the Tamarack Tennis Camp was thriving, drawing clientele from all over the country to play on the Kenneys' clay courts.

A profound love for nature, particularly forests, had drawn Bode's father, Woody Miller, to the area. Relieved to bail out on an unfulfilling medical career in 1974, he found more joy and purpose giving tennis lessons around New England, which was how he met Jo Kenney, the eldest of Jack and Peg's five children. The summer Woody came to work as an instructor at Tamarack, Jo had come home from Boston University to help her parents run the camp.

The Vietnam War was raging and they were passionately opposed to it. Woody found a novel way out of the draft. Playing tennis in 1966, he'd injured his elbow trying to hit a backhand volley; now he deliberately aggravated it until his elbow was so messed up that the army was forced to reject him.

Jo and Woody were both independent-minded people, but they saw themselves as part of the back-to-the-land movement that flourished amid America's countercultural upheavals in the 1960s. Their guiding text was *Living the Good Life*, Helen and Scott Nearing's 1954 manifesto on self-sufficiency.

In 1974, Jo and Woody set out to build the cabin in the woods where Bode would spend his childhood. This might have been an ambitious plan even if they'd chosen a less extreme climate. The winters in Franconia were mercilessly long and cold and the summers could seem tropical there in the evergreen forest.

They were inspired by the distinctive house that Jo's parents had built elsewhere on the property—a tall, angular structure. They aimed to build something smaller farther up in the woods, on a steep slope made irregular with ridgelines. Hiking up to it, one passed through a second-growth forest of cedar, ash, hemlock, birch, maple, poplar, and balsam fir.

They selected a relatively level spot about three quarters of a mile from the road, close to a small mountain stream that fed the Ham Branch of the Gale River. When they thinned the woods, saving many of the logs for building material, they noticed that the knoll in the center of the clearing looked like the head of a turtle poking out from its shell. They named the place Turtle Ridge.

The first house they built was a two-story dwelling, 12 feet by 15 feet, with a trapezoidal façade that dropped right down to the edge of the stream. Their first winter there was 1974–75, the year that Bode's sister Kyla was born. Bode arrived in 1977, and two other siblings followed: Genesis Wren Bungo Windrushing Turtleheart Miller and Nathaniel Kinsman Ever Chelone Skan Miller. The house expanded with each addition to the family, winding around a central stone chimney and then stretching up along the edge of the stream. It came to resemble something from a Doctor Seuss book—multifaceted and shaggy, with alcove porches and roofs sloping in every direction. The interior was a cozy warren of skylighted lofts, irregular passages, and hand-built staircases. The log posts holding it up—debarked spruce trees that had grown within a few hundred feet of the house's location—were worn smooth. Their living brothers and sisters stood a few feet from the windows, making Turtle Ridge feel like the world's ultimate treehouse. A giant boulder incorporated into the floor plan domed up in the middle of the house, a glacier-deposited piece of furniture.

A log across the stream was their bridge to an outhouse (more than once, the spring runoff washed it away). Nearby they built a sauna, and after working outside in cold, damp weather, it was a luxury to climb inside the structure, which looked like a little spaceship in their yard.

Just as city kids know the outline of every crack and bulge in the sidewalk on their street, so Bode and his siblings learned every contour of streambed and footpath radiating out from the house. The brook spilling past their door pooled and dropped through a scalloped bed of metamorphic rocks. It was lined by ferns and moss, and some of the pools were wide enough to skate on in winter. Jo and Woody let their children play in the streambed, believing that the only way a child could discover his or her balance was to challenge it.

Bode and his siblings were encouraged to explore the world around them and their place in it. There was no television and Jo homeschooled them. Visitors would come by to help out with some project, stay for dinner and a session in the sauna. The family would make trips down to the road for groceries and supplies or to do laundry. At the center of their world were Jo's parents, accepting people who also loved sports and children. Bode came of age in a milieu that reflected not just the activist spirit of the Flower Power generation but also old-fashioned New England thriftiness. Mixed in with all that was a sense that sports were a serious endeavor—the family business, in a way.

The goal of moving into the woods had been to simplify their existence. This sounded romantic, but it took doing. Years later, stories about Bode's upbringing would unfailingly note the lack of plumbing and electricity, but the more consequential thing, in the long winters, was the absence of an oil furnace; the house was heated entirely by a wood-burning stove, which required constant attention. They often fell short of their goal of having a full winter's supply of firewood cut, split, stacked, covered, and seasoned, and would scavenge dead wood from the forest.

The main access to Turtle Ridge was a crooked old logging road too steep and overgrown to ever think of driving on it. The path was lined with hemlocks and ladyslippers. In the winter you could ride a sled down it all the way to the road. Ideally, after a heavy snowfall, the sledders would follow the same track, deepening and smoothing out a channel in the snow. Bode and his siblings became adept at the descent, using the trail's banks and pitches like a bobsled track to maximize their speed.

Bode's parents had no doubt that this trail was where Bode developed the foundation of his skiing abilities—not just on the descent, but while hiking up it in the winter, when the trail got icy and slick, requiring just the kind of balance and recoveries that would become Bode's specialty.

Jo would also point to the brook that rushes past the cabin, where she let Bode and her other children run barefoot over the rocks. It was important to allow children room to test their own boundaries, she would say. She spoke of the groundedness great skiers had, which she defined as "feeling that connection between your body and the earth, and having respect for both of them."

CHAPTER 6

The Blueprint

Since 1974, the United States Ski Team has been based in Park City, Utah, a former mining town tucked cozily into a sun-soaked valley high up on the gentler side of the Wasatch Mountains. Long and slender ridgelines drop steeply into canyons where elk still occasionally roam through the aspen glades and wildflower meadows. In winter, storms roll across the Nevada desert, collect moisture above the Great Salt Lake and slam into the 12,000-foot-high Wasatch Front, depositing the world's lightest and driest powder.

The winter's snow was still clinging to the three ski areas that surround the town in early April 2009, when the US team's coaches convened at headquarters to design their master plan for the coming winter. It was an annual ritual, a weeklong gathering where the coaches hashed out rosters, staff, schedules, budgets, and goals. This year the planning session was especially charged, with the Vancouver Games just ten months away. For three years, the team had been plotting to avenge the Torino debacle, raising the stakes for every member of the organization.

The US Ski Team is an evolving thing, a coed fraternity that slowly changes as athletes cycle through it, some staying for a decade, others for less than a year. To compare it to other elite American sports franchises, you have to understand a few salient facts. It has no owner. It doesn't pay salaries to the athletes on its roster. It can't trade those athletes away. And it isn't part of any nationwide league in which rival teams challenge it on a more or less equal basis.

The team, in fact, is the most visible piece of the USSA, the only organization the US Olympic Committee recognizes as the sport's national governing body. Unlike most other national ski associations under the FIS umbrella, USSA has never received substantial funding from its national government. Instead, every year the team's administrators work to gather millions of dollars from corporate sponsors and private donors.

The donors, who might otherwise give their expendable millions to a university or charity, get a tax write-off and, for the right price, can go beyond the crowd-control fences at the races, perhaps raising a champagne flute with the team staff during one of the intimate toasts that follow a World Cup victory. The corporate sponsors pay USSA for the right to put their logos on ski team uniforms and to use the skiers' likenesses in their company's advertising materials. The companies pay big money to be the official airline of the US Ski Team, or its official credit card or granola bar.

Each of the team's athletes signs an agreement granting USSA the right, with some restrictions, to raise funds by selling the athlete's "name, picture, likeness, voice and biographical information." An addendum identifies specific companies to which USSA promises categorical exclusivity; if in a given year Pepsi were to be the team's cola "partner," no individual athlete could strike up a personal endorsement deal with Coke. For the team's few stars, the agreement is a hindrance (it helped spur Bode Miller's drive for independence), but for the vast majority of the team, signing the agreement each year is a no-brainer. While the athletes don't earn a salary from USSA, the season-long training and racing program the team provides is worth several hundred thousand dollars to each skier.

While Olympic amateurism in its pure form is a thing of the past, and while top skiers like Lindsey Vonn can make millions, the earning potential drops fast. Most team members collect only a pittance, cobbling together prize money and endorsement deals with small companies. Being on the road up to ten months a year eliminates any hope of holding a steady job. Some racers and their families stage their own fundraising efforts. Others manage to squeeze in summer college classes. Most make it well into adulthood earning only a few thousand dollars a year.

It all seems unfair at first glance, given the $30 million in gross revenue USSA might pull in each year from its benefactors. But then you see what the team spends on the racers, which is what the coaches figure out at the April planning meetings in Park City. With spreadsheets and dry-erase boards, calendars and maps, the coaches carve up the alpine budget into thousands of necessary expenditures.

The costs begin running up in the summer, with training camps in the wintry southern hemisphere. Dozens of athletes fly to New Zealand and Chile and stay in hotels for two or three weeks. Joining them there are not just coaches but physios—the team physiologists who help remedy nagging injuries and monitor conditioning programs. Those staffers need salaries as well as travel expenses. So do the equipment technicians (the ski companies only provide that service to the top athletes).

If you are a coach, you can expect big bills for baggage fees, van rentals, fuel, food, and training space. You need hardware like gates, fencing, timing equipment, and walkie-talkies. You need video cameras and software to analyze the footage. Inevitably, your skiers get hurt and you need to book them short-notice flights home for medical care. Sometimes a snowstorm or a heat wave makes the training lousy, and you have to move the whole team to another mountain. And that's just summer. When October rolls around the team goes to Europe, where the costs skyrocket.

From October to March, the US team foots the bill for dozens of athletes to tour the world, often staying in the most exclusive resorts. The FIS subsidizes accommodations on the World Cup tour, but between races the teams are on their own, leaving the Americans often staying in chalets or airport hotels while their European competitors dash home.

There are highway and tunnel tolls, gasoline is heavily taxed, and cell phones are always roaming. Even when the coaches plan the trips well, a dearth of snow at one mountain or a surplus of wind or fog at another forces organizers to cancel a race at the last minute or reschedule it for a different date, a different mountain. The teams suddenly have to modify ten or more flight reservations. The endless and often thankless job of managing these logistics falls to the US team's coaches. When asked about their biggest challenge, they frequently point to the conflicting priorities of supporting the team's veterans and preparing the team's future stars. How do you know when to shift resources to a nineteen-year-old with great promise?

In April 2009, the men's team coaches were all rooting for Scott Macartney, a thirty-one-year-old Dartmouth College graduate from Washington state. In January 2008 he had spent more than a day in a coma after a hideous crash at Kitzbühel, but came back the next year and had been on track to revisit the Streif course in 2009 when he blew his knee out at Wengen. Now, in 2010, he was finally going to get his chance to get back on the courses that threw him and possibly compete in the Olympics.

But then, there was a strong imperative to bring the next generation along—guys like Travis Ganong, a twenty-one-year-old rookie out of Squaw Valley. Ganong was ranked 176th in the world in downhill. His chances of being one of the four downhillers the US team would enter in February's Olympic downhill were slim. In 2014 he might have a shot; for that, he needed experience.

There were enough resources for the men's team to take both Macartney and Ganong on the downhill tour, but Jeremy Transue was another story. Transue was from Hunter Mountain in New York's Catskills, where his father was the mountain manager. He was twenty-six, but in his seven years with the team, Transue—known to all his teammates as "Worm"—had undergone ten surgeries, mainly to his knees. He'd made it unscathed through the 2008–09 season, just barely requalifying for the team, and Vancouver was a long shot at best. Sasha Rearick had given him a motivational ultimatum: if he wasn't finishing in the top thirty in December, he would be left at home in January, healthy or not.

All these permutations made selecting the members of the national team the most delicate task of all for the coaches at the April conclave in Park City. While the majority of the roster would be veterans, others would be newcomers, called up from the more than three hundred USSA clubs that formed the US Ski Team's development pipeline. These were ski teams based at mountains, ski academies, and, very occasionally, colleges and universities. The best racers they put forth are ranked in the same FIS system that dictated Olympic qualification and national team selection criteria.

Alpine skiing is brutally mathematical. Advancement is sorted through a unified points system in which every new racer starts with 990 FIS points in each discipline, which are shed through good results. As junior racers climb through the intermediate tiers—the regional races, college circuits, the Europa Cup—there are weekly opportunities to lower their FIS points. A complex formula ensures that results are weighted according to the strength of the field of competitors.

Generally speaking, if you have your FIS points under 50 by the end of high school, you stand a decent chance of racing for an NCAA college team—a good one if your points are under 25. If you are a seventeen-year-old racer with under 30 points, you are probably getting at least some free equipment through sponsorships, as companies bet on your projected success and marketing value.

The FIS points system, continuously updated on the organization's website, ranks racers against every other FIS athlete in the world, including the best skiers on the World Cup circuit, who have close to zero points and have long since shifted their focus to accumulating World Cup points for the tour's standings.

Qualifying for the US Ski Team is largely about getting your points below a certain level in more than one discipline. The cutoffs change over time, but generally a racer needs to get his or her points under 20 to make the US team. Like schoolteachers resentful of the tyranny of grades and test scores, ski coaches across the country struggle to persuade ambitious young racers that, although FIS points are a necessary yardstick, it is far better to focus on underlying skills than outward measurements.

At least one American world champion's points were marginal at best before age eighteen. In 1996, the year Bode Miller qualified for the US Ski Team, his FIS points in downhill were 92.61. He had never been picked for the FIS world junior championships or invited to train with the national team. His unlikely avenue to the US Ski Team was the first chapter in his legend, and a cautionary tale that true talent doesn't always reveal itself in the ranking lists.

Bode Miller's unlikely path to the US Ski Team began at Cannon Mountain, an old-school ski area in Franconia Notch. Though his earliest skiing took place on the sloping field behind his family's tennis camp, Cannon's steep trails became his second home growing up. When Bode and his siblings were little, their mother often dropped them off there to ski on their own in lieu of day care. Jo figured they'd burn off energy, encounter the natural world, and either make friends or be their own company.

Learning to get an edge into the snow was a matter of survival at Cannon, where the winding trails were often glazed with ice. Bode was making do with borrowed or hand-me-down equipment, skis that were too long for him and boots that were so big he had to pay strict attention to his balance lest he tip forward or backward, fall on the ice, and slide into the trees. Often he was forced to use his whole body to make a turn, jumping up to unweight himself and twisting his lower body to swing his skis around so they were pointing in the other direction.

Most of this improvising was unsupervised. For a few years, Miller was part of the Franconia Ski Club, a USSA racing team, but the first in a lifetime of clashes with coaches brought that to an end, and Miller learned to ski on his own, coaching himself through the complex negotiations between his body and gravity that formed the foundation of his skiing style. It was in those years, he would later say, that he discovered his turn.

Naturally, the discovery happened while he was skiing fast. A lot of the time he spent at Cannon, Miller was crouched low in the classic tuck position, his arms outstretched and his crappy skis rattling on the hard snow, moving so fast that the wind dragged tears from his eyes and froze them in the corners of his goggles. The ski patrollers at Cannon, having witnessed the human wreckage of too many collisions, were on alert for Bode, ready to chase him down and confiscate his lift pass for recklessness.

But the speed wasn't just about thrills; Bode found that the faster he went, the better he understood the physics of skiing, because these concepts announced themselves in his flesh. Skiing fast, as all skiers learn, amplifies the natural forces at work in the sport. Your legs thrum with the kinetic friction of your skis displacing snow. You struggle to keep your arms and torso from twisting in the sluggish, resistant air. All these forces combine in infinite permutations on every fast run. Bode learned early that if he could suppress his fear enough to listen to them, and adjust his body and his path to anticipate their effects, he could use them to do things that most skiers never imagined.

When Bode was fourteen, he lost the chief sponsor of his nascent skiing career: his grandmother, who died of brain cancer in 1992. Peg Kenney had supported her grandson's downhill truancy, buying him season passes at Cannon each winter and letting him partly repay her later with money he earned from summer jobs repairing tennis courts. Her death came at a turbulent time in the Miller household. Jo and Woody had split up, and Woody went away for a bit, leaving Jo to raise the kids at Turtle Ridge. She was piecing together various streams of income, helping run the tennis camp in the summer and in the winters sewing buttonholes on nightgowns for a local clothing company. Her annual income didn't exceed $10,000 a year.

In part because Bode was still crazy about skiing, Jo took a receptionist job at Cannon, where one of the employee perks was free season passes for the entire family. Bode continued to ski daily (and snowboard too), bombing around the mountain with an older crowd and catching rides back home at the end of the day. The future world champion might have languished in that milieu if not for the creativity of John and Patty Ritzo, old friends of the Kenney clan. While teaching and coaching skiing at a nearby prep school years earlier, Ritzo had watched Bode skiing at Cannon and saw promise in the boy's self-taught technique. Five years later, he was the headmaster of Carrabassett Valley Academy in Maine; remembering Bode's funky turns and knowing that resources were dear at Turtle Ridge, Ritzo called Jo and told her he was in a position to offer Bode a scholarship.

CVA was a ski academy. Students carried full course loads in the fall and spring so that their winter schedules could accommodate training and racing. Located near the town of Kingfield, at the base of Sugarloaf Mountain, CVA was a top feeder program for the US Ski Team. It was expensive, but Ritzo suggested a living arrangement that would save Bode from boarding fees as well as adjustment issues; he could live 20 miles from the campus with Sam Anderson, another scholarship student, who lived with his mother in a woodstove-heated log cabin accessible in the winter only by snowmobile.

In his freshman year at CVA, Bode was exposed for the first time to the kind of sophisticated instruction that most top ski racers had encountered at a much younger age. For the first time, he was training alongside a group of older peers whose varied abilities placed them on every step of the US skiing development pyramid. Some had sponsorships from ski companies. Others had raced in the national championships. They wore coats and fleeces embroidered with the names of USSA's elite regional teams. They had raced around the country, sometimes in Europe, always under the close supervision of coaches who alerted them to bad habits of body position and timing.

At CVA, skiing was a regimented endeavor. Every day during winter, a fleet of vans and buses shuttled students up to nearby Sugarloaf, where roped-off trails were reserved for their training courses. A group of older boys preparing for speed races in Montana might train downhill from 7–9 a.m., then return to the school as a group of girls set out for slalom training in advance of a weekend series in Vermont. In the evening, groups would reconvene to analyze video, with coaches slowing down the tape of each run to a frame-by-frame crawl.

With his secondhand equipment and self-generated carving technique, Bode stood out for the wrong reasons. The freeze-frame images of him were among the most ungainly. With his arms swinging wildly and his weight rocking back on his heels, he was the antithesis of Alberto Tomba, whose disciplined, forward-driving style his classmates sought to mimic. What Bode had going for him, coaches and classmates would later recall, was an ironclad confidence derived in part from his natural athleticism. Bode excelled on the soccer field and tennis courts, could dunk a basketball, was adept on a skateboard, and could throw a football on a level plane with either hand. He was hardwired for sports, and few things illustrated it more clearly than his instant mastery of one of the school's autumn conditioning rituals: upstream runs through the riverbed of the mostly dry Carrabassett River.

The river runs were perfect training for ski racing. The idea was to jog over the boulders and cobbles while keeping your sneakers dry and your shins unbloodied. After running along for a mile in this way, leaping with downcast eyes, you entered a sort of trance. As your field of vision narrowed to the rocks scrolling by, your ankles learned to instantly gauge the wobbliness of each weathered stone, feeling out its angularity or slickness. It was not unlike skiing, in which the muscles and joints in your legs provide not just stability but intelligence, a constant stream of information for the brain to compute. Going fast activated something powerful in one's deepest cognitive faculties. It was an instinct that Bode had honed in lieu of instruction from others.

From the beginning of his time at CVA, Bode owned the river runs. No one could compete. A coach would drive the kids down Route 27 and drop them off; they would all scamper down into the riverbed; the run would start; and Bode would jump out into the lead. In a minute or two he would disappear around a bend, way out in front of everyone, reaping the harvest of truant days playing in the streambed back home at Turtle Ridge.

Elite teenage sports academies can induce peculiar neuroses, in part because ambitious children tend to fixate on the measurements of achievement, the imperfect systems of ranking and scores, and interpret those measurements as ends in themselves. At CVA, Bode Miller never fell victim to that mentality, and in fact went toward the other extreme, paying little attention to concrete results. He devoted his energy to experimenting with equipment and taking tuck runs down Sugarloaf when the ski patrol wasn't looking. He played around on classmates' snowboards. He developed his own notions of technique and line, and argued on behalf of them with his coaches.

Bode was far from the best skier at the school, but he was the most analytical. As they rode the chairlift together during training, his roommate Sam Anderson recalls, Bode would study the tracks in the snow and theorize about them. Bode would ski lines that he couldn't physically pull off yet, rather than ski where everyone else did. After a race, Bode would break down his run, talking about all the things he'd done wrong. His analysis was often an entirely different interpretation of his mistakes from what his coaches would point out. What Anderson remembers most was Bode's granite self-confidence, his ability to tune out critics. "It was incredible how he never let that bother him," Anderson recalls. "He had this unwavering certainty about what he was going to do."

Bode improved while at CVA, and by his junior year he even won some important races, but he retained his tendency to lean back, and even denied that it was a bad habit. Every day, coaches advised him to move his weight forward, insisting that was the only way to maintain stability and initiate a turn—the crucial moment when a ski begins bending. Miller countered that leaning back was an effective way to carve; by moving his weight back onto his heels, he could put bend in the tails of the skis.

Luckily for Miller, one of his primary coaches at CVA was Chip Cochrane, a former World Cup downhiller from northern Maine who saw Miller's potential and allowed him the leeway to invent his own style. Witnesses to their relationship remember them arguing stubbornly but respectfully on van rides. Cochrane could see that Bode had grown up in a more intimate relationship with the mountains than the average skier, and had received minimal formal education in skiing technique.

"Chip is probably maybe the second most independent person I've met in my life, Bode being the first," John Ritzo recalls. "A lot of coaches prior to that tried to fit Bode into the more traditional model. Chip didn't. I think he saw the potential Bode had, but I think he also saw that Bode had his own ideas."

By Bode's senior year at CVA, he was convinced that skis shaped more like snowboards would help his skiing as much as any of the reconfigurations of stance his coaches were recommending. He needed more sidecut. The term essentially means that the ski has an hourglass shape; instead of a long rectangle, uniform in width from end to end, a ski with sidecut is wide near each end but narrow in the middle, where the skier stands on it. Skis had been built with sidecut for decades, but usually only with a minimal amount, especially race skis, where sidecut was thought to be a destabilizing factor.

Snowboards were another story. CVA had a snowboarding team, and Miller—who was a skilled boarder himself—couldn't help seeing how snowboarders seemed to spring from one turn to the next. It was easier for them to get their boards to bend and track through a turn than it was for most of the skiers to do the same. Something was helping them handle the centrifugal forces that built up at the apex of the turn.

It was clearly the equipment, Miller thought—particularly the standard snowboard's hourglass shape. If you clicked into a snowboard, sat down on the snow and extended your legs down the slope so the snowboard rested upright on its edge, you could see how the board was narrowest in its midsection. The edges along each end of the board would be in contact with the slope but, because of the sidecut, a crescent of daylight would be visible in the middle where your feet were attached. As you pushed your feet down on the middle of the board, you depressed the middle of it until the whole edge was touching the snow, and the board was bent in an arc perfect for carving.

Miller searched around for skis with radical sidecuts, but few existed. The only ones on hand were K2 Fours, a recreational model designed for intermediate skiers as an instructional crutch. The skis were short and lightweight, the exact opposite of racing skis, and when Miller took them up on the mountain, the K2 Fours did exactly what he expected. As his speed mounted and he tilted the skis up on edge, their tips and tails gripped the snow, and the skis bent and took off.

Miller soon mounted each ski with an EPB plate, a foot-long strip of layered rubber and metal under the foot, between the ski and the binding. It was meant to dampen vibration, and also to make the ski heavier. When Miller tried that combination, he knew it would work. He decided to race with the whole kooky assembly at the Junior Olympics, a season-end championship that featured the best hundred juniors in the eastern United States in four races: downhill, super G, giant slalom, and slalom.

Miller won three of the four races and was second in the fourth. He used the K2 Fours in the super G and won by 2.02 seconds. He used them in the giant slalom and won by 2.11 seconds. The victories guaranteed his invitation to the US national championships, to be held a few weeks later on the same slope at Sugarloaf. Starting thirtieth in the slalom there, Miller wore his torn-up old speedsuit and a pair of K2 slalom skis with tip deflectors. He finished third. According to the objective selection criteria, that meant he was on the US Ski Team.

Two months later Miller failed to graduate from CVA, spurning a senior English assignment while he pursued his skiing dreams.

————

Thirteen years later, there were no such surprises for the coaches selecting racers for the US Ski Team during their April planning session. After consulting the rankings lists, the athletic budgets, and the plans for the upcoming season, the US Ski Team coaches chose thirty-six of America's finest alpine ski racers as members of the 2010 national team.

Within that group were about two dozen skiers who would go to the Olympic Games in Vancouver, but in April 2009 it was impossible to say which members of the team would make the cut. Olympic team selection would come at the end of January 2010, and would be based on how the athletes had performed on the World Cup tour up to that point.

The thirty-six members of the 2010 US Ski Team included twenty men and sixteen women from fourteen states. Some came from ski racing families—great dynasties like the Cochrans of Vermont—while others had parents who barely skied at all. Six athletes had already won World Cup races, and eleven had competed in previous Olympics. The oldest man was thirty-one-year-old Scott Macartney, and the youngest was eighteen-year-old Will Gregorak of Colorado, born in 1990. The oldest woman was Sarah Schleper, who at thirty was the mother of a little boy, and the youngest was Alice McKennis of Glenwood Springs, Colorado, who on August 19 would turn twenty.

Generally speaking, all of the athletes were beautiful people, extremely athletic and outdoorsy. Some were humble despite real accomplishments, and others were cocky even though they hadn't really proven themselves yet. They came from small communities where their talent earned them local fame. Their families, rich or poor, had generally made great sacrifices and done creative things to get them there. Some had parents that had hovered over every step of their child's development, practically chasing their kids down the race courses. Others had parents who had kept a distance, dropping them off at the bottom of the race hill with a bagged lunch and a tube of Chapstick.

A press release was prepared, listing the names and ages and hometowns of each of the athletes. For the third year in a row, Bode Miller's name was not on the list.

Sasha Rearick, the head coach of the US men's team, had never been an outstanding ski racer himself, mainly because he grew up in Lakeville, Connecticut, a few hours north of New York City, and didn't encounter high-level competition until boarding school at Gould Academy in western Maine.

It was there that Rearick decided to become a professional ski coach and set out to gather all the education and credentials he would need. He went to Western State College, in Gunnison, Colorado, where he took business and sports science classes while coaching a junior team at nearby Monarch Mountain. In his last two years at Western State, he coached the college team. After graduation in 1999 he set out for Tignes, France, where he enrolled in a prestigious ski instructors' training program. When he returned to the US, he got a job coaching at the Green Mountain Valley School, a top ski academy in Waitsfield, Vermont. There he met his future wife, Katrin Barnerssoi, a former member of the German national ski team.

When the Salt Lake City Games ended in 2002, a wave of coaches left the US team, the usual high turnover that comes at the end of an Olympic cycle. Sasha was offered a vacant assistant coaching spot on the team's staff. He and Katrin moved to Park City, and in the years that followed Rearick worked in various capacities for the US Ski Team, often supervising strength and conditioning programs. He spoke fluent French and German, and mastered the new software that allowed users to combine multiple streams of race video to analyze which lines were faster. By 2006, he was coaching the men's team's up-and-comers on the Europa Cup, a gritty FIS circuit that was skiing's equivalent of Triple-A baseball.

In the spring of 2008 Rearick replaced Phil McNichol as head coach of the entire men's side of the US Ski Team. The first year went pretty well, and once team selections had been made for 2009–10, Rearick and his fellow coaches began to work out a detailed plan for the following Olympic winter. Rearick spent a good deal of April at the ski team's offices in Park City, sitting at a table with his assistants, working over a series of meticulous spreadsheets that mapped out the 2009–10 season. By the end of the process, Rearick would know everything from who would bunk with whom in Slovenia in late January to who would fly home to Squaw Valley for Christmas and who would stay in Europe at the team's apartments. There was a special spreadsheet for February, when the team would focus its energy on the Winter Olympics in Vancouver. There were also blank cells in the spreadsheets. It was impossible to know, for instance, when Ted Ligety, in a knee brace since his crash at nationals, would be rehabilitated enough to ski again.

In Rearick's mind, the biggest question was Bode Miller. Two years after Miller's contentious divorce from the team, Rearick wondered if it wasn't time for an olive branch. Rearick and Miller had known each other for years, and Rearick admired Miller's intensity. In his first year as head coach, Rearick had even invited Miller to train with the team that fall, and no one in Park City questioned him for it. Rearick thought he was in a unique position to broker Miller's return, largely because, as Europa Cup coach, he hadn't been party to the acrimonious disputes that drove a wedge between Miller and the ski team and led to Miller's 2007 departure.

Rearick had floated this idea publicly in February at Val d'Isère, when he was the subject of a profile in the Austrian magazine *Sportwoche*. In the story, Rearick said he hoped to rebuild the team's relationship with Miller, and was even unopposed to the idea of Miller's traveling in a motor home. The headline of the article called him *"Obama im Schnee"*—a reference to his being a perceived peacemaker, unburdened by the previous regime's disputes.

At Val d'Isère, Rearick spoke briefly to Miller, suggesting that the two of them talk it over at the World Cup finals a month later. But then Miller vanished, and nobody on the US Ski Team staff had heard a thing from him since. After Miller's announcement on March 3 that he was suspending his season, his only public statement had been the *HBO Real Sports* appearance, in which he had accused the US Ski Team of driving athletes out of the sport.

Rearick had sent a number of text messages and voicemails to Miller, but hadn't heard back. Now that the team had been named, he decided to call Miller and assure him that there would be a spot for him on the US Ski Team should he decide he wanted to come back. It was a long shot, Rearick knew, but he did it anyway. He thought not having Miller in Vancouver would be a historic waste.

"Whatever you end up deciding, Bode," Rearick said in the voice-mail, "I want you to know that the door is totally open."

CHAPTER 7

The Cruelest Month

Lindsey Vonn didn't take a lot of vacations from her ski career, so she made the most of the one she got in mid-April of 2009, when she and Thomas flew to Mexico for a week-and-a-half stay at a resort near Cozumel. They were joined there by the German skier Maria Riesch and her boyfriend, a sports agent named Marcus Höfl.

The previous month had been a whirlwind for Vonn. After the World Cup finals, she had flown home to Utah. It had been months since she'd been to the house that she and Thomas owned in Park City, but she'd barely had time to drop her bags before she was off again on a victory lap orchestrated by her primary sponsor, Red Bull, which flew her to New York City for a media tour. For three days, Vonn stayed at a midtown hotel while she made visits to NBC, CBS, ESPN, CNN, Fox Business, *Rolling Stone,* the Associated Press, the *New York Times*, and the *New York Daily News*. The schedule had her bouncing all around Manhattan in a black car, carrying her skis and her World Cup trophies for photo shoots. After an appearance on the *Today* show, she took the elevator up to the executive suites at Rockefeller Center and met personally with Dick Ebersol, the legendary boss of NBC Sports, which was gearing up to make her the face of the Olympic team.

A few days later, she was on a plane to Alaska for nationals. From there, Vonn should have been free to flee for the beaches, but earlier in the season she had agreed to travel to Switzerland for a pro-am event organized by the Danish beer company Carlsberg, a major World Cup sponsor. Every year, Carlsberg promised big appearance fees and wild parties to lure a bunch of the tour's best skiers to the resort of Verbier, high above the upper Rhône valley. It was a fun event, even if it required another transatlantic flight.

Travel fatigue meant that for about ten days in Cozumel, all Vonn could do was rest. She and Maria played a little tennis, but otherwise Vonn spent her time on a dock in front of the hotel. More than once, Lindsey went snorkeling by herself. And inevitably she sat with Thomas and discussed the plan of attack for the coming season.

There was a running joke between Lindsey and her husband that she had stolen his speed when they fell in love. Thomas Vonn's own World Cup career had been on an upswing in the summer of 2002, when he and Lindsey started dating. From that point forward, his results suffered while Lindsey's improved at a steep, steady pace. When Lindsey had her breakout year on the World Cup in 2004, scoring her first podium at Cortina and her first victory at Lake Louise, Thomas had gotten progressively slower until the US Ski Team cut him loose.

A native of Newburgh, New York, Thomas didn't start racing until he was twelve, and by then he was far behind his peers. At sixteen, he made his way to the Northwood School in Lake Placid, where he could train on the Olympic hill at nearby Whiteface Mountain. In 1997, he made the US Ski Team, but he was cut from the roster after half a season. He enrolled at St. Lawrence University, where he dominated the NCAA college circuit and was renominated to the national team at twenty-two. Stubborn and obsessed with his equipment—frequently switching brands and forever tinkering with the bevel of his edges and canting of his boots—it sometimes seemed to his teammates that he believed the only thing separating him from the World Cup podium was equipment.

Thomas Vonn raced at the Olympics in 2002 and was living in Park

City that summer when his romance with Lindsey blossomed. They started hanging out between out-of-town trips (Lindsey attended German-language immersion classes at Dartmouth College and both of them went to train at a New Zealand ski camp). When they were back in Park City, they spent nights at the bowling alley and afternoons working out at the US Ski Team gym. It was a season of cookouts and waterskiing. To Lindsey, Thomas was the cool older guy who had raced at Kitzbühel, gone to college, and had finished ninth the previous winter in the Olympic super G. Lindsey would later say it only took about two months of dating for her to fall in love.

She was seventeen and he was twenty-six, and while Thomas's teammates teased him about "robbing the cradle," the love affair presented Lindsey with far bigger problems. When her father learned about the relationship and the age difference, he was vehemently opposed to it—and he let Thomas know. However, there was little Alan Kildow could do, in part because he and Lindsey's mother were separating. Lindsey sided with her mother, ultimately forbidding her father to attend her races. When he ignored that edict, appearing at the world championships in Bormio in 2005, a terrible confrontation ensued. Their full-throated argument in a hotel left Lindsey in tears.

Lindsey wouldn't speak to her father for years after that. She would say she had "dissolved" her relationship with him. Meanwhile Thomas, retired from racing, went on the road with his girlfriend for the 2005–06 season, driving Lindsey from race to race in Europe, schlepping bags and introducing himself wryly as a "professional spectator" or "chauffeur." In fact, Lindsey found a huge benefit in having a constant companion who understood racing—who knew what it took to get psyched up for a race, or to take a gate to the chin. He offered her consolation, motivation, and organization.

Pretty soon, Thomas was advising her on her gear—the thickness of her boot soles, the way they ramped her foot forward or tilted her ankle to one side. Lindsey had never needed to obsess over equipment, but with Thomas on her side it was another arrow in her quiver. Lindsey was amazed by Thomas's ability to geek out over the minutiae of the sport, and grateful for it when she needed to unplug and let someone else worry about the gear. When he clashed with her serviceman, she took Thomas's side, and the serviceman was soon gone.

Thomas proposed in Austria on New Years' Eve as 2006 ticked over into 2007. Nine months later, on September 29, 2007, they married in Deer Valley, Utah. Light snowfall was dusting the aspens, and the tables at the reception were labeled with names like "St. Moritz"—the mountains where the couple had happy memories of racing as teammates. From then on, whenever Lindsey was on snow, Thomas was with her. On race days they inspected courses together, sliding slowly down the slope and analyzing the combination of turns, pitches, and snow. In training sessions he filmed her runs, noted her times, and offered sometimes blunt observations about her line. When they bickered, their arguments were sometimes esoteric; was it the quality of the snow crystals or the mounting position of her bindings that was delaying her turn initiation? But they were a unit, and Lindsey respected Thomas's assessments, thankful for frank communication that was rare between an athlete and a coach.

People in US skiing didn't know what to call Thomas; he was Lindsey's husband, coach, business manager, and press agent all at once. At various times, she would describe him as her manager, motivator, and mental trainer. Thomas sometimes said he was her Dick Cheney, helping his wife wield the new power she obtained as she emerged as a star in the sport. The label fit, given how success had inverted some of Lindsey's relationships within the sport. The US Ski Team and certain sponsors needed her more than she needed them, and managing that political capital was a burden; Thomas had seen up close how exhausting it had been for his old teammate, Bode Miller, to manage his new clout without feeling like he was being a jerk.

To liberate his wife, Thomas stepped in as the heavy. In more and more conversations, as diplomatically as possible, Thomas told a coach or administrator or sponsor representative that the negotiation was over. Lindsey, through him, was dictating the terms. Not everyone liked it, but that wasn't the goal.

On April 29, Julia Mancuso had fully expected to be on the north shore of Maui, spending early summer as she normally would, kite surfing or stand-up paddleboarding. Instead she was in Utah, sitting around a table with a bunch of her US Ski Team teammates, all of them feeling betrayed by the French.

Two weeks had passed since Mancuso's agent, Ken Sowles, had forwarded her a letter from Bruno Cercley, the new chief executive of Rossignol. Dated April 16, the letter requested Mancuso's attendance at the April 29 meeting at the company's North American headquarters in Park City. Sowles told her that everyone who skied on Rossignol had received the same letter, and that the company's World Cup race director, Angelo Maina, would also attend.

"The current economic climate compels us to introduce various action plans," Cercley's letter said ominously. Though he was vague on the details, Cercley claimed that the worldwide economic downturn had injured Rossignol severely enough that the company's future was "under threat if nothing is done."

Now here they all were, sitting around a conference table. Lindsey and Thomas Vonn were there, as was Ted Ligety, still on crutches after his knee injury a month before. Sowles and a few other agents were present, along with Rossignol's race department representatives from the US, trying hard not to look dispirited.

As Mancuso and the others sat around a conference table, Cercley informed them that the company was unilaterally cutting their retainers in half that summer. It was a global arrangement, Cercley said. He and Maina were on a worldwide tour, informing all of Rossignol's racers of the changes.

To the athletes, the move was shockingly cold-blooded. At this point in the year, it was too late to switch to another company. If Rossignol had announced its plan even a month earlier, the skiers could have gone to the other companies that supplied gear on the World Cup tour. But by late April those other companies had already finalized their rosters, settled their budgets, and begun building the next season's skis.

As Cercley talked, all the athletes realized how badly Rossignol had left them hanging. Even if they could convince Head or Atomic to let them test their skis, where could they do it? The snow that remained in the northern hemisphere was spring snow—wet slush that froze solid at night and melted back into slush by mid-morning; skiing on a surface like that wouldn't give you a feel for how new and unfamiliar skis would perform on World Cup snow. The next meaningful testing opportunity wouldn't be until the teams went to New Zealand and Chile in August, awfully late to be trying out new brands.

Like Julia Mancuso, Lindsey Vonn had been on Rossi since she was a little girl. Her father had negotiated her first sponsorship deals with the company, and she had resisted the temptation to jump to Atomic in the mid-2000s, when for a time that company became the Ferrari of ski brands. When the American athletes met outside, everyone was stunned and angry. Lindsey and Thomas were already considering finding a new supplier and there was even talk of going after Rossignol. The company had doubly damaged them all, Thomas pointed out, by publicly announcing the salary cuts. Every other company had received a signal that it was safe to lowball the Rossignol skiers if they came looking for a contract.

Ligety was offended but also resigned to it, knowing his injury precluded him from doing any ski testing in the summer. But it was obvious that Mancuso was in no position to stand up to Rossignol either. At the time Rossignol had chosen to scrap its agreement with her, she was in the worst slump of her career.

Julia Mancuso had won the giant slalom at the Torino Games in 2006, a day after retired Picabo Street had chastised her on the *Today* show for wearing a plastic tiara on the mountain. The tiara became Julia's talisman. She named the lingerie line she started "Kiss My Tiara."

Her best season came the following winter, when she won four

World Cup races and collected 1,356 points to finish third in the overall standings. At the time, it was the best season-long performance by an American woman since 1984.

Her mysterious slump began in 2007–08, when her speed deserted her as quickly as it had arrived. Her coaches and the ski media had no shortage of theories about it, the primary one being that Julia had been distracted by the opportunities. She had started a lingerie line, and in 2007 posed in her underwear and ski boots for one of her sponsors, then lost control of the digital images. In the summer of 2008, she went to the Beijing Olympics for NBC, and that year she also climbed Mount Kilimanjaro with a friend, British racer Chemmy Alcott, as part of a charity fundraiser. She also spent a lot of time in the Maui surf.

Another theory, espoused by her father, was that the hip surgery Julia had undergone in 2006 had compromised her skeletal alignment, leading to back pain that sometimes made her tentative on snow. The pain made her feel disconnected from her body, as if the fine sense of balance she'd always taken for granted was gone.

Whatever the cause, the 2008–09 season had been even worse. A nonfactor at the world championships, Mancuso had finished outside the top ten in twenty-two of the twenty-four World Cup races she started. At the finals, she had closed out the season with a mere 285 points, her worst World Cup performance since 2004. In terms of rankings, she was a worse skier at age twenty-five than she had been at twenty.

Mancuso herself felt that at least part of the blame lay with the US Ski Team; some of her favorite coaches had departed, particularly Trevor Wagner, a laconic westerner who had coached her during her childhood at Squaw Valley and graduated with her to the national team. In his absence, she was convinced the solution was a more per-sonalized program. She was the only all-around skier on the team besides Lindsey Vonn, who had a unique advantage in her husband, Thomas. It took a lot of care and attention to manage a career when you were doing every single race on the World Cup. One wrong move—lost luggage, a missed flight—and the whole enterprise went off the rails.

The problem was unique to Mancuso. Most of her teammates specialized, but Mancuso was always bouncing back and forth among the disciplines, and things seemed to slip through the cracks. The US women's team was split, with separate coaching staffs for the tech and speed squads. The Austrians had a separate squad for four-event skiers. Other all-rounders on the tour—such as Tina Maze of Slovenia and Anja Pärson of Sweden—were from smaller teams that had no choice but to design the program around their one big star.

The US Ski Team was still learning to be flexible, with Mancuso coaxing them along. She had brought in a personal coach, but the US team coaches seemed to dislike the arrangement. At the end of the 2009 season, Julia had campaigned for the national team to assign one coach to her, to approximate the unified program that Lindsey had with Thomas.

This had taken a great deal of salesmanship, partly because of the dynamics of the US women's team, which was coached entirely by men. On the men's team, she'd noticed, athletes were always mouthing off, asserting their needs, and making demands. But on the women's team, she felt, it was hard to be respected for your own ideas, especially if you'd joined the team when you were a fourteen-year-old kid.

As Mancuso left the Rossignol meeting and headed back to Maui, she knew at least one thing was going her way for the next season: she had convinced the US team to make Chris Knight her personal coach. Knight, a tech coach from New Zealand with whom she had a great rapport, was open-minded and respectful.

Rossignol's cuts were something she would just have to accept. In the off-season, her focus would be on getting healthy. The pain in her back was severe enough to warrant MRI tests, which showed a compressed disc in her lower spine. All those rattling rides over rock-hard ice had crushed the soft tissue between her vertebrae. Nothing was structurally dangerous, the team doctors had said. She could keep skiing.

Mancuso knew that she had to focus on her body. She would forgo traveling and be extra disciplined about her physical therapy, working with a chiropractor three times a week and doing Pilates to strengthen her trunk muscles. In the end, it would be up to eight hours of therapy a day, in addition to the regular gym workouts and kite surfing.

—————

Rainer Salzgeber, the race director for the Austrian ski company Head, didn't know quite what to think when he received a call from Thomas Vonn in early May wondering if it was too late in the season for Lindsey to join the Head team.

Salzgeber's office was just a few steps from the ski room at Head's factory in Kennelbach, Austria. The facility was one of the last artifacts of the company's heyday in the 1960s. Half a century after the American entrepreneur Howard Head invented the world's first metal ski, the business he founded had evolved into a globally diversified and publicly traded sporting goods company that manufactured most of its products in Asia. But World Cup skis were handmade in Kennelbach, where a team of engineers and expert skiers constructed about 3,000 pairs of race skis a year.

The clamor of hydraulic machinery and the smell of heavy-duty glue pervaded the place as Rainer Salzgeber received the surprise call from Thomas Vonn. The skiers might be in their off-season, but the ski companies were in overdrive in April and May. Salzgeber was closely monitoring Head's ski presses at Kennelbach, which were busy cranking out skis for the racers to use in New Zealand and Chile later in the summer. Among the hundreds of skis cooling on racks, Salzgeber hoped, were a few specimens that would carry Head athletes to the podium at the Vancouver Olympic Games.

It is a science and an art to glue together the components of a ski: wood core, metal edges, layers of fiberglass and plastic. You have to bake and compress them and get a consistent result, somehow giving each ski the exact amount of flexibility it needs. It has to be sturdy enough to withstand the torque a World Cup racer puts on it, but supple too. Fast pairs of skis are precious, mysterious things, and they have an expiration date—after a certain amount of use, the wood and glue between the layers cracks and the skis grow soft and lifeless.

Salzgeber was prepared to hand out bonuses exceeding 100,000 euros to some of the Head racers if they won Olympic gold, along with their base salary and other bonuses for World Cup wins and titles. Like all the big ski companies, Head fervently believed that the success of their high-performance race gear would boost retail sales for mass-produced products. For the companies that provided skis on the World Cup circuit—Atomic, Rossignol, Head, Völkl, Fischer, Dynastar, Stöckli, Salomon, Nordica, Blizzard, and Elan—it was an article of faith that if a top racer won World Cup races on your equipment, consumers would notice.

The game was to build fast skis and get exposure for the brand when the racers took their equipment with them onto the podium and into television interviews. While there were prohibitions on the location and size of commercial logos athletes could wear on their suits and coats during a World Cup race, ski brands were virtually unregulated.

The racers knew it too, which is why, when they crossed the finish line with a strong performance, their first reaction was to lift a ski and put the company's logo within view of the camera. A racer might prolong the company's exposure by kissing the ski, strumming it like a guitar, or, in one case that drew an admonishment from the FIS, putting it between their legs and making thrusting motions with their hips.

Each of Head's downhillers might start their summer training sessions with perhaps fifty pairs of skis, and slowly winnow the number down to a dozen or so to take into the season. One or two would become favorites. Companies spend millions to locate the perfect wood and the fastest plastic for the base. They have analytic software to guide them on how quickly or slowly to let the glue dry, and how to taper the ski's wood core. When an engineer leaves the employ of one company, another might give chase and hire him; Head had recently done that, snatching up Bernhard Riepler after he moved on from Atomic. When a racer's skis go missing at a race, fears spread that a rival company has taken them and sawed them open to study the cross-section of materials inside. Salzgeber and his colleagues were always there at the end of every race to safeguard the skis. As soon as a racer comes through the finish, a ski company rep steps up with a pair of the company's latest ski-shop model for the athletes to lean up against their shoulder during interviews and hold high over their heads on the podium. As the photographers take the images for the next day's newspapers, the actual race-winning skis are often already on their way back to the guarded race room for a tune-up.

For Salzgeber, an overture from the number one female skier in the world was obviously welcome. It was also highly unusual. Almost nobody switches brands in the summer before the Olympics. Salzgeber knew all about the contract disputes roiling Rossignol. The worldwide economic crisis had sharply reduced the number of ski vacations people were booking, and Head had taken its own steps to ease the budget shortfalls. Salzgeber had recently asked his racers to contribute to the costs of bringing their ski servicemen to the southern hemisphere. But Salzgeber couldn't be sure where the Rossignol cuts had left Vonn; he had to consider the possibility that Vonn was using him to get better terms from another factory.

The companies spent millions to stay respectable in racing, paying fees to the teams merely to have the right to approach the athletes and negotiate contracts. A top racer with a good agent could make well over a million dollars in a season from their ski supplier. Bode Miller had excelled at the game, moving from company to company throughout his career, leveraging his results for bigger and bigger contracts, and taking with him the accumulated knowledge of what worked and what didn't.

When Rainer Salzgeber got off the phone with Thomas Vonn, he called Heinz Hämmerle. While he was technically Hämmerle's boss, he had great respect for the waxroom wizard. Hämmerle, who had grown up close to Kennelbach, had begun working for Head in the early 1980s. He had seen it all. When Salzgeber told Hämmerle that Lindsey Vonn was "knocking on the door" with Head, Hämmerle thought it was a joke. He assumed that Vonn was just using Head to get better bargaining power with Rossignol. But he was also intrigued by the idea of working with Vonn, in part because he was still angry at Miller for vanishing at the end of the year.

———

Sasha Rearick hadn't heard back from Bode Miller either, and by the first of May he figured that Bode had decided not to race in the upcoming season—certainly not for the US Ski Team. It made Rearick sad, but he saw an opportunity. With summer training camps approaching, Rearick still had one position to fill on the men's team staff: head coach of the Europa Cup team. Rearick, having once held the position himself, knew how critical the job was to the team's long-term goals. These skiers would be the 2014 Olympic team; he needed someone he could trust: someone thrifty, organized, and capable; someone who'd been there. Naturally he thought of Forest Carey.

For the previous two years, Carey had been a coach on Team America, and he was one of Miller's closest confidants. The two had known each other since the early 1990s, when Carey was the big man on campus at Carrabassett Valley Academy and had loaned Bode skis.

When Rearick reached him, Carey had just gotten back to the US from a long, unexpected surfing vacation. After Miller vanished in mid-season, Carey suddenly had time on his hands. He'd gone to Nicaragua, where he owned land.

Carey was flattered by the offer. Rearick trusted him to take athletes to these gritty places on a shoestring budget and bring them back with their bodies and spirits more or less intact. Carey himself had gotten chewed up in the rough transition to European racing and believed his career had been mismanaged. He knew he could do better for these racers.

But before accepting the offer, Carey called Miller. He knew not to try to pin Miller down on what would happen in the next year, but he needed to make a decision. On May 15, the men's team was heading out for a nine-day training session on the late spring snow at Mammoth Mountain, California.

Carey reached his old classmate and employer and caught up. They shared the worldview that can come from growing up in northern New England forest-industry towns, where an economy built around wood and paper products had once flourished. The disappearance of those industries left a vacuum in their communities that the local ski area had helped fill. There was still a good measure of real, chronic poverty where they came from, but Miller and Carey had both managed to carve out careers in skiing that were still going, sixteen years or more after they'd become friends.

That was in the background when Carey asked Miller what he should tell Rearick.

"If I turn down the ski team job," he said, "would you be ready to hire me next season?"

There was a brief silence while Miller thought about it.

"Don't count on me," he said.

Carey hung up and called Rearick back and accepted the job.

"What about Bode?" Rearick asked.

"I don't know if he'll ever ski again," Carey told him.

PART 2

Training Days

May–October 2009

CHAPTER 8

Taking Wing

The international arrivals hall of the Munich airport is bright and civilized. The Americans stumble into it less than an hour after the final descent of an overnight transatlantic journey, nudged awake, perhaps, by the gentle intonations of a Lufthansa captain or flight attendant: *"Guten Tag, meine Damen und Herren."*

Travelers emerge with their luggage and stamped passports into a polite crowd of expectant faces. Immediately ahead is an open-plan restaurant where, even an hour or two after sunrise, customers are being served soft white sausages and tall glasses of cloudy Erdinger *Weissbier*, the Bavarian mainstay. The eyes of the breakfasters shift calmly from the perpetual soccer broadcasts to the big, old-fashioned flight status board overhead, which lists scores of flights and updates itself every minute with a soft flutter of shifting digits.

In late May 2009, this was the starting point for the first step on Lindsey Vonn's road to Vancouver: a six-week early-summer physical training block in Austria, coordinated by Red Bull energy drinks.

Vonn had entered Europe this way dozens of times, and the scene was as familiar to her as any peak or valley in the Alps. Off to her left as she entered the terminal was a short cluster of benches where, a decade earlier, when she had started traveling with the US Ski Team, she and her teammates would regroup while the coaches brought the cargo vans around to the curb. Now her routine was to cross the marble floor of the terminal and a wide outdoor plaza to an Audi showroom where a representative of the company (an enthusiastic World Cup sponsor that doted on top athletes) would hand her the keys to the sleek new car she would drive down to Austria.

In the terminal, hanging in a window of a magazine store, was a remarkable poster that few fans of Alpine skiing could resist stopping to examine. An intricate, hand-painted map of the Alps, it showed the entire mountain range as if viewed from the stratosphere above Hamburg or Helsinki, looking slightly south, so that the boot of Italy stretched away toward a curving horizon. Here was the cradle of the sport: a wall of rock hundreds of miles across, stretching from the Balkans to Lake Geneva and then curling down toward the Mediterranean near Nice. In the middle of this wrinkled crust was a long, wide spine of sharp peaks—the glacier-capped massif that divides Italy from the rest of Europe but for tunnels, some high mountain passes open only in summer, and softer side entrances on the shoulders of the range around Slovenia and Monte Carlo.

The Alps are sometimes called "the water tower of Europe." Every spring and summer since the last ice age, huge pulses of snowmelt drain out of these mountains, flowing thousands of miles in every direction, providing boundaries for nations and empires. These rivers nourish the agricultural systems and hydroelectric turbines that sustain the lives of nearly a billion people, from the Black Sea to the French Riviera.

One of these great waterways is the Inn River, which begins life in the glaciated peaks of western Austria, flows down through the city which is named for it, Innsbruck, and then drains east through the region that had become Lindsey Vonn's adopted home over the previous ten years.

The race for the Olympic gold medal started there, in the summer, in the weightroom.

Physical fitness was survival for Vonn; she believed that tenacious conditioning would save her from serious injuries. Stamina, strength, flexibility, reflexes—any one of these trainable physical proficiencies could help her avoid the kind of violent crashes that marred her early career. Vonn had set aside six weeks of early summer for this trip, where she would sweat and grunt her way through a punishing physical training regimen designed by a team of professionals using the latest advances in sports science.

The program was one of the career-enhancing perks that came with Vonn's endorsement of the Austrian energy drink company Red Bull, her primary sponsor since 2005. In addition to paying her millions, Red Bull supported her World Cup quest through the Red Bull Athletes Special Project (ASP), a personalized support program overseen by Robert Trenkwalder, an Austrian former downhill coach. The ASP program included other Red Bull athletes, but mainly it revolved around Vonn, supplying her with the services of a full-time personal trainer, Martin Hager, a former conditioning coach of the Austrian ski team, and also Oliver Saringer, a Red Bull physiotherapist who had worked with soccer players and specialized in a massage technique called lymphatic drainage. The plan was for the two of them to travel with Vonn through much of the World Cup season.

The arrangement was the brainchild of Red Bull's visionary cofounder and chief executive, Dietrich Mateschitz, an Austrian who had discovered the drink on a trip to Thailand and launched it in Europe in the 1980s. Almost from the beginning, Mateschitz, a former ski instructor, had made sponsorship of adrenaline-fueled extreme sports central to the company's marketing plan. The company not only sponsored competitions and athletes but devised unique stunt shows that usually involved people jumping off things with the Red Bull logo prominently displayed on their parachutes and helmets. In 2012, Red Bull coordinated Felix Baumgartner's record-setting jump from the stratosphere, allowing spectators to follow online as Baumgartner plunged from a helium balloon 24 miles above the New Mexico desert, reaching estimated speeds of over 800 miles per hour.

In Austria, Red Bull fielded strong teams in Formula 1 auto racing and soccer, two of the nation's three most popular sports. World Cup ski racing fit perfectly with the company's image, and in 2004 Red Bull became the main sponsor of the Hahnenkamm races at Kitzbühel, placing its ubiquitous logo—two bulls colliding head-on against a yellow and blue background—on every possible surface, from course fencing to the racers' bibs. The company erected viewing platforms along the trail, a lounge near the start, and a giant, inflated archway over the Hausberg jump, the entrance to a critical section of the race.

When it came to putting logos on the racers themselves, Red Bull had to walk a tighter line. According to FIS rules, any logo on a skier's downhill suit has to represent a sponsor of their national team and be confined to a small patch. The only space on their bodies that athletes themselves can rent out is a 50-square-centimeter space on the helmet. This space, the so-called "headgear sponsor," was an accommodation the FIS made in 1985, as IOC amateurism rules were lifted.

Though small, the headgear space is strategic; the logo worn there will appear in every television interview, action photo, and podium celebration in which a racer participates. Top skiers rent out their foreheads in seven-figure contracts, and even the tour's up-and-comers can make a quick $10,000 by advertising anything from ski resorts to banks, potato chips, nonalcoholic beer, and energy bars. Bode Miller made a small fortune in 2005 and 2006 wearing the logo of Barilla pasta.

As Red Bull grew, largely because of its global popularity as a vodka mixer, the company jumped in as headgear sponsor for some of the top ski racers on the World Cup tour, including Aksel Lund Svindal, Erik Guay of Canada, and American downhiller Daron Rahlves. When Vonn's headgear contract with Vail Resorts expired in the fall of 2005, her agent brokered the lucrative deal that eventually made Red Bull as important to her career as the US Ski Team.

After that, Vonn wore the Red Bull logo on her person any time there was a camera nearby. At press conferences she would put a can of it on the dais near her microphone. In finish line interviews, as she moved along a fence talking to film crews, she often carried an over-sized Red Bull waterbottle, and when she got to the print journalists she would unfailingly mention the extensive and creative support the company gave her, which was no exaggeration. In return, Mateschitz paid Vonn a salary and bonuses, and showered her with favors and support, like the occasional use of a company jet, a German language tutor, the registration and design of her website, and even a job for her younger sister. Vonn signed deals with a host of other companies as Vancouver approached, but it was fair to say that Red Bull was her chief source of sponsorship income. Not everything the company proposed appealed to her, though.

One odd component of Red Bull's athlete support system was the Diagnostics and Training Center, a state-of-the-art workout facility in Thalgau, a peaceful village on the eastern outskirts of Salzburg. Part laboratory and part gymnasium, the DTC was housed in a secure, non-descript old tin oxide factory beside a small stream. Hundreds of Red Bull athletes made use of it. A receptionist verified their identities via a video camera before buzzing them in through a locked door.

As soon as Vonn signed up with Red Bull, the company began encouraging her to go there, and she had since made several visits to Thalgau, where the services offered included blood-lactate measure-ment, strength testing, and psychological counseling. But she was ambivalent about the place. While it might have appeared a perfect training resource for her in many ways, she avoided it during most of her trips to Austria and almost never listed it among the favors the company did her.

The reason was the DTC's Bernd Pansold, the elderly German doc-tor who oversaw the Thalgau facility. From 1975 to 1989, Pansold had played an instrumental role in East Germany's infamous, state-sponsored program to dope unwitting young athletes with anabolic steroids. In 1998, a German court had convicted him of aiding and abetting assault on young female Olympic swimmers who suffered ghastly permanent damage from the drugs Pansold had approved. He had collaborated closely with the Stasi, the GDR's notorious secret police, and their records, seized after the Berlin Wall fell, showed that he'd overseen programs in which girls as young as thirteen were given oral steroids and told they were taking vitamins.

At the time of his indictment in 1998, Pansold was living in Austria, working at a training facility in Obertauern frequented by Hermann Maier and other Austrian downhillers. In the scandal that ensued, the Austrian team frantically distanced itself from Pansold, as did Maier. But one person sought Pansold out, despite the court conviction: Dietrich Mateschitz. In 2001, Mateschitz personally recruited Pansold to establish and run the facility in Thalgau, where his title was *Leistungsdiagnostiker*—roughly translated as "performance analyst." Red Bull athletes were encouraged to consult with him there, as were trainers like Hager.

Vonn made a few visits a year to the DTC, but mainly steered clear of it. Some of her competitors and the FIS knew of Pansold's position there, and Thomas Vonn was concerned about the optics of a strong relationship with the facility. Instead, Lindsey chose to work out at the training center of Austria's leading professional soccer team, FC Red Bull Salzburg, near Salzburg's Wolfgang Amadeus Mozart Airport. There she would train to the point of total exhaustion, something she couldn't afford to do during the ski season because as an all-rounder she needed to conserve energy for races. In Salzburg, Red Bull had everything Vonn could want: natural and artificial fields, ice baths, a swimming pool, and an indoor quarter track. Often she felt as if she was the only woman in the building.

She and Hager also worked out near Innsbruck at the Hotel Schwarz, a five-star resort and spa. There she could lift weights, use the pool, or go through any number of balance drills she had learned or designed herself over the years. She might crouch in her tuck position with each foot on a squishy rubber ball, or sprint through a set of cones, stooping to touch each of them as she went by. She might walk across a slackline, a piece of nylon webbing pulled taut between two anchors, locking her eyes on some grounded object ahead of her while every muscle down to her feet and ankles worked to hold her body steady. Vonn pumped a lot of iron (low weight, high reps), but many of her workouts took place on a simple stationary bike with a heart-rate monitor, riding for hours in an effort to raise her anaerobic threshold. Hager and others would periodically take small blood samples to measure her lactate levels and make sure she wasn't overtraining.

This was how Vonn passed most of June, often spending six hours a day working hard, then receiving a massage from Saringer and eating a 5,000-calorie diet for fuel. She spent a lot of this time considering the Rossignol situation. They were demanding she sign a new contract, and she was not responding until she and Thomas knew if they could work something out with Head. She also relaxed, using Austria's sweet summer evenings for some of the last downtime she'd get all year. That month Vonn joined Twitter, watched Wimbledon, and submitted to a few interviews for magazines and television programs getting the jump on their coverage for Vancouver, now only eight months away.

The wagon trains of persecuted Mormons that lurched past Park City in the late 1840s passed through canyons nearby and established their Zion in the saline basin 20 miles to the west. As Brigham Young and his progeny built their temple and began to colonize the intermountain west, prospectors and outlaws claimed Park City, turning it into a den of relative sin.

If the town still enjoyed that identity a century later, it was because ski bums had replaced silver miners. Three major ski areas adjacent to the town brought another wave of young people who veered frequently from the codes of abstinence and industry that prevailed in the surrounding territory. The jetsetting Sundance crowd, the incomparable Wasatch powder, a real estate boom—there was fun to be had in Park City, and in the early summer, when the US Ski Team was back in town, they often knew where to find it.

The US Ski Team threw what could arguably be called a $22-million party on July 17, 2009, inviting some of US skiing's biggest supporters to gather at the official dedication ceremony for USSA's palatial new head-quarters on five acres of grassy hillside on the edge of town. The official address was 1 Victory Lane. The team's staff had begun moving in months earlier, thrilled to escape from cramped old offices on Kearns Boulevard. But the July gathering was the real celebration, attended by the FIS secretary general Sarah Lewis, decorated alumni of the US Ski Team, and Bob Beattie, the seventy-six-year-old godfather of American ski racing.

The building was an architectural gem. In addition to ample office space and a gym full of sophisticated machines, the facility contained a sports science lab and a rehabilitation center for injured athletes. In one big hall there were ramps and trampolines for freestyle skiers to use when there wasn't snow outside; they could fly into the air, perfect their aerial tricks, and land softly in pits of foam. It was far more impressive than the home base of any other ski team in the world, and even out-shone the US Olympic Committee's aging facilities in Colorado Springs.

The building also stood as a monument to the fundraising prowess of Marolt and others who had spent years drumming up the money for this Xanadu. When Marolt came to the team in 1996, USSA had such serious cash flow issues that the coaches sometimes had no firm idea in the spring what their budget would be in the fall. Marolt tamed the budget and cultivated new supporters.

One of the special challenges of Marolt's job was the dual nature of the organization. On one hand, he was the president of a small, elite sports team comprised of dedicated professionals; on the other hand, he ran a nationwide youth sports program based on mass participation. Marolt knew he couldn't rely on USSA's membership base to fund the World Cup teams; the organization's future was staked on keeping the sport's costs low, including membership dues. The parents who wrote those annual checks were also typically volunteering with their child's ski team, doing weekend duty as start referee, or printing race results. Their kids often played other sports too—sports that were cheaper, and safer.

Instead of stressing that resource, Marolt would fund the US Ski

Team's modernization by soliciting donations from wealthy individuals and striking up sponsorship deals with name-brand corporations. A lifelong passion for the sport guided him with the sales pitch he always kept at hand.

"It's pretty simple," Marolt might say to a prospective donor. "We're not trying to put a man on the back side of the moon. What we're trying to do is put men and women on podiums."

Marolt plowed most of the money he raised into athletic programs, especially for the alpine team. In the late 1990s, USSA launched a sports science program. In the early 2000s, the teams got apartments in Europe. Marolt asked the top coaches to keep wish lists handy, so that as soon as a donation came in it could be steered toward a new initiative to help athletes get an edge. In his first four years at the team, he nearly doubled the annual athletic budget to $9.9 million.

Marolt would bring the donors and sponsors back around to show them exactly where their money was going, giving them a sense that they were part of a grand experiment. He made supporting the team fun, whether that meant getting donors into World Cup parties where they could meet their favorite ski team alumni, or bringing them out on the hill to observe training, or flying them to Kitzbühel to dine at quaint restaurants with the head coaches. He knew the sport and could interpret it well for people who didn't.

He wasn't universally loved. Some people in the skiing community saw hypocrisy in the "Bode Rules" he instituted in 2006. Others resented his compensation, high for a nonprofit where budget decisions were so fraught; by 2004, Marolt's salary was $559,880, and continued to grow after that. Other detractors accused Marolt of being detached from the practical realities of running the team, but they couldn't deny he made record sums of money for USSA, nearly doubling its revenue between 1998 and the year ending April 30, 2009, when the organization reported $23.7 million in net revenue.

The global financial crisis had hurt the team, however, and in January 2009 USSA had laid off approximately 20 percent of its staff and slashed salaries—but the Center of Excellence was already bricks and mortar. Some thought it too opulent for a nonprofit, but those voices were muted at the dedication ceremony as Marolt saluted the generous donors who had made the project possible and promised that it would help create a new generation of champions for the US Ski Team.

Every member of the team was skiing for his or her own aspirations, not those of Bill Marolt, and yet there was no question that the organization's CEO was counting on them to come back from Vancouver with some hardware. The 2010 Olympics, more than any other event, would be a referendum on his leadership. Marolt had done his part. It was up to the athletes to do theirs.

CHAPTER 9

Working the Angles

In the last week of July, his knee ligaments finally restored to stability after his crash at nationals, Ted Ligety started packing for an extra-long trip to New Zealand, where he expected to spend the better part of a month on snow at Round Hill and Coronet Peak, working his way back to top form. Among the heaps of gear he laid out were Day-Glo helmets and goggles from Shred, the equipment company he had founded after winning Olympic gold in Torino. Fluorescent ski gear had briefly been in vogue in the early 1990s, when Ligety was learning to ski, and he had made it his company's mission to bring back the neon.

Ski racing wasn't a year-round sport, but the season was at least nine months long, and by August every national ski team of consequence would be on snow in New Zealand, Chile, or Argentina. It was always winter somewhere. They went to Portillo, La Parva, Termas de Chillán, Bariloche, and Ushuaia. They went to Mount Hutt, Coronet Peak, and Treble Cone. They stayed for two weeks or a month, moving into hotels and lodges, renting whole swaths of mountain for what turned out to be some of the most focused training they got all year.

There were skiers coming back from injury, easing their way into the gates. There were downhillers who wanted to work on giant slalom, and slalom skiers trying out downhill.

Summer training was a chance for team bonding—drinking pisco late into the Chilean night, or bungee jumping in New Zealand. But it was mainly work, with the US Ski Team's sports science wizards often on the hill to enhance the training with high-tech gadgets that helped the racers measure their performance in new ways. They played with ski-mounted GPS units, or high-definition cameras with extreme shutter speeds. For a skier like Ligety, who spent the winter crossing over between the technical events and the speed events, it was often the only time he got to focus exclusively on his turns. With Ligety there wasn't much room for improvement.

At age twenty-four, Ligety had acheived an almost total mastery of the science of carving turns. While Miller might have had more artistry, and Svindal was bigger and brought more power to the mountain, Ligety had come closer than perhaps any racer in the world to absolute efficiency. Not a single movement was wasted.

Growing up in the Wasatch, Ligety learned to carve on the hardest ice on the Olympic slope and float softly through cold-smoke powder, an education that gave him a diverse set of skills. If you asked any ski coach to explain his proficiency, their answer would rely heavily on the two most important terms in alpine ski racing: technique and tactics. The first concerns biomechanics, and the second the line a racer takes through a course. The two concepts are inextricably linked. Although every ski racer's approach is different, all strive for the same ideal: to find the perfect combination of technique and tactics. Only when these two fundamentals of skiing competence align can a racer hope to harness all the power of the fall line.

Technique is dictated by the potential and limitations of the human body. As the racers turn around the gates, they must position their bodies in ways that help them withstand the extreme forces that arrive as speeds mount. This requires not one ideal stance but a fluid set of movements. Body shape and joint alignment are part of it, but technique is an expression of all the things a racer has learned, or unlearned, or has yet to learn. It incorporates their physical capabilities, as enhanced by training and inhibited by injuries, and also the capabilities of their equipment. In a skier's technique, you can see years of skiing on Minnesota ice or Utah's packed powder.

Tactics is the broad term for the choice of path a racer takes down a course, as dictated by the course setting, terrain, snow quality, and other variables. The shortest distance between two points is a straight line, but sharp corners are impossible on a steep and icy surface. Athletes stretch their turns into rounded arcs, weaving in and out of the fall line, able to see only two or three gates ahead at a time.

Tactics aren't only about making rounded turns or going straight; they often have to do with the direction a racer points when passing a gate. One may take a high line, rounding the top of the turn in order to swoop under a gate like a driver swinging wide to the right before jack-knifing left into a narrow parking spot; another may go deep, staying in the fall line and waiting to pass the gate before completing the turn. Different tactics have their own risks and rewards.

Racers are capable of refining the shape of these turns even as they make them. Every racer takes a different line, but certain strategies work better than others, which is why ruts tend to develop along the optimal path. Smart tactics might mean taking a risky line when a racer knows it will be easy to rebuild momentum, and skiing more conservatively when a mistake will have lingering consequences.

Certain tactics demand certain techniques, and certain techniques permit different tactics. Very few people possess a combination that allows them to turn cleanly and precisely in such a limited amount of space at such high speeds. (In World Cup giant slalom, for instance, a racer might turn 45 times in 75 seconds, at speeds of 40 to 60 miles per hour.)

Of the people who can do it, a few hundred of the very best compete in the World Cup every winter. Only on that circuit do they find the world's most challenging slopes, where constant terrain changes, tricky gate placement, and highly engineered surfaces make every turn a tactical and technical problem to be recognized and solved in a fraction of a fraction of a second.

There was no disputing that Ligety had adopted some of Bode Miller's tricks in these areas, having seen them up close at the 2002 Olympic giant slalom, where Miller won silver and Ligety was a seventeen-year-old volunteer course worker. The shaped-ski revolution Miller led had begun five years earlier, and Ligety didn't really know anything else. The curvy skis dramatically sped up the learning process for carving. On the World Cup circuit, the established racers had to adjust or get out of the sport. The most daring, strong, and adaptable racers radically changed their tactics, diving in on a tighter line where before they had needed big, rounded arcs. For several years, the marks racers created on World Cup courses changed from a single deep rut to a serried array of hash marks as skiers experimented with different lines through the course.

A key element of technique is angulation—the ability to get one's skis tilted way up on edge, which corresponds with the ability to fluidly rearrange one's body in something very different from the natural stance of an upright person. Because the world's best racers move so quickly and confidently through the angulated phase of a turn, it's hard to see how extreme it is without the help of the action photographers along a race course. Occasionally one of them will get a shot of Ligety coming straight on toward the camera as he passes a gate. At that moment, Ligety's shoulders may be level and his leg, the one all his weight is balanced on, extended so far out to his side that it is almost horizontal. At that moment, Ligety's skis are tipped on edge to such a degree that someone standing on the side of the course can read the manufacturer's logo on their bases.

When World Cup racers assess each other's technique, skiers like Ligety are often described as making "big angles," meaning that Ligety creates big angles not just with his skis but with his whole body. If you watch his upper body as he comes down a course, Ligety might seem to be standing up straight, but often his legs are extended out to his side, creating a sharp angle at his waist.

That technique gives Ligety enormous power to carve turns, but it is sometimes difficult to pull off on a rugged course, where the tilted ski can pop out of its groove, forcing Ligety to go down on his side.

———

On July 28, after two weeks at home in Utah, Lindsey Vonn flew to New Zealand, where she and the rest of the US Ski Team women planned to train at Coronet Peak. The guys from Head were waiting for her with a quiver of new skis. She was leaning heavily toward abandoning Rossignol for the Austrian company. But she wasn't certain yet.

Though offended by Rossignol's unilateral contract renegotiation, Vonn still had affection for people at the company and its quaint little factory in Voiron. She had skied on Rossignol since she was a little girl. Moreover, starting from scratch with an unfamiliar company would be one of the riskier moves she'd made in a carefully plotted career; it had the potential to throw her skiing so far off she wouldn't be able to adjust in time for winter.

Like all the racers, Vonn had long planned to use the summer training block in the southern hemisphere to tinker with her skis, her boots, and the bindings that joined them. Moving the bindings forward and back a fraction of an inch, or customizing a boot to make a racer's stance more knock-kneed or bowlegged—the tiniest modifications can profoundly affect a skier's performance. Modern racers are endlessly searching for the right vibration-dampening plate to go under their bindings. Every one of these variables impacts the others in infinite permutations. Changing one element might require changes to all the others. The collective term for these refinements is the set-up, and racers agonize over it. It determines how readily you can engage your edge for a carved turn, or drift across the snow's surface when you need to. And it is essential to get one's set-up dialed in before the winter arrives, because the FIS uses costly and embarrassing disqualifications to enforce its meticulous equipment rules for the World Cup.

By 2009, the FIS World Cup had rules for each discipline governing the minimum length of a ski and the minimum width of its waist. No more than 93 millimeters of material could come between a racer's sock and the snow; boot soles could be no thicker than 43 millimeters and there was a 50-millimeter limit on "stack height"—the combined thickness of ski, dampening plate, and binding. The most controversial rules limited the curvature of the ski—the hourglass-shaped sidecut that empowered Bode Miller's early career—which the FIS had gradually restricted.

Whether these equipment rules had achieved the FIS's stated goal of making the tour safer was uncertain, but there was no question they had intensified the relationships between racers and their servicemen, who typically worked for the factories. This was another reason why it was practically unheard of for a top skier to change suppliers before an Olympic season. Like every racer, Vonn knew that while the wax a serviceman put on her skis some January race day was crucial, it wasn't nearly as important as his July and August assistance with the set-up. To quiet her anxiety, Rainer Salzgeber had raised the possibility of her working with Heinz Hämmerle, suggesting that Miller's former serviceman could be hers if she followed through on the switch.

To the extent that Vonn was considering a switch, the only real alternative she saw to Rossignol was Head. In the previous four years, the company had become a juggernaut on the World Cup, luring top skiers like Hermann Maier away from Atomic and Anja Pärson from Salomon. In 2007, Bode Miller had made the jump. The company's downhill skis were clearly fast, but Vonn felt confident in their slalom construction too, in part because her friend Maria Riesch was a longtime Head skier; Maria, like Lindsey, was big and strong and successful in slalom events.

Thomas Vonn was overseeing the negotiations, ignoring Rossignol's deadlines while trying to work something out with Rainer Salzgeber. Like the other companies, Head was prepared to pay its racers fixed retainers along with performance bonuses, and Head's budget for the 2009–10 season was already drawn up. Salzgeber didn't have room to pay Lindsey the hundreds of thousands she was likely to make elsewhere. Thomas proposed a solution: a back-loaded, multiyear contract.

If Lindsey earned nothing in the first year, her compensation should increase correspondingly in 2010–11, the winter following the Olympic season. By then, Thomas argued, some of Head's current athletes would presumably have moved on to retirement, including Maier and Pärson and Miller—if Miller wasn't already retired. And Lindsey's going without salary in 2009–10 could only help the Vonns prove damages if they ever decided to sue Rossignol.

An outline was in place as Lindsey arrived in New Zealand. A five-year Head contract had been drafted, with an annual 425,000-euro base salary and bonuses for every kind of win—120,000 euros for an overall title, 4,000 euros for a national championship win, and 40,000 euros for each World Cup win. The bonuses would be capped at 575,000 euros. If Lindsey skied at her current level, she'd make a million euros from Head in the years leading up to the 2014 Games.

Lindsey floated above it all, firmly in control but by necessity detached; although it was an indignity—the world's number one skier forced to race for free in the most important season of her career—she had to find skis that worked. She couldn't think about money now. In three months the competition season would begin, and after that there would be very little time to test gear. As soon as she got on snow in New Zealand on August 1 she would need to start testing the skis, getting a feel for their flex and responsiveness—what the guys back in the factory called their running behavior.

She also got a feel for her new relationships. She immediately liked Heinz Hämmerle, finding him friendly and easy to talk to. But their time was limited. The camp was only two and a half weeks long. Vonn got to work, taking run after run, winnowing the quiver down, taking notes on the different models—how they acted in different parts of the turn, in different types of snow.

From the first run, the speed skis felt solid, and even more so when Hämmerle gave her a pair of the men's skis. When she got up over 70 miles per hour, speeds where even little ripples and ridges in the surface can be jarring and distracting, the skis were quiet and smooth. Part of that was the length and stiffness of the men's skis, but they also turned extremely well, responding to the subtle pressure she applied to different parts of the skis by shifting her weight, leaning against different sides of her boot cuff, or kinking her lower body just so, adjusting the angle of a knee or ankle or hip.

Seeing that Vonn was comfortable on the men's skis, Hämmerle brought out the beefiest skis of all. The intricate details of their construction defied his or anyone else's ability to describe, but the code numbers printed on them indicated that these were not just men's skis: these were Bode Miller's skis. Hämmerle was still in possession of about a half dozen of them, and since no one had heard from Miller, he had kept them.

Now he wanted Vonn to try them. Rainer Salzgeber had approved the transfer; the skis technically belonged to Head, and it was company policy that they were controlled by the servicemen. Not that Hämmerle said any of that; he simply nodded to the skis, which leaned with dozens of others against the wall beside his tuning bench.

"This is a good pair, but it may be too stiff for you," he said.

Vonn took them up on the mountain and had no problems. In fact, she liked them better than anything else she had tried. After a few runs, she decided to make it official. She talked to Thomas, who followed up with Salzgeber. Send over the contract; Lindsey is making the jump.

CHAPTER 10

Coming in from the Cold

At the start of the second week of September, Sasha Rearick was at the Center of Excellence, making some final preparations for the camp the men's speed team was about to stage in Chile. A film crew would be there at Portillo, and among Rearick's duties was integrating them into days of high-speed training runs and nights in the big old hotel that constitutes pretty much the entire resort. The ramp-up for the Olympic season had begun, and Rearick's organizational skills were already being tested. His wife was pregnant with their second child and was due sometime around the Winter Olympics, less than five months away.

Then Bode Miller called. Rearick would later do his best to pinpoint the date, and thought September 10 marked the first of what were several long telephone conversations in which Miller asked what steps would be involved if he were to return to the US Ski Team. In the previous week, Miller said, he had finally come around to the idea of racing another season on the World Cup tour and making a go at the Olympics in February.

Miller apologized for not responding to the messages Rearick had sent him in the spring. He explained his silence; he'd needed a complete break from the sport. Only by renouncing all of his ties to the ski world had he been able to reduce the possibility of retirement to the simple question of whether he was motivated to race. Now, he told Rearick, he was certain that he was. That spring and summer, Miller had spent as much time as he could with his daughter. The vertigo of rookie parenthood had called for his undivided attention.

"I had let everything come to a total stop," Miller would later recall. "There was no momentum carrying anything on. The team wasn't behind me, momentum-wise, because I'd been separated from the US team for two years. They didn't have any responsibility and had no right to really even ask me what my program was."

That Miller thought of it as a matter of "rights" was telling, and it was no misperception. The governing bodies that run Olympic sports in the United States do so under a set of rules endorsed by Congress that were intended to protect the rights of amateur athletes from the abuses that would otherwise occur in a system in which those governing bodies have monopolistic power. The Ted Stevens Amateur Sports Act required the USSA and every other national governing body recognized by the US Olympic Committee to select athletes as objectively as possible.

But for Rearick this wasn't about rights so much as an opportunity. While Rearick could theoretically have decided to turn Miller away, the thought never crossed his mind. He was ecstatic to work with Miller, a skier who had made a career-long habit of doing things that no one in American skiing had even thought possible before.

And this was one of those things. Rearick looked to the calendar. Nobody he could think of had willingly waited this long to commit to a competition season. The team's budgets had been set months earlier; plane tickets had been purchased and hotel rooms booked. Most of the guys on the team had gotten more than twenty days on snow. Even the injured Ligety had done more training. In a few days, the men's speed team would be en route to Portillo for a two-week block of downhill and super G training. The first World Cup race of the season was about six weeks away, the Olympics six months.

What Rearick wanted to know was what kind of shape Miller was in. On that subject, there was good news and bad news; the good news was that Miller's ankle had fully healed. The injury early in the season before that had trailed him through the winter had turned out to be serious: it was broken, Miller said—with cracked bones apparent in images of the ankle joint. Continuously aggravated through the season, without a chance to heal, the damage had actually deformed his foot.

The bad news was that, outside of some golfing and volleyball, Miller hadn't done much conditioning over the summer. Mostly, Miller confessed, he'd been moving at the pace set by his eighteen-month-old daughter. But as he and Rearick talked about fitness, they circled back to a shared memory they had of a dryland training camp led by Rearick years before in Wyoming, and a particularly grueling workout in which Miller had pushed Rearick up a hill in a wheelbarrow. "Intensity" was a word they kept using for what the next four months would require, and that set the tone for the rest of their conversation. Rearick didn't need to tell Miller that nothing like this had ever been done before. The experimental nature of it excited both of them. The world's best racers had a huge head start on Miller, but Rearick knew that Miller thrived in an underdog role far better than he did as a favorite.

A lot had changed since May 2007, when Miller had walked away to form his own team. Rearick told Miller that he didn't really mind if Miller wanted to travel the tour in his motor home. In fact, Rearick said, it had always seemed like a good idea to him. He had encouraged the team to adopt the concept of having a mobile home in Europe to serve as a kitchen and gathering place at the bottom of the mountain.

What mattered, Rearick told Miller, was effort. Getting back into racing shape would require an intense remedial conditioning program—all the same pain and suffering Miller usually put himself through, but in a compressed time frame. The basic idea would be to reach peak performance by January, for the biggest races on the men's tour, Wengen and Kitzbühel, just before the Olympic team was selected.

Before the conversation was finished, they were already designing Miller's season. Portillo was out of the question, as was the season-opening giant slalom in Austria; Miller was too out of shape for all that. Besides, he didn't even know where his skis were. But the team was going to Europe in early October, to train on snow there ahead of the opener. Rearick proposed that Miller come along and train on the glaciers as the rest of the guys prepped for the race. The priorities would be to get fit, test skis, and find a set-up that worked.

Down the road, there was a World Cup slalom in mid-November in Finland. Rearick and Miller agreed that if he was ready by then, it would be a safe place to start. If not, they would target the first down-hill and super G of the World Cup season, at Lake Louise in late November. From there on, it would be a full World Cup schedule, a race a week at least, until the Olympics. When it came to Vancouver, they agreed on one goal: minimizing distractions. The degree of attention America paid to their little sport in an Olympic season jumped at least a hundredfold, and it took a disciplined, unified plan to keep doing things as normal. Rearick promised Miller that he would work to insulate him from media intrusion as much as possible.

Come out to Utah next week, Rearick told Miller, and do some physical testing at the Center of Excellence. There are also some people here you'll need to talk to. And with that, Rearick hung up and walked upstairs to the executive offices, where he found Tom Kelly, the team's vice president for communications. Kelly, who had been at USSA for twenty-three years, was one of Marolt's most loyal aides.

Rearick asked Kelly to clear some space in his schedule in the following week to meet with Bode Miller.

"He's coming here?" Kelly asked.

"He's coming here," Rearick said.

"He's thinking of coming back?" Kelly asked.

"He's coming back," Rearick said.

In the third week of September, while some members of the US men's team were visiting a wind tunnel to test out their new downhill suits, and Lindsey Vonn was on a circuit of promotional events, Bode Miller went to the Center of Excellence to finalize his rapprochement with the US Ski Team. Lowell Taub, Miller's agent from Creative Artists Agency and a driving force behind Team America, was along for the trip.

While Taub cooled his heels at the ski team offices, his client and friend met with Bill Marolt, Tom Kelly, and the team's vice president for athletics, Luke Bodensteiner. All of them thought Miller seemed upbeat, refreshed, and positive about the Olympics. It was a cordial meeting, with everyone ready to make it work. Marolt proposed that Miller call the US Olympic Committee and notify the organization of his new plans. A phone call was arranged between Miller and USOC chairman Larry Probst, which went fine.

It wasn't that USSA needed USOC's permission to reinstate Miller; he would have to qualify for the Olympics, just like anyone else. The goal was to notify all the stakeholders in the Vancouver campaign so that no one was surprised when the news broke. In 2006, the USOC had been irritated enough by Miller's perceived mischief that it vowed to educate future Olympic team members about ambassadorship.

After the meetings, Sasha Rearick ran Miller through a series of physical tests in the gym downstairs. The results confirmed that Miller was seriously out of shape, falling far short of his previous benchmarks in power and aerobic efficiency. Come winter, he would be skiing himself into shape, so he might be strong by January if he didn't get hurt.

Meanwhile, Marolt got on the phone with perhaps the most important stakeholder: Bob Beattie.

Beattie had been a mentor for Marolt since the elder man had recruited him to the NCAA champion University of Colorado ski team in the late 1950s. In 1961, when the USSA tapped Beattie to prepare a team for the 1962 world championships in Chamonix, France,

Beattie took his team, Marolt included, to the big European races. He later persuaded US skiing to extend his mandate through the 1964 Winter Olympics. This was the origin of the modern US Ski Team. Before then, the team had been an ad-hoc squad that was formed and disbanded for every Olympic and world championship season. After success in Innsbruck—two of his protégés won the US's first ever men's Olympic alpine medals—Beattie had gone on to help conceive the World Cup tour, commentate on countless races for television, and serve as a trustee of the team. Novelist and screenwriter James Salter had used him as a model for Gene Hackman's character in the film *Downhill Racer*.

Beattie—or "Coach," as he was called—had a particularly close relationship with Marolt. They talked regularly, Marolt calling the older man at his handsome home near Aspen for advice and perspective. Beattie had once even bailed Marolt out of an Austrian jail. The incident had occurred at the 1964 Games, when the twenty-year-old Marolt and some friends had stepped out of a party in downtown Innsbruck in the wee hours of February 6, in search of a way back to the Olympic Village.

About a block from the bar, Marolt spied a Renault bus with the keys in it and decided to take his friends for a little ride. He went the wrong way down a one-way street and was pulled over. Accounts would vary about the confrontation that ensued. Police claimed Marolt refused to leave the vehicle and, when one officer reached in to pull him out, kicked the officer's hand hard enough to break a finger. Marolt's version, memorialized in a letter that later went to the US Olympic Committee and the vice consul's office at the American embassy in Vienna, was that he merely shuffled his feet to free his legs.

Either way, Marolt spent the night in a jail cell with two other Americans. Beattie didn't learn about it until the next morning, when he boarded the team bus heading for a training session and noted Marolt's absence ("Uh, maybe he's in jail," one of the skiers said).

Marolt was in custody for more than forty hours, during which time the preliminary charge of car theft was reduced. The owner of the vehicle came forward to say the Americans had permission to use it, and Marolt's three-month probationary sentence was suspended.

For decades afterward, the episode was a piece of lore that the two men could joke about in familiar company. But that changed after Miller's 2006 contretemps with the US Ski Team, in which Miller's penchant for partying had driven Marolt into the role of a disciplinarian. Now the legend of Marolt's 1964 arrest threatened to make him look like a hypocrite. He was inclined to give others the second chance he had been given.

Beattie had always been somewhat skeptical of the team's management of Bode Miller, whose grandfather Beattie had known decades earlier—back in New Hampshire, where Beattie grew up, and where he brought the World Cup to Cannon Mountain in its inaugural year.

Beattie was a great fan of Vince Lombardi, and had run the ski team in a similar style; it was many things, but it was not a democracy. The philosophy of personal sacrifice for the good of the team worked in the 1960s. Marolt, however, knew this approach wouldn't work with Miller, or with most modern athletes. Marolt tried to be flexible and sometimes regretted making the effort, according to those in his inner circle. His reward for giving Miller unprecedented freedom had occasionally been to suffer disrespectful critiques of the team's leadership. But over the years, people at USSA had learned to joke about it, as had Marolt. It was just Bode being Bode.

During the past decade, most people had accepted that insight, but Beattie wasn't one of them. The coach was protective of the US team and of Marolt. While he had enjoyed watching Jack Kenney's grandson bring so much excitement to the sport, Beattie had his reservations about this comeback. He was worried that Miller was going to turn on the ski team again. When Marolt called him to say that Miller might be coming back, Beattie said he was ambivalent about the whole thing.

"I'm not sure, Bill, what I would do," Beattie told Marolt. "But if I were you, and I didn't have a great men's team, it would be a no-brainer. One of the best ski racers the sport's ever produced at my fingertips. I would take a chance. But I would be suspicious. I am suspicious. I wish everybody well. That's the nicest thing I can say."

Rainer Salzgeber was in Vancouver scouting Olympic accommodations for Head's reps when Bode Miller called to inform him that his eleventh-hour return to skiing was official. Salzgeber had stopped in British Columbia on his way back to Austria from Chile, where he and Lindsey Vonn had finalized the contract that would make her a Head skier.

Now here was Miller, wanting to know if Salzgeber could outfit him with gear and service by October. Salzgeber, who hadn't heard from Miller since the spring, was stunned. He couldn't immediately think of any World Cup racer who had returned to skiing so late in the year unless forced to do so by injury. Salzgeber was overjoyed at Miller's decision, but it wasn't convenient, especially now that many of Miller's old skis were in the possession of Lindsey Vonn.

It was yet another eccentric move from Miller, whom Salzgeber had admired since the day in November 1997 when he saw Miller at Park City in his first World Cup race. Back then, Salzgeber was a skier on the dominant Austrian machine and the US Ski Team was an outright joke in men's tech events. Then Miller came down the giant slalom hill, starting sixty-ninth to finish eleventh—a spectacular result considering the ruts Miller had skied in. Salzgeber could still see the intensity—the kid was pushing so hard, wearing a pair of K2 skis that weren't even World Cup race skis. It was ugly, for sure, but some of the turns showed a genius that Salzgeber had been unable to forget.

Miller's star had risen as Salzgeber's fell; after Salzgeber retired from ski racing in 2001 and went to work for Head, he remained fascinated by Miller's skiing—the inimitable tactics and technique that could only work with the right equipment. He watched as Miller moved restlessly between ski contracts (from K2 to Fischer to Rossignol to Atomic) and read all the stories about Miller's intimate relationships with the factories. Here was a true test pilot.

When Salzgeber became the race director at Head, he resolved to recruit Miller to the brand. In the spring of 2006, after Miller's Torino debacle, Salzgeber succeeded in wooing him away from Atomic. Miller's experience with four different companies had given him an extraordinary understanding of ski equipment that was deeply valuable to Head's engineers, who used Miller's feedback to build faster skis.

Now Miller needed Head, and Salzgeber promised to do his best. They planned for him to come to Kennelbach in October, prior to the team's training camp, to get fitted for new boots. Hämmerle was off-limits, but Salzgeber promised that Miller would be in the capable hands of another serviceman, Guntram Mathis, with whom he had worked before.

The key contribution Head could make was something the factory prided itself on: quick turnaround. How rapidly and accurately the company could replicate a piece of equipment to meet a skier's specifications was a defining element of any top skier's success. Without off-season training, Miller was going to be finding his set-up as he went.

***

"No sportswriter has any feel or passion," Miller once said. "They just want to fill up their shit with quotes from other people."

Tom Kelly, who spearheaded USSA's communications department, figured on this sentiment for his starting point now that the time had come to make Miller's return public. Kelly had no idea how the news would be received by the American sports media, whose cyclical interest in skiers was just perking up in September. With a few exceptions, the American media had had zero interaction with Miller since Torino. For the two years he ran Team America, Miller's unofficial policy had been to avoid most face-to-face contact with journalists, walking past the cameras and the notepads and turning down almost every formal interview request. Kelly had to wonder if the Bode Miller who was coming back for 2009–10 would act and speak differently, or remain true to himself, or find some way to do both.

After his meetings in Park City, Miller had returned to California.

When Kelly called him there to propose a simple press release, followed by a conference call with members of the media, Miller surprised him by suggesting they do something in person. Kelly arranged a press conference at the Staples Center in Los Angeles on September 24, where Miller would announce his intention to race in the upcoming season.

About forty members of the media responded to the invitation, with many more telephoning in to listen through a speakerphone sitting on the dais, where Miller sat wearing a green baseball cap and a week's growth of facial hair. Sasha Rearick was there, with Kelly acting as the moderator. When Miller took the microphone, he made reference to a quarterback who was notorious for his inability to make retirement last.

"I can relate to Brett Favre," Miller said. "You know, you enjoy your sport, you dedicate your life to it. And you can see how it would be nice to walk away and try something new. And then you walk away, and there's obviously a big hole left where that sport was, where, you know, especially in my case, it's my main form of expression."

Miller was relatively easygoing during the question-and-answer portion of the gathering. The most meaningful question may have come from David Leon Moore of *USA Today*, who asked whether Miller had any apologies for his Olympic effort in 2006.

It was a fair question, and one that in other circumstances Miller might have confronted with less diplomacy. On this day he answered that anyone can look back on any area of their life and wallow in regret, but that he was looking forward to the season in front of him.

"Actions are going to speak more loudly than apologies," Miller said. "Your actions carry a lot more weight."

There was a flurry of print media reports about Bode Miller's return, many of them charged with excitement at the prospect of having Miller back for another season skiing on some of the same high Alpine mountains in winter that Lance Armstrong climbed in summer (Armstrong had commenced his own star-crossed unretirement the year before).

The two men, their careers coinciding almost exactly, had been called, in France's national sports daily, *L'Equipe*, "les deux faces de l'Amérique." While Armstrong enjoyed far more adoration and wealth at home, Miller was recognized in the Alps for having an abundance of panache—a claim never made for Armstrong, much to his chagrin. One man was bent on total world domination, the other was preoccupied with an extreme form of authenticity.

In a 2005 *Rolling Stone* article, Miller had called out Armstrong as a doper, though such was the power of the Armstrong myth that the backlash forced even Bode Miller to distance himself from his honest comments, and even make a small contribution to Armstrong's cancer awareness foundation.

Miller was perhaps a perfect ambassador for his home state's "Live Free or Die" ethos. He had grown up beside one of New Hampshire's proudest locales, Franconia Notch, a dramatic granite gorge that until one foggy morning in 2003 had been home to a famous rocky outcropping that jutted out of a 1,200-foot-high cliff to produce what looked like a human face in profile. The Old Man of the Mountain was an iconic New Hampshire landmark, adorning the state's license plates and road signs.

Not long after the craggy face crumbled from its perch on May 3, 2003, robbing the area of a tourist attraction, a reporter had visited Miller and was surprised to find he was pleased that the rock formation—noted in the writings of Daniel Webster and Nathaniel Hawthorne—was now a pile of rubble.

"I think it's awesome. I totally support that. It should have fallen off years ago, I think," Miller said in that interview, amid the leafy bachelor-pad comfort of his house. "I mean, they had it chained up there. It was all man-made and manufactured. If you went up there and saw it, it was like a travesty to nature. That's one of the things that's supposed to be cool about it—that it's not man-made."

Miller had been up to it for a close inspection and knew it was being held on by cables and other artificial props. Its collapse provided him the occasion to joyfully call out a false idol.

"That's the kind of thing that anxiety and stupid human nature tends to screw up," Miller said. "If it had been left entirely alone, maybe it would have crumbled off and turned into, you know, an eagle or something, sitting on the cliff, and it would have been the 'Old Eagle on the Hill' or whatever. But now with this it crumbled off and it just looks like the side of the mountain now. Maybe we shot ourselves in the foot. I think it should have been gone a hundred years ago. It doesn't make it cool when they strap it on there. It was a strap-on old man."

CHAPTER 11

Back to Work

Every October, the national teams of the World Cup converge upon the glaciers at the roof of Europe for their final training camps ahead of the first World Cup races in Sölden, Austria, at the end of the month.

The racers ski on fields of snow that the glaciers refrigerate from underneath. Hundreds of acres wide, these snowfields partly melt away every summer and typically begin growing again in September with the winter's first storms. When they do, the ski areas expect and rely upon an influx of dozens of ski teams that rent training space for a week or two. The greatest number of racers usually congregates at Pitztal, a high ski area at the end of a deep, long valley in the Tyrol region of Austria. It is just one valley over from Sölden, where the race hill, according to World Cup rules, is off-limits in the days leading up to the competition.

It can get crowded up there, so Pitztal appoints a "slope boss" to apportion training space, and this *Pistenchef* sometimes assigns all the teams to one slope in loosely defined lanes. It is a sight—ski racers from all around the world weaving through parallel courses tucked so closely together that it isn't always obvious to a casual observer which gates are part of which course.

The amount of available space on the glaciers declined dramatically in the first decade of the twenty-first century thanks to record-breaking warmth that broiled the Alps, especially the deadly heat wave of 2003, continental Europe's hottest summer since 1540. After that ordeal, the Pitztalers and Söldeners looked upon the rapid diminishment of their glaciers with a new alarm. These were old farming communities that had spent a century transitioning away from agriculture toward a tourism economy, and their indispensable assets were the ancient glaciers that sustained their ski areas.

In 2004, as part of a University of Innsbruck experiment, Pitztal unrolled several huge spools of white, fleece-like insulation over key sections of the glacier. Initially the hope was to preserve a few critical areas where the glacier's disappearance would disrupt the flow of skier traffic between the various sections of the mountain. The experiment worked; though awkward and costly, the program helped Pitztal save a few meters of snow and ice each season on the endangered slabs.

In 2009, one of the first ski teams to arrive at Pitztal was Finland. When they took the main lift, the Pitz-Panoramabahn, for their first day of training on September 28, they could see the glacier's demise up close. Their assigned section was a groomed run that skirted the base of the Vorderer Brunnenkogel, a sharp peak that looms over the ski area. So much of the glacier had melted over the summer that fields of naked boulders were visible everywhere around the base of the peak.

Glacial retreat is a self-reinforcing cycle. Snow and ice reflect the sun's rays, but as warm temperatures expose dark rocks amid the glaciers, those black surfaces soak up the sun's energy, heating the nearby ice and exposing more rocks. The Finns could see one of these new boulder fields at Pitztal, a tapering peninsula of rock extending into what had traditionally been a ski run. The Finns' course ran parallel to that strip, about 100 meters from its edge. The fact that there would be no fence in between bothered no one, including the team's best giant slalom skier, a twenty-two-year-old racer named Marcus Sandell.

There had been a light snowfall the night before, and on Sandell's first run down the training course the snow felt a little tricky, as if there might be a hard crust on top of softer snow. About a third of the way through the run, when he was traveling about 50 miles per hour, his edge caught on this surface and jolted his leg so violently that it spun him around 180 degrees. Still upright but skiing backward, he careened away from the course and toward the strip of boulders he'd seen that morning.

The best strategy for self-preservation might have been for Sandell to deliberately fall, but with the first GS of the season less than a month away, he didn't want to risk injury. With his momentum undiminished, he spun himself around and discovered he was no more than 30 feet from the edge of the run. Moving at about 40 miles per hour, Sandell decided to try to jump across the rocks. From his angle of approach, Sandell couldn't tell how wide the strip of rocks was until he reached the edge of the snow. As he leapt, his landing area came into view: about 100 feet of black, sharp boulders.

Sandell doesn't remember the impact. Coaches who saw the accident later told him he bounced several times across the rock field before sliding onto the snow on the other side. The first thing Sandell remembers is lying on that snow with all the wind knocked out of him, desperately heaving to fill his lungs with air. There was a strange sensation in his abdomen, and his first thought was that he'd broken his ribs. After about thirty seconds his team's physio showed up, and then more people, and soon someone called for a helicopter. By the time it arrived, Sandell was breathing a little better but his body felt worse and worse, particularly in his stomach area. Paramedics hooked him to an intravenous painkiller drip, which brought some relief. The helicopter took Sandell from Pitztal to a hospital in Innsbruck, where doctors rolled him into a body scanner to identify the damage. For Sandell, the pain, terror, and confusion were unprecedented. When he saw his team's physio standing beside him, Sandell screamed at him to tell the doctors to give him something that would knock him out, which they did.

When Sandell woke up, a doctor informed him that they had removed his left kidney, which had been ruptured badly in the fall. He had also lacerated his spleen, and more than three liters of blood had flooded into his abdomen. He had also broken bones in his hand, nose, and spine. Without the helicopter, the doctors said, Sandell would almost certainly have died. The salvation of his spinal cord had probably been the back protector he was wearing under his race suit, a plastic shell that had printed an outline of its shape onto his skin in an oval of blue bruises.

Would Sandell's accident have happened twenty years before? Certainly not in that place; the boulders that nearly destroyed him were buried deep under glassy glacial ice in those days—ice that hadn't been precipitation for at least a thousand years. But the main reason a ski racer training at Pitztal would have probably been safer in the 1980s was the skis. The skis of 2009 were springy, touchy things, with extraordinary propulsion built into their layered core and voluptuous curves. Modern skis give racers unprecedented control, but when they are thrown off balance—when one of the sharp steel edges along the tip digs into the snow without the racer's absolutely undivided attention—the skis have the power to send racers hurtling across the landscape in violent spins unlike anything seen before the 1990s.

To compensate, the FIS lines race courses with high fences and massive airbags, and has also put limits on equipment, strictly regulating the allowed curvature of skis. The efficacy of these rules is fiercely debated on the World Cup tour, but as the limits are adjusted and readjusted it is more important than ever for the world's best racers to train in the off-season and familiarize themselves with their gear, even if there is barely enough snow to ski on.

⁂

On October 1, 2009, the US men's tech team departed for Europe (the speed guys were still down in Chile). From their scattered homes, they joined up at various airport terminals until they all converged in Munich, their arrival marking the team's forty-fifth season in Europe— that was, if you went by the acceptable definition of 1964 as the watershed moment when Bob Beattie made the team a permanent but self-renewing institution.

Though the team had a much stronger footing in the Alps by now, some dislocation still defined the racers' experience. Central Europe remained a foreign land. It demanded that they adapt to little breakfasts, incomprehensible languages, and bathtubs without wall mounts for the shower nozzle. The gas stations might have an Erotik Mart built in. The pizza you ordered might have an undercooked egg in the middle of it. There would also be sparkling highways with long tunnels, high tolls, and no speed limits; liters, meters, and military time; and the constant math of time zone dislocation, and when to connect with girlfriends and parents and even children, six or eight or nine hours behind them. This fish-out-of-water feeling eroded the confidence of many a young American racer.

Disorientation faded over long drives in fleets of Audis, minivans, boxy diesel cargo vans, and even mobile kitchens, heading into the Alps with upbeat, savvy Sasha Rearick leading the way. This time their destination was Saas-Fee, Switzerland, a town of restricted automobile access. A train took them up the final climb to the enchanting settlement of cozy lodges and pubs. As darkness fell, it seemed that this town, a glowing refuge amid a cold blackness, was at the roof of the world, but for the spotlights of a few lonely snowcats on midnight grooming jobs, maybe at work on the hill itself. It suggested an impossible steepness, another world up above the little town. The Americans finally fell asleep under plush duvets and woke up sledgehammered by jet lag. In a day or two, they'd be training to perform in the big show.

For the Americans—and Canadians, and to some extent the Scandinavians as well—survival on the World Cup tour requires overcoming this sense of not belonging that for some racers seems to extend to the podium. Every young American racing in the Alps needs to confront this vague sense of anomie, punctuated by bolts of the natural fear and inspiration that such dramatic mountains can provoke in any living person.

Bode Miller had been at it for thirteen seasons, in hundreds of ski towns in every corner of the Alps, from his first FIS race at Alpe d'Huez in 1996 to this. It was just around the corner from the Matterhorn, and was surrounded by glaciated peaks over 4,000 meters high. That month, Aksel Lund Svindal was training there, as was Switzerland's hot young phenom on the women's tour, Lara Gut.

Rearick was taking his guys there after calling around and learning that training space was limited in Pitztal. He had prepared for this by not overpreparing, deliberately leaving the US men's team's October plans vague. Settling on Saas-Fee, Rearick booked training space and hotel rooms and flights for the team's athletes and staff. With any luck, Rearick hoped, Miller would get his first day on snow on October 3, when his teammates were getting their thirtieth. Even Ligety, despite his injury, had managed by that point to get in thirty-two days of summer skiing.

Dawn revealed a vast and varied wilderness, and the effortlessly hospitable old innkeepers of Europe. Hardships of travel aside, the American ski racers knew how lucky they were that this was their sport's arena. Whereas most American ski areas were an industry grafted onto a mountain town after World War Two, the ski culture in Lech or St. Moritz predated the concept of tourism itself. An inexpensive ticket got you access to a sprawling system of minimally engineered runs with no significant closures. After a few runs, you could stop off at a low-slung, heavy-timbered lodge a few thousand feet above town and enter to find waiters in lederhosen serving beer and noodles while a tuba and accordion played softly in the background. Remove your boots and gloves and leave them warming near the fireplace. Order strudel and an espresso, and admire the stuffed marmot and deer-antler chandeliers.

For someone as seasoned as Miller, all of this was unremarkable, and yet he knew he would have missed it tremendously had he not come back to the tour. He'd grown gills for exactly these currents, and sometimes seemed practically addicted to the tour. One of the most distinctive records Miller had set during his career reflected his umbilical tie to the World Cup. Between 2002 and 2006, Miller had started in 136 consecutive World Cup races, a streak so unlikely and unprecedented that nobody even realized it was a record until Miller broke the streak on January 28, 2006, choosing a round of golf in Dubai with his brother Chelone, over the Garmisch-Partenkirchen downhill.

On October 7, Lindsey Vonn finished an interview for Austrian television at the Hotel Schwartz, near Innsbruck, got behind the wheel of her new Audi RS6, and headed west on the highway in the direction of Liechtenstein. High mountains rose steeply on each side of her as the pristine roadway passed through a valley dotted by castles and small medieval villages.

Before reaching the Arlberg Pass, Vonn turned off the highway and steered her way through a familiar set of intersections and roundabouts to the road that would take her south, up a long valley to Pitztal, where she would join the US women's team for their final block of training ahead of the October 25 season opener at Sölden.

Her last day on snow had been September 18, in Chile, and the three weeks since then had been a blur of airports, publicists, and the perquisites of moderate fame. After returning to the US, Vonn had set out on a promotional tour that took her through Los Angeles, San Diego, Colorado, New York, Boston, Chicago, and Minneapolis. During that whirlwind she'd thrown out an opening pitch at Wrigley Field, strolled the red carpet at the Emmys, chatted up wealthy USSA benefactors at a gala ski team fundraiser in Boston, appeared live on the *Today* show in New York, and visited a Bronx film set to watch the shooting of an episode of her favorite TV show, *Law and Order.*

She had finally flown to Europe on October 4, attending an event in Munich on behalf of Vail Resorts. On the 6th, she went to Austria for the television interview, and now here she was at last making her way up this Tyrolean valley. The road skirted a river that was a milky greenish-blue from the fine-ground rock sediment embedded in the glaciers the river drained.

Her plan was to start training slalom at Pitztal on the 10th. Slalom, the event that had been her first love back at Buck Hill, had taken a backseat in her career to the speed events, but it was still a necessity.

She needed to keep her skills sharp if she wanted to threaten for the World Cup title, particularly in the combined events.

Compartmentalization was the key to such a schizophrenic lifestyle. The red carpets and backstage schmoozing were fun, but they were work too. Most of the appearances fulfilled requirements in her contracts with her sponsors and the ski team itself. But now Vonn needed to switch her thoughts back to skiing, and focus her mental energy on making the final adjustments to her new equipment set-up with Head.

The whole enterprise depended on the reliable team she'd built around herself to manage the diverse priorities in her busy life. She was alone on the race courses, but most of the rest of the time she was accompanied by an entourage that helped insulate her from distractions, maximize her performance, and seize opportunities that came up, whether that meant getting her to the French Open in a sponsor's corporate jet or making sure the cuffs of her ski boots positioned her lower legs at the perfect angle.

Thomas had recently started calling their group the Vonntourage, and had even snatched up Internet addresses in case they ended up using the name for commercial purposes. As she headed into the competition season, the Vonntourage gave Lindsey the chance to participate in the US Ski Team's programs when it suited her or break off on her own when she needed a more customized training session.

Other racers on the US Ski Team could rely on the team's coaches— Lindsey did too—but those coaches were thinking of the divergent interests of all the team's racers. Vonn knew that her private team entirely and uninterruptedly focused on her needs. She had extra eyes and ears on the slope, not only watching her ski but gathering crucial information about the wider ski world. Where was the good snow for training? What were the best hotels and airports to use for the next race?

The beauty of being the number one skier in the world was that everyone wanted to train with her, which allowed her to raise the intensity level of her own training. If Vonn wanted to go train with Maria Riesch or Anja Pärson, a former overall winner from Sweden who had also won races in every discipline, she could. Or she could stick with the US team at Pitztal, which was what she did this month, arriving just in time for a huge snowstorm that made it impossible to train. The chalet-bound teams lost another day to fog.

Still, she had to be grateful just to be healthy when she heard about what had happened to Lara Gut, the eighteen-year-old who had finished runner-up to her in both speed races at the world championships in Val d'Isère. A journalist texted Vonn with news that Gut had fallen and dislocated her hip over at Saas-Fee. It looked like Gut's season was over before it began. She would have to wait for the 2014 Olympics.

Vonn responded to the journalist's text with one word: "Ouch."

Austrian skiing began the 2009–10 ski season with the loss of one of its national heroes: Olympic great Toni Sailer, who swept up the three gold medals at the 1956 Winter Games in Cortina d'Ampezzo, Italy. Handsome and entrepreneurial, Sailer had converted a brilliant ski résumé into a career in movies. He also coached the national team and spearheaded the Hahnenkamm races in his hometown of Kitzbühel.

Sailer, who had died of cancer on August 24 at age seventy-three, was the model for all the Austrian ski idols who followed. And none of them, with the exception of Franz Klammer, had earned the prominence and esteem of Hermann Maier, the indestructible champion who came out of nowhere in 1996 to supplant the Italian Alberto Tomba as skiing's most visible worldwide personality.

Maier enjoyed one of the greatest careers the sport had ever seen, and it finally came to an end on October 13, less than two weeks before the 2009–10 World Cup season was set to begin. That day the thirty-six-year-old champion called a news conference in Vienna, where he tearfully announced his retirement. Although he'd collected fifty-four World Cup wins between 1997 and 2008, four overall World Cup titles, and ten medals from the Olympics and world championships, the statistics didn't begin to illustrate the spectacular and unusual trajectory of his career.

A burly, blond country boy from the mountains south of Salzburg, Maier had gotten a late start on the record books. When he was fifteen years old, a painful knee disorder, paired with his father's hospitalization following an accident, led Maier to drop out of one of Austria's elite ski academies, the Skihandelsschule in Schladming, in 1988 and start working as a bricklayer's apprentice. In the winter, while his former classmates qualified for provincial race teams and began competing internationally, Maier worked as a ski instructor, while setting his own training courses after hours and studying books on skiing technique. He entered local races when he could afford to and devoted himself to physical conditioning.

Maier was a twenty-three-year-old outsider in 1996 when he finally got a shot at the Europa Cup, where four quick victories convinced the Austrian national team to give him a World Cup start position. Within a year, Maier was winning, first in super G, then in downhill and giant slalom as well. He won a record thirty-two of the first 100 World Cup races he started.

Muscular and fearless, Maier was a new terror on the tour, snorting and frothing like a caged bull in the start house and bursting onto the course with an aggressive technique. Leaning forward against the cuff of his boots, Maier loaded a huge amount of power into his Atomic skis and swatted gates out of the way as if they were twigs, often battering them with the thin, yellow helmet he wore.

Maier was a clear favorite heading into the 1998 Winter Games in Nagano, Japan, but crashed off one of the downhill course's biggest jumps, springing straight up into the blue sky, spinning his arms in a vain effort to right himself. Maier was in the air for nearly two seconds, flying more than 130 feet before he landed on his head with a sickening crunch. His body bounced and cartwheeled through several layers of safety netting, hurtling into the soft powder on the side of the race venue and finally coming to a stop. Maier suffered a bruised sternum, a dislocated left shoulder, bruises on his lower back and a sprained right knee. But the look on his face as he pushed himself back to his feet wasn't one of fear or even of great pain, but rather of disgust. Remarkably, Maier came back to win the Olympic super G three days later and, a few days after that, the giant slalom too.

Maier left those Olympics with fame that transcended the sport. His crash, immortalized on the cover of *Sports Illustrated*, earned him an invitation from Jay Leno to *The Tonight Show*, where he appeared alongside Arnold Schwarzenegger—a real-world Hans and Franz—and embraced the inevitable nickname "the Herminator."

Over the next few seasons, Maier ruled the sport. In 1999–2000, he won ten races on his way to amassing 2,000 World Cup points, a new record, and the next year he won thirteen races, tying the record for victories in a single season that the Swedish technical specialist Ingemar Stenmark had set in 1979. Then, on August 24, 2001, Maier was riding his customized motorcycle near the town of Radstadt when he collided with a car driven by a German retiree, crushing Maier's lower right leg. The seven-hour surgery that followed involved the insertion of a 15-inch titanium rod with four metal pins and extensive skin grafts, where flesh from his arm was transplanted to his mangled shin.

All of Austria followed Maier's recovery with the kind of fascination Americans had reserved for the Apollo 13 astronauts out of touch behind the far side of the moon. Maier missed the 2002 Winter Olympics, and didn't struggle back into racing until the following season. Then, in January of 2003, he returned to the World Cup, winning the super G at Kitzbühel and tying Bode Miller for the silver medal at the world championships in Switzerland a few weeks later. He went on to prevail in a tight race for the overall World Cup in 2004.

Maier was a changed man after the motorcycle accident. Gone were the malevolent start house snarls, replaced by a soulful stoicism. In interviews he was more reflective than before, advocating greater restrictions on equipment for young racers. Rather than vying for the overall title, he tailored his seasons for success at big events like the 2006 Winter Games, where he won two medals. His final World Cup victory came in the super G at Lake Louise on November 30, 2008. He finished the 2008–09 season twenty-sixth in the World Cup standings (eighth among Austrians), and underwent arthroscopic surgery to repair torn cartilage in his right knee.

At the Vienna news conference where he made his announcement, Maier said he'd felt strong in the pre-season training on the glacier near Sölden, but this time the strength was urging him to slow down; he said a desire to ski for the rest of his life whenever he wanted to had overridden his desire to race another season, at another Olympics. He thanked his family, sponsors, coaches, doctors, and teammates. And at the end of his statement, he noted that the Austrian mountains might still contain a *verstecktes Talent herumtreibt*—a "hidden talent hanging around."

To Bode Miller, who was a careful student of ski racing history, Maier's retirement was not just a farewell to one renowned racer but to a whole era of skiing—one whose passing Miller had already begun to mourn.

Miller had come onto the World Cup in 1997, in the middle of what in retrospect he believed to have been one of the most competitive periods in World Cup history. Although Miller had an abiding respect for truly old-school ski racing—the days of leather boots, wooden skis, and minimal safety netting—he had come to believe that the late 1990s and early 2000s had been a high-water mark for the sport.

A decade later, Miller believed that the World Cup, especially the downhill, had gotten tamer. The courses were set to slow racers down and the equipment was restricted by more and more regulations. Some people wrote this off as nostalgia. They said that Miller's memory was distorting things, arbitrarily glorifying an era that only a dwindling few of his peers had witnessed up close.

But Miller believed that Austrian rivals Hermann Maier and Stephan Eberharter, and the Norwegian duo Lasse Kjus and Kjetil André Aamodt, were more authentically aggressive and daring than the current generation. He had watched those guys work themselves into an animalistic state in the start house and lunge onto the courses with an almost irrational disregard for a safe outcome.

Miller believed that Maier, at his peak, wasn't even thinking about winning races. He wasn't trying to earn 100 points in the overall chase, or collect a check for 100,000 Swiss francs. The only thing Maier was emotionally attached to, Miller believed, was accessing some deep part of himself that saw a path down the race course that was just out of reach—just beyond the limit of what had looked possible.

It was artistry; you couldn't fake it. It offended Miller when his peers on the World Cup imitated Maier's start house routine and then skied cautiously. A ski racer still had to live within some physical limitations: of course, you still had to train; you had to be physically fit, have a fast pair of skis and a fine-tuned setup; you had to inspect the course on the morning of the race. But the point of all that often tedious preparation was to be able to trust your body and skis to keep up during the race, while you disengaged your conscious mind and just skied.

If Maier knew he wasn't able to do that in October, he knew he wasn't going to be able to do it in February. Mentally, Miller felt up to the task, but the other components weren't yet in place.

And Miller didn't need anyone to tell him how important it was to bring his abilities in line with his ambitions; he only had to recall the sad story of 1984 Olympic downhill champion Bill Johnson, a living ghost who haunted every member of the US Ski Team.

A cocky Californian whose schoolteachers had considered him brilliant, Johnson was a fanatical ski racer. Dislocated by his parents' divorce, Johnson fell to breaking into homes and stealing cars, got caught, and was facing three felony charges in 1977 when an Oregon judge remanded him to a ski academy with the promise of five to ten years in jail if he slipped up.

Johnson went on to make the US team, where he clashed repeatedly with then–Alpine director Bill Marolt. After four penurious years in which he was dropped off the team and fought his way back, Johnson perfected his tuck and scored a pair of superfast Atomic skis, and in 1984 took a surprise win at the Lauberhorn downhill, becoming the first American man to win a World Cup downhill. A month later, Johnson predicted his own victory at the Sarajevo Games, as Franz Klammer famously dismissed him as a *Nasenbohrer*, or nosepicker. But Johnson prevailed, getting the first gold Olympic downhill medal of any sort for an American.

Johnson won two more World Cup races that year, but his career fizzled amid injuries and acrimony. After his 1990 retirement, his life became a streak of personal tragedies (his infant son drowned in a hot tub). Divorced and impoverished at age forty, Johnson attempted a foolhardy comeback, suiting up for North American FIS races against athletes half his age. A former teammate, Doug Lewis, believes Johnson was overmatched by the modern shaped skis, which were easier to turn but much more squirrelly.

Johnson survived twenty races before the downhill he entered on March 22, 2001, at The Big Mountain, Montana. Midway through the race his skis split apart beneath him and he crashed face first into the hard snow. The impact rotated Johnson's brain within his skull, and he nearly choked to death on his lacerated tongue.

Doctors were able to save Johnson's life, but his brain was so severely injured that he claimed he was unable to remember the 1990s. Ravaged by seizures and increasingly immobile, Johnson lived out his middle age in the care of his mother at their home near Mt. Hood, Oregon.

PART 3

The White Circus:
The 2009–10 World Cup

October 2009–February 2010

CHAPTER 12

A New Beginning

Since 2000, the World Cup season has kicked off at Sölden, an Austrian town at the end of the 25-mile-long Ötz Valley, southeast of Innsbruck in the heart of the Tyrol region. The races—a pair of giant slaloms, one for men and one for women—take place on the Rettenbach Glacier, a slab of ancient, bluish ice. The area gained international renown in 1991, when a pair of hikers found the body of a 5,300-year-old caveman half protruding from his icy grave.

The 2009 races were set for the weekend of October 24–25, but it is traditional for the national teams to arrive at Sölden a week early, to spend the mornings skiing on the glacier and the afternoons and evenings in town, participating in a dizzying series of press conferences, presentations, and parties that the ski manufacturers, race sponsors, and the FIS organize. The week has a back-to-school atmosphere, as racers and coaches and journalists exchange a summer's backlog of gossip and news about the upcoming tour.

Bode Miller was often the object of greatest fascination, and was especially so this year, after his mysterious hiatus. Even though he would be skipping the race, the Austrian media found things to say and write about him. It was noted, for instance, that he was reintegrating with the US team, staying in hotels and not his famous motor home. One of the vehicles was for sale online for the equivalent of about $155,000, and a story in the *Kleine Zeitung* had pictures of the vehicle's interior, including both the beloved game console station and a bookshelf that reflected the wide range of his omnivorous reading.

During the week of the opener in most years you can walk around Sölden in a light sweatshirt; with the ground not yet frozen, the air often carries the scent of manure from nearby farms. But winter is only a short drive away. A steep and twisting road rises up from the town, through evergreen forests and into the U-shaped valley that the Rettenbach carved out before its upward retreat. There, a set of switchbacks takes drivers up into a barren moonscape of boulders to a wide basin amid the rocky peaks. A parking lot and a sun-bleached ski lodge sit at the edge of the snow.

Even in diminished form, the glacier is imposing, spilling out of a bowl in the mountains like a frozen Niagara. Blinding white snowfields are wrinkled with crevasses that yawn open to reveal ice churned full of rocks; the glaciers atop the Alps don't just cap the mountains but digest them as well, swallowing boulders around the margins and carrying that debris slowly downward, grinding away at the earth.

At various places on this wilderness of seracs, smooth trails have been plowed out and maintained for the skiers. The one that race teams covet most for training sessions is known as the Icebox, a run that skirts a peak that casts almost perpetual shade. The snow there can be compact, almost chalky, and it does not forgive the unprepared; at 10,000 feet above sea level, the air is thin, compounding the racers' fatigue as they make laps on a simple T-bar lift that serves the pistes.

Meanwhile, a few thousand feet away, the Sölden race hill awaits, featuring one of the steepest uninterrupted descents on the World Cup. According to the tour's rules, racers may not ski upon the competition slope in the five days leading up to the event. And so the racers could only look on from a distance in the last week before the 2009 season began, as organizers put the finishing touches on the race slope, erecting a temporary stadium around the finish line and stringing fences along the edges of the run. A team of coaches and volunteers was dispatched to harden the surface, spraying it with water and using snowcats outfitted with tillers to churn the snow into a denser form.

Miller trained with the US team at the Icebox, but would not be racing in the 2009 edition of the Sölden race. This came as a disappointment to the mostly European journalists on hand, who associated the race with one of Miller's classic demonstrations of artistry.

Back in 2003, Miller had come onto the long, mercilessly steep pitch that makes up most of the lower half of the Sölden course, and instead of linking clean arcs down the mountain's face, he intentionally skidded on half the turns. For every turn he carved cleanly, the next one saw him tip his skis up on edge and grind out a little spray of snow. He then reengaged his edge in a carved turn that swept in under the gate.

It was a little ugly, but it was undeniably fast. Miller had figured out that on a hill that steep and icy, a little bit of old-school skidding was actually faster; what time he lost to friction fighting gravity he more than gained back by the shorter path he took through the turns. Skidding on one turn allowed him to go straighter down the fall line while carving the next. It wasn't until much later that Miller revealed he had prepared his equipment differently for just that strategy, tuning one of his skis in a way that made it easier to skid—to perform what he called a "speed control turn."

In 2003, with giant slalom skis not yet heavily restricted by FIS equipment rules, the top racers worshiped the ideal of carving cleanly arc to arc, but Miller dared to be heretical, and his skidding at Sölden proved to be a winning strategy. In every subsequent year, other racers tried to mimic Miller's novel tactics on the pitch, with some success, but the original experiment had made Miller a legend on the Rettenbach.

Injuries come to Alpine ski racers the way colds come to kindergarten teachers. Every day on the World Cup a racer might break a hand on a passing gate, dislocate a shoulder in a crunching fall, or stretch some ligament or tendon beyond its tolerance simply by leaning in one direction while a ski shoots off in another.

Knees get the worst of it, and to spend any time around the tour is to become numb to the frequency and severity of the violence skiing does to the joint. Knee injuries aren't even considered serious until there is a rupture to the most important piece of tissue connecting the bones of the upper and lower leg, that tiny twist of gristle at the very core of the knee: the anterior cruciate ligament.

It took roughly half an hour for the new World Cup season to find an ACL to destroy. The victim was the twenty-third racer to start down the women's giant slalom course, twenty-five-year-old Nicole Hosp of Austria, the overall World Cup champion in 2007, who had spent the previous ten months rehabilitating from a complex injury to her left knee.

This time it was her right. About 27 seconds into her run, Hosp was setting up for a turn to her left when she made a simple mistake, leaning too far in that direction and thereby losing pressure on her right ski. As she realigned her stance Hosp overcorrected, shifting all her weight to her right ski. At that exact moment, her edge found its grip on the surface, the ski locking into a slicing track. All of Hosp's momentum was now suddenly driven into her right leg. Her knee, bent and slightly twisted, buckled underneath her, and Hosp felt a fiery jolt of pain as it unhinged and she went down.

The 11,000 fans on hand for the race saw her slide to a stop on her back as coaches rushed to her aid. A helicopter arrived to take her away, and as Hosp disappeared over the horizon, headed for a sugeon's table near Innsbruck, fans of the popular racer could lament the lonely road she faced, with two knees wrecked in ten months. Her peers had no choice but to push such thoughts from their minds as the race resumed. The season's first World Cup points would go to the skiers who could best compartmentalize distractions like a course delay for a helicopter evacuation.

The winner, after two runs, was Tanja Poutiainen of Finland, whose combined time of 2 minutes, 24.96 seconds was 0.01 seconds faster than that of Kathrin Zettel of Austria. Lindsey Vonn was a respectable ninth (GS was her weakest discipline). By the next day she was back in the United States, starting a crucial block of training in Colorado. When racers like Hosp went down with an ACL injury, it could only motivate racers like Vonn to keep training—to hone her reflexes and build her strength.

The first racer out of the gate in the first run of the first men's race of the 2009–10 season happened to be the oldest man on the start list, thirty-five-year-old Didier Cuche, a Swiss farm boy from the French-speaking side of his country. His name was pronounced *Did-yay Koosh*. It was his 298th World Cup race.

Short and stocky, with a big head he kept shaven, Cuche was intense yet playful. His signature move upon completing a race run was to detach his right ski and kick it twirling into the air above him. He would let the ski make one full rotation before catching it in his gloved hand and giving it a kiss. It was clearly a dangerous trick, but if anyone could risk handling those sharp metal edges it was Cuche, who happened to be a trained butcher.

On October 25, after completing his first run in 1 minute, 9.89 seconds, Cuche executed a perfect ski flip. Then seventy-three other racers from twenty-three nations came down the Sölden course, and none of them could beat his time. The person who came closest was American Ted Ligety, who was 0.36 seconds off Cuche's pace. The other four Americans at Sölden were thirty-first, thirty-second, thirty-seventh, and fifty-fourth. They were done for the day; only the top thirty would get a second run.

The standard schedule continued. The gates were repositioned, pulled from the snow and reconfigured into a new course. While the racers ate a catered lunch in a guarded lounge, fans wandered around to find sausages and beer, collect autographs, or even ski along the edge of the course. Austrian television broadcaster ORF carried an unhurried halftime report from an on-site studio. Servicemen hustled to tune up the race skis. Just after noon, the best thirty skiers of the day headed up the gondola toward the start.

Suspense was built into the technical events; in slalom and GS, the second-run start order sent the thirty top first-run finishers onto the course in reverse order. Ligety would go twenty-ninth, and Cuche would go last. The format was designed to keep television viewers watching to the very end. It also shook up the field, giving newcomers an opening. If a young guy saddled with start number sixty-four in the morning could overcome the ruts to finish twenty-third, he would start eighth on the second run and show what he could do on a fresh track.

Ligety had done exactly that four years earlier, but 2009 was different. He was now a race favorite, even with his knee injury the previous March. He'd won four World Cup giant slaloms, took the discipline title in 2008 and a world championship bronze medal in February. At Sölden, he'd finished second in 2007 and third in 2008. Now he wanted the win.

With just five racers left at the start of the second run, the course was deteriorating and an overcast sky made it harder to see the ruts. Benjamin Raich went down the hill and took the lead with the fastest combined time. Then Italy's giant slalom specialist Max Blardone did the same, besting Raich. Just before Ligety's turn, Carlo Janka of Switzerland went out of the start and knocked Blardone and Raich into second and third. Ligety's first-run advantage over Janka was only 0.15 seconds.

Ligety went out of the start house, gave it full gas across the flats, and took an aggressive line down the face. He made a few small errors, but he attacked, and when he crossed the line and looked to the scoreboard he'd beaten Janka again. First place was his, with only Cuche left.

Cuche took his place in the start, muttered some last instructions to himself and pushed onto the course. He skied conservatively at first, nearly lost his footing once, and then committed to the fall line as horns blared in the stadium. At the final timing interval, about 20 seconds from the finish, his margin over Ligety was down to a single hundredth of a second. But right there the course dropped onto the flats, and Cuche, tucking when he could, and slightly heavier than Ligety, maintained his momentum through the final dozen gates and lunged for the finish line to win in 2 minutes, 21.45 seconds, 0.6 seconds faster than Ligety.

Second place aside, Ligety had put to rest some of the speculation about whether his knee would interfere with the Vancouver Olympics.

From the minute he finished the race, Cuche was chaperoned by anti-doping collection officers, whose job was to stay by his side up to and including the moment Cuche produced a urine sample that would be marked with a serial number, sent to a laboratory, tested rigorously, and stored in a refrigerator for up to seven years, in case science caught up with the undetectable substances and methods that fuel modern doping.

Ligety was tested too. As a rule, the FIS collects urine and some-times blood from the top four finishers in every World Cup race, along with others selected mostly at random. The skiers generally saw it as invasive overkill; in 2009, alpine skiing still remained almost totally unspoiled by the doping scandals that had swept through other sports. What few doping troubles did arise in alpine ski racing usually involved lesser-known skiers whose medications contained an obscure stimu-lant, or who stayed out too late partying. Rainer Schönfelder of Austria had tested positive for Etilefrine, something he blamed on an inhaler. Mirko Deflorian of Italy had been disciplined for having metabolites of cocaine in his system. The sport's most conspicuous positive test had come at the 2002 Salt Lake City Games, when the IOC revoked Scottish slalom skier Alain Baxter's bronze medal after he tested positive for levomethamphetamine, a prohibited stimulant he said he'd inadver-tently ingested through a Vicks nasal inhaler.

The only real star of the sport to get into serious trouble was Aus-trian downhiller Hans Knauss, who in late 2004 tested positive for a metabolite of the steroid nandrolone. Knauss blamed a tainted nutri-tional supplement and sued the American company that produced it, winning an out-of-court settlement. He got his two-year ban reduced by six months, but the suspension killed his career.

The Knauss case had prompted Bode Miller to deliver a famous denunciation of what he saw as the hypocrisy and ineffectiveness of the anti-doping system. Miller's calm and colorful diatribe came at the World Cup opener in 2005, when he arrived at Sölden as the reigning World Cup champion. More nuanced and clever than some of the soundbites that proliferated, Miller's subversive take was clearly shaped by a childhood milieu in which cannabis was a constant presence, and its restriction by law was understood to be an overreaction.

Miller sat with journalists in the lobby of the Hotel Central at Sölden that year and spun out a takedown of the World Anti-Doping Agency. He made a provocative case for the legalization of erythropoietin, or EPO, the endurance-boosting anemia drug that had all but destroyed cycling's credibility. Miller said EPO wouldn't make a ski racer faster—but safer, perhaps. Miller pointed out that the increased red blood cells spawned by EPO would carry more oxygen to muscles in the final 15 seconds of a race, when athletes become uncoordinated and their judgment suffers.

"That's one of the things that's so hard about skiing is that you're recruiting such big muscle groups all the time, and by the bottom you can't think right because you have no oxygen in your blood, and no blood in your brain," Miller said. "You have to make four or five decisions every second in skiing, every turn. Conscious decisions, plus there's another hundred that are instinct. And when your brain starts to slow down, as if you're holding your breath for two minutes, it makes it damn hard to make those decisions."

Miller pointed to a logical fallacy in one of the central themes of the anti-doping enforcers: protection of an athlete's health. If that were the priority, Miller said, the use of EPO should be legal for ski racers because "you'd have less chance of making a mistake at the bottom and killing yourself."

Miller went further, and took some criticism for his words, but he competed in a sport relatively immune to doping. The banned substances and methods couldn't turn an above average athlete into a champion, as they can in endurance races or tests of strength. Winning an alpine ski race called for a more diverse set of skills and strengths; explosive power and endurance were important, but they couldn't compensate for a lifetime spent practicing technique and tactics.

Eventually a drug will arrive perfectly tailored to corrupt alpine skiing. Some even believe it already has, in the form of Zoloft and other antidepressants and anti-anxiety medications. Freed from the shackles of fear, ski racers who take those drugs, which are not banned, may have a distinct advantage over rivals, as some of those racers may learn when they go off the drugs and find they lack the confidence to take the same risks as before.

After Sölden, the World Cup teams scattered to training sites around the world. The next races weren't for three more weeks: a pair of slaloms in Levi, Finland. The Americans returned to the United States, where snowmaking had been underway in Colorado for two weeks.

October hadn't paid off for reigning overall World Cup champion Aksel Lund Svindal of Norway. A week before the Sölden race, on October 18, Svindal had jolted his left knee skiing over a rut while training at Saas-Fee with the Americans. When he returned to town he could walk on it, but when he got back on skis the next day, the pain returned. Svindal packed up and went to Germany to see a doctor, but the MRIs were clean, so he went to Sölden and raced. The bumpy conditions were unbearable, and he had pulled out midway through the second run.

Until that moment, Svindal was confident he could defend his World Cup title. It had been a productive summer, training with the Canadians, Swiss, and the Americans, but the mysterious new pain in his leg was a major problem. To Svindal, it felt like the injury was in the meaty muscle running up his shin, right where it attached to the bone. After Sölden, Svindal went to another doctor, who noticed that the bones in his lower leg were separated—nothing was broken, but the fibula was loosened from the tibia. The doctor advised a four-to-six-week break, with physiotherapy and exercises to keep the blood circulating. That meant no races until Lake Louise at the end of the month, where Svindal would ski with his leg taped up.

October training had taken its toll on Miller too, who just before the Sölden race had decided he needed to do something about his aching left knee, which had acted up periodically ever since he tore his ACL in a crash at the 2001 world championships. He'd had four surgeries on that knee by then, and had trouble keeping count of how many came after that. At least eight. His upper and lower leg bones had ground together in so many ice-slapping landings that the meniscus and cartilage between them showed permanent deterioration.

Normally rest and ice did the trick, but the compressed physical conditioning program was making that hard. Miller, who had just turned thirty-two years old, had been working weightlifting sessions into his afternoons after gate training, and that hadn't left him much time to recover. So while his teammates were racing at Sölden, Miller made a visit to the private clinic of Christian Schenk, a surgeon based in Schruns, Austria. Schenk performed a debridement procedure on Miller, removing bone chips and pieces of cartilage that were floating around within the joint.

LINDSEY VONN (USA): ÅRE, SWEDEN
By age 24, Lindsey Vonn was already one of the most decorated ski racers the US Ski Team had ever produced. She finished the 2008–09 winter season primed for maximum performance on her sport's biggest stage, the next season's Olympic Winter Games in Vancouver, Canada. (Agence Zoom)

BODE MILLER (USA): ALTA BADIA, ITALY
The 2008–09 season was Bode Miller's worst outing in nearly a decade. Injured, dogged by negative media attention, and having broken company with the US Ski Team, Miller at 31 found his focus drifting from a sport to which he'd devoted his life. After abruptly disbanding his private team, he seemed to retreat from friends and colleagues, voicing doubt about participating in the Winter Games. (Agence Zoom)

JULIA MANCUSO (USA); VANCOUVER, CANADA

The US Ski Team's unprecedented success in Alpine skiing in the 2000s was driven by racers like Julia Mancuso of Squaw Valley, California, born in 1984 like her archrival Vonn. The team selected both girls at age 13 and groomed them for success on the annual FIS World Cup tour. (Agence Zoom)

TED LIGETY (USA); BEAVER CREEK, COLORADO

Ted Ligety of Park City, Utah, became the world's best giant slalom skier by perfecting the art of carving. Like most great racers, his obsession is the World Cup, a circuit where the planet's best ski racers face the most challenging courses, exacting surface preparation, and deepest traditions. (Agence Zoom)

LINDSEY VONN; CORTINA D'AMPEZZO, ITALY

The FIS Alpine skiing World Cup, a season-long tour that incorporates the oldest and most challenging downhill courses, began in the winter of 1966–67. But a sport that grew out of central European mountaineering culture more than a century ago is now proving vulnerable to climate change. (Agence Zoom)

ERIK SCHLOPY (USA); SÖLDEN, AUSTRIA

Beginning in the late 1990s, technological advances in skiing equipment allowed top racers to harness greater forces. The new gear contributed to a rise in speed and a spate of violent crashes that spurred organizers to alter courses and restrict equipment. (Erik Schlopy was unhurt in this 2003 crash.) (Agence Zoom)

BODE MILLER; BORMIO, ITALY

Ever the showman, Bode Miller in 2005 nearly completed a perilous downhill course on one ski after losing the other at 80 miles per hour. Fans loved his iconoclastic style, but Miller often clashed with authority—including the sport's global governing body, the International Ski Federation (FIS). (Agence Zoom)

BODE MILLER; SESTRIERE, ITALY

Bode Miller attained global notoriety in 2006 for his disastrous outing at the Torino Games. Despite the highest expectations, he earned no medals. He failed to finish the super G but managed to stay upright even after this mistake, which tore his ski out from under him at 60 miles per hour. (Agence Zoom)

AKSEL LUND SVINDAL (NORWAY); KITZBÜHEL, AUSTRIA

The Hausberg jump marks the beginning of the final 2,000 feet of the annual Hahnen-kamm downhill, graveyard of ski racing careers and the scene of ski racing's ultimate initiation rite. Merely finishing the treacherous Streif course is said universally by downhillers to be one of the purest thrills in the sport. (Agence Zoom)

T. J. LANNING (USA); WENGEN, SWITZERLAND

Tens of thousands of fans attend the great downhills of the Alps, where the racers often follow nearly the same courses that have been used for generations. Here T. J. Lanning starts the 79th Lauberhorn at Wengen, Switzerland, in the shadow of the iconic Eiger peak. (Agence Zoom)

THE BERNESE OBERLAND

The Lauterbrunnen valley in the Swiss Alps is a cradle of Alpine ski racing. There in Mürren, in 1922, Sir Arnold Lunn of Britain developed the fundamental rules of slalom that later became the basis of Olympic and World Cup racing. The historic Wengen downhill is staged nearby, its final sections visible on the left middle foreground of the above photograph. (Agence Zoom)

EASTON, NEW HAMPSHIRE

Bode Miller's childhood home was Turtle Ridge, a cabin his parents built off the grid in 1975 on the forested side of Kinsman Mountain near Franconia, New Hampshire. The nearby streambed and three-quarter-mile path down to NH 116 gave Miller and his siblings plenty of opportunities to test the limits of their balance.

TINA MAZE (SLOVENIA); GARMISCH-PARTENKIRCHEN, GERMANY

One of Lindsey Vonn's chief rivals is Tina Maze, who hails from the tiny Slovenian village of Črna na Koroškem, close to the Austrian border. Like many other skiing champions, she built her own private, personal team. (Agence Zoom)

MARCEL HIRSCHER (AUSTRIA); WENGEN, SWITZERLAND

Modern racing skis are wide at each end and narrow under the racer's boot. When tipped up on edge and pressured, this hourglass shape—known as "sidecut"—causes the ski to bend and carve a smooth arc in the snow, distributing pressure and enhancing speed. (Agence Zoom)

CORTINA D'AMPEZZO, ITALY

US Ski Team coach Chris Knight and racer Laurenne Ross inspect the women's World Cup downhill at Cortina d'Ampezzo. An inspection period comes ahead of every ski race, giving athletes an opportunity to study the course and the surface they will later descend at speeds that can exceed 90 miles per hour.

BILL MAROLT; WENGEN, SWITZERLAND (1962)
Leading the US team into the 2010 Olympics was Bill Marolt, a former racer and coach who raised unprecedented funds for the team as its chief executive from 1996 to 2014. With his "Best in the World" slogan, Marolt dramatically raised the stakes for the team's athletes at Vancouver. (Image courtesy of the University of Colorado.)

BODE MILLER; BEAVER CREEK, COLORADO
Racers strive to apply pressure primarily to the inside edge of the outside ski, bracing against powerful forces that build up as the ski tracks through the snow, which is rarely as smooth and level as it looks on television. (Agence Zoom)

BODE MILLER; WENGEN, SWITZERLAND

Slalom is the most technical of Alpine skiing's four main disciplines, with racers weaving through gates set so closely together that the racers don armor and punch the gates out of the way. Bode Miller qualified for the US Ski Team as a slalom skier and, though he later evolved into an all-rounder, remained enamored of slalom long past an age when most racers abandon the discipline. (Agence Zoom)

MARIA HÖFL-RIESCH (GERMANY); OFTERSCHWANG, GERMANY

One of Lindsey Vonn's main rivals going into the 2010 Olympic season was German all-rounder Maria Höfl-Riesch, who was also Vonn's best friend on the World Cup tour, though their relationship was not without occasional tension. (Agence Zoom)

JULIA MANCUSO; WHISTLER, CANADA

The 2010 Olympic courses at Whistler, two hours north of Vancouver, presented a uniquely challenging race venue. Cycles of warm temperatures, heavy snow, rain, and freezing temperatures made the surface especially rugged, even with 2,000 volunteers working to prepare the slope. (Agence Zoom)

LINDSEY VONN; WHISTLER, CANADA
No American has won more ski races and titles than Lindsey Vonn, whose 67 victories on the World Cup tour (as of September 2015) put her second on the all-time wins list behind only one racer, Ingemar Stenmark of Sweden, who won 86 races. (Agence Zoom)

BODE MILLER; BEAVER CREEK, COLORADO

Dubbed "the eternal crash pilot" early in his World Cup career, Bode Miller later
honed his recovery instincts and became the most watchable ski racer on the
tour. "Everybody is waiting," explains Franz Klammer, "saying, 'I have to watch,
Bode is still to come. What will he do?'" (Agence Zoom)

CHAPTER 13

Pure Speed

For some ski fans, the 2009–10 World Cup season began not at Sölden in late October, but in the Canadian Rockies at the end of November, with the tour's first super G and downhill at Lake Louise, Alberta. This was the start of the speed season; the Lake Louise race was the first of eight men's downhills on the season's calendar, six of which would precede the Olympics.

On November 24, the downhill teams started arriving in Calgary and making their way up to the resort near the town of Banff. The Austrians had spent a few days training at Sun Peaks, a resort in British Columbia, getting acclimated to the time zone. The Americans were arriving from Colorado, where there was already good snow. Bode Miller had snuck in a trip to San Diego for an early Thanksgiving dinner with his daughter.

The whole World Cup family—skiers, coaches, race officials, media people, and equipment reps—took up residence in the Chateau Lake Louise, a grand old hotel built a century before by the Canadian Pacific Railway. Their training runs over, the skiers could step outside, don their ice skates, and play pickup hockey games on the frozen lake amid the splendor of the Canadian Rockies.

Lake Louise was the only Canadian stop on the World Cup, and the downhill was known as the least fearsome course on the men's tour. Most of the racers were too gentlemanly to say it on record, but a knock they privately made against Lake Louise was that it was a women's course. (In fact, the women's tour would visit the resort the following week, and race on a slightly adjusted track.)

One guy not prone to show any disrespect for the Lake Louise course that week was twenty-five-year-old T. J. Lanning, a self-professed redneck from Montana who was living proof that talent and courage were insufficient virtues for downhillers who didn't also possess luck.

Ten years earlier, Lanning had been the most promising junior ski racer in the United States, if not the world. When Lanning was little, his parents moved to Park City and signed him up for the local ski team. Big and strong for his age, he had excellent coaching and access to an ideal training environment as his home slope was groomed for the 2002 Winter Games. By age twelve, Lanning was unbeatable within his age group, and coaches had him train with older kids. Ted Ligety, who was four days younger and lived only a few houses away, would later recall that every twinkling accomplishment he made was invisible within the sunlike glare of Lanning's talent.

At sixteen, Lanning was wearing the uniform of the US Ski Team, where there was a difference of opinion about how to manage his career. Some coaches wanted to put Lanning in Europa Cup races to let him mature gradually, while others argued for advancing him directly to the top level. Bode Miller was in the latter camp; seven years older than Lanning, Miller could see that the kid had pure speed. Like Miller, Lanning crashed a lot, but when he didn't he was fast. Miller wanted to train with him. By his eighteenth birthday in 2002, Lanning was the number one giant slalom skier in the world in his age group, and began racing World Cups.

A depressing series of injuries followed. In a 2003 crash at a Europa Cup in Switzerland, Lanning tore the ACL in his left knee and deeply lacerated his tongue biting down on it while he tumbled. After losing most of a year to surgery and rehabilitation, he was training slalom when the tip of his left ski caught the base of a gate and stopped, jamming his foot forward against the inside of his ski boot, fracturing a bone and straining a ligament in his ankle.

Lanning fought his way back again, but chronic lower back problems led to surgery and rehabilitation. Finally back in top form in 2006, he took a too-direct line into the last turn of the Birds of Prey downhill in Beaver Creek and careened off the Redtail jump, spinning like a detached helicopter blade toward the woods. The upper part of the net snagged him and whipped him around a few times before bouncing him back onto the course with a broken nose, broken finger, and torn meniscus in his knee. While other ski racers had comparable injury résumés, Lanning always came back with undiminished hunger for speed. In the 2007–08 season, he won a Europa Cup downhill and the national downhill championship in Sugarloaf, Maine. His next year's World Cup campaign went well until January, at the Hahnenkamm.

On the US Ski Team, downhillers are considered rookies until they've raced the famed Streif course at Kitzbühel. By 2009, Lanning had been racing downhill for nine years, but his serial injuries had kept him away from the big one. When he finally got his chance to run the Streif on January 24, he attacked the course fearlessly. He seemed headed for a top fifteen finish as he entered the fabled final 20 seconds of the course: the Hausberg jump and the long, bumpy traverse toward the final schuss. Like any racer, Lanning was aware of the carnage that occurred there every year, including unspeakably violent crashes that had ended the careers of two great downhill champions, Patrick Ortlieb and Todd Brooker.

But Lanning, betrayed by his indomitable confidence, took a too-direct line, underestimating one of the hulking knolls along the traverse. Launched into the air at 80 miles per hour, Lanning was unable to position his body to land in a powerful squat; instead, he came down on one extended leg, which crumpled instantly. Like so many other racers through the years, he cartwheeled into the netting, with a shredded ACL and damaged cartilage in his right knee.

Ten months of rehab later, Lanning was back yet again, old and young at the same time, hoping to fulfill his early promise, maybe even at the Olympics. Lake Louise was a course he knew well, and he was ready to let it rip.

⸻

Lanning was one of nine young men the US Ski Team had brought to Lake Louise for the first downhill of the winter. The other eight were Bode Miller, Scott Macartney, Marco Sullivan, Steven Nyman, Erik Fisher, Andrew Weibrecht, Jeremy Transue, and Travis Ganong. Only four of them would be racing in the Olympic men's downhill in February.

Sullivan liked his chances. An amiable twenty-nine-year-old from Squaw Valley, whose uncle was a respected ski coach there, "Sully" was an avid powder skier who had a soft touch for the snow but hadn't found the psychological abandon required for lots of victories. He had won his first and only World Cup downhill in 2008 in Chamonix, but had missed the 2006 Olympics with a knee injury.

He'd be competing for a start spot with Nyman, a tall, thoughtful twenty-seven-year-old from Provo, Utah. In 2002, at an age when Mormon men are expected to go on an LDS mission, Nyman gave ski racing one more year and did well enough that the US Ski Team coaches made him their discretionary pick for the world junior championships in Italy. There Nyman won the slalom, a victory that qualified him for World Cup finals, where he finished fifteenth, earning a spot on the US Ski Team. His home mountain was Sundance—the resort owned by Hollywood's downhill racer, Robert Redford—and naturally Nyman gravitated to downhill. In 2006, he became the first American to win the downhill at Val Gardena, the classic Saslong course.

Scott Macartney and Erik Fisher were westerners too, but the northeast would not be unrepresented on the downhill team. Andrew Weibrecht, the smallest athlete on the team, had grown up at the Mirror Lake Inn, the historic hotel his family owned in Lake Placid, New York. Weibrecht was short but barrel-chested enough to look like a bowling ball rolling down the slope, making big angles with his legs. His reputation for fearlessness was cemented in 2007 in a kamikaze attack on the Beaver Creek downhill, when he started fifty-third and finished tenth while skiing through a snowstorm. They called him Warhorse.

The oldest and most experienced of the American downhillers was Miller, with seven World Cup wins in the discipline. He had been coming to the World Cup races at Lake Louise for ten years, and a pair of wins there in 2004 were his first World Cup victories in speed events.

The youngest racer, competing in his first World Cup ever, was Travis Ganong of Squaw Valley. In another era he would have carried the Rookie Rock, a giant stone new members of the team were forced to pack on tour. The current era's initation ritual involved hairstyling; for his first World Cup race, a member of the men's team was obliged to get a haircut (invariably a hideous one) from the skier on the team who had most recently scored his first World Cup points.

At 5 p.m. sharp on November 23, as hundreds of volunteer course workers scrambled to prepare the course for race day, the coaches gathered in a hotel ballroom for an important pre-race tradition, the *Mannschaftsführersitzung.*

These gatherings—the team captains' meetings—came the night before each race on the tour, and indeed at every alpine ski race at lower levels too. Topics of discussion included the schedule, snow conditions, safety concerns, the weather forecast, and the next day's start order. It was traditional to serve hors d'oeuvres and drinks, and it was not uncommon to see great theater—arguments, walkouts, and lectures in multiple languages.

It was part of the World Cup's charming intimacy that the meetings were open to the public. The coaches of every team sat in rows facing a dais upon which sat members of the race jury, a representative of the local organizing committee, and, presiding over it all, the race director, a man from the FIS who erred on the autocratic side in part because there was at least a century of downhill tradition to defend.

What many historians regard as the first downhill ski race took place in Switzerland on January 7, 1911. After climbing for eight hours the previous day and spending a night in a remote mountain hut, the twenty competitors started en masse, scrambling across a Swiss glacier and down a mountainside that later became the Crans-Montana ski resort. By modern standards, the Roberts of Kandahar Challenge Cup was a chaotic affair. There were no gates marking the course, and racers could choose their own adventure down an unfamiliar slope. The winner reached the designated finish line in 61 minutes.

The organizer of the event, Sir Arnold Lunn, went on to codify alpine skiing's rules and force the FIS—then concerned exclusively with cross-country skiing and jumping—to recognize the gravity-driven new sport. In an article he wrote for the *Atlantic Monthly* in 1949, Lunn lamented the demise of mass starts like the one on the Plaine Morte glacier thirty-eight years earlier. The modern-day racers of the 1948 Games had started at regular intervals, Lunn wrote, relying on an "elaborate system of artificial timing" that may have prevented collisions but robbed the spectators, Lunn said, of the "dramatic interest" at the finish line.

Mass starts weren't as anarchic as they might at first sound. In fact, the 1911 race's start procedure sounds rather dignified, according to Lunn's description. On the morning of the race, the competitors gathered on the mountaintop. Waking at their hut, they prepared for the descent by adjusting their tweed coats and packing away their tobacco pipes. When everyone was ready, Lunn wrote in the *Atlantic*, the race began "when the oldest competitor gave the word go."

In the decades that followed, as downhills like Kitzbühel and Wengen became annual traditions, courses began to follow strictly defined tracks that varied less and less from year to year. As consensus identified the fastest path through the gates, ruts developed in the race line and it became advantageous, almost always, to go early in the start order. The FIS rules governing start order grew ever more complex, combining the meritocracy of world rankings with the serendipity of a random draw. By 2009, the system on the World Cup—and therefore also at the Olympics—was both convoluted and elegant, a little different for each alpine discipline, and subject to change every few years. In downhill, the top thirty or so start positions were the ones to watch most closely.

The formula generally worked like this: first the top seven down-hillers in the world were matched in a random draw with start numbers sixteen to twenty-two; next came a second draw, this one pairing the downhillers ranked between eighth and fifteenth with bibs eight through fifteen; finally a third tier of downhillers, those ranked fifteenth in the world to thirtieth, drew for bibs one through seven and twenty-three through thirty. Pretty much everyone else, the thirty or fifty other racers filling out the start list, started according to their rank.

In this system, the best racers got a relatively fresh course, but could count on the guidance of the tracks of a few guinea pigs who went before them. Television broadcasters and educated viewers knew that they could usually (but not always) turn away after racer thirty, or even twenty-two. And ambitious racers in the third tier—hungry upstarts and reenergized veterans alike—could get lucky and pull a good number. Sometimes it was better to go early, and sometimes it was better to go late. It depended on the snow, the sunlight, and a half dozen other variables.

The draw itself took place the night before the race. On the World Cup circuit, it sometimes happened during the nightly meeting of the coaches in a local gymnasium or concert hall, where impartial race officials or honored volunteers pulled numbered ping-pong balls out of a hat, and coaches took the bibs back to their team under their arms. More often, the World Cup organizers made the bib draw part of an elaborate public presentation in a town square, with the athletes swooping in on zip lines to receive their bibs, or high-fiving their way to a stage through a gauntlet of local schoolchildren.

The skies were overcast the next day and the fresh snow was mostly pushed out of the track by the time the race started at 11:30. The eighteenth racer down the course, Didier Cuche, crossed the finish line with the fastest time, 1 minute, 50.31 seconds. Starting two behind him, with bib twenty, was Bode Miller, who used up 1:52.42, crossing into fourteenth place but sure to get bumped down by later racers.

The US Ski Team coaches, spread out along the course and communicating by radio, looked down at their lists at the eight other Americans who were still to come. Sullivan, Lanning, and Fisher would go twenty-three, twenty-four, and twenty-five, then Nyman twenty-ninth and Macartney thirty-fifth. Transue would go fifty-seventh, Weibrecht sixty-second, and Ganong seventy-first.

Sasha Rearick was standing toward the end of the course, bundled up in a black US Ski Team uniform at the bottom of a section called Gunbarrel. As word came that Sullivan was on course, Rearick was watching where the race line had deteriorated from the traffic and listening to the split times through an earpiece. The voice of a colleague with an eye on a television monitor listed Sullivan's times at each of five interval stations—0.07 seconds off Cuche, then 0.30, then 1.53, then 2.14. At the final interval, right above Rearick's position, Sullivan's time was 1 minute, 39.69, a full 2.73 seconds off Cuche's pace.

Sullivan's coaches watched the splits with growing disappointment. Of anyone on the team, Sullivan was usually the least likely to overpressure his skis on soft snow. Carving, after all, is not the only important element of downhill racing. Another skill is gliding, the act of letting the edges unlock from their arcing turns and drift over the snow. Gliding is considered more of an instinctive gift—like writing, people say it can't be taught but it might be learned. (And it can even be lost; after Hermann Maier's motorcycle accident he never regained full sensation in his maimed leg, which compromised his gliding ability. For years after his return, he obsessively searched for a customized boot fitting that would bring back the magic feelings in his shin.)

Sullivan was a good glider, and he had the chance to thrive on a milder course like Lake Louise, but he crossed the line three seconds slower than Cuche, and almost a second behind Miller. By then Lanning was already on course, the wind blowing snow in front of his path.

When he came into view of Rearick, he was on track for a respectable result, but the light was bad. The timing system clocked his speed at 124.3 kilometers per hour—a little over 77 miles per hour. Rearick pivoted and watched as Lanning passed by him, entering a long turn to the right.

There was a ripple in the snow that Lanning couldn't see, or maybe a limit to the innate balance that had survived all those crashes. Whatever it was, Lanning's skis did something funny, and although he successfully shuffled his weight to recenter himself, he was now aiming straight for the gate at full speed. Lanning stood up out of his tuck just in time to plow into the panel, which wrapped around his lower leg and yanked it backward before ripping off the poles.

Still going 70-plus, Lanning careened off the course. As his skis hit the soft snow they slowed and he went headfirst into the ground. He began somersaulting through the snow and one of his ski poles catapulted into the air, his glove attached to it. Lanning's right ski came off but his left ski stayed attached, leaving his knee ligaments to accept the burden of leverage it created as his 200-pound body cartwheeled across the slope. From above, Rearick saw Lanning disappear within a cloud of snow that kept him hidden until he tumbled to a stop near the fencing.

Lanning had hardly stopped moving before the pain overwhelmed him. Hips, knees, neck—his whole body felt broken. Sitting up, Lanning felt something wrong in his hip. Looking down, he saw the lower half of his left leg was pointing in the wrong direction, the ski still attached. He turned to look up the hill for help, and when he did his head felt oddly balanced on his body, like he was a bobblehead doll. Panic set in, and Lanning started to scream.

Rearick was the first on the scene, followed shortly by Craig Faulks, a doctor traveling with the US team who had been above on the hill and skied down. They found Lanning clutching his right knee, the one he'd destroyed the year before at Kitzbühel, even though the other one was dislocated. A medical team was soon at Lanning's side. While they waited for a helicopter, Faulks reached out and prised open the release on Lanning's bindings, freeing his ruined left leg from the ski that had mangled it. One of the medics had said that Lanning had broken his leg, but Faulks saw that Lanning's knee was completely dislocated. He told the young skier to look at him and count to three, and then pulled the leg back into a normal position.

As relief rushed in, the screaming subsided, and it was Rearick who asked Lanning about his neck. Then someone reached out and stabilized it. Only later would Lanning learn that he'd fractured several bones in his neck, including cervical vertebrae C5 and C6. These were big, strong bones whose shattered fragments could have easily sliced through the soft spinal cord they were meant to protect, leaving Lanning paralyzed or dead. Despite the carnage, luck in a way had been on Lanning's side.

After the evacuation team took Lanning away, the race went on, but nobody caught Cuche. Bode Miller finished twenty-ninth. The best American result came from Andrew Weibrecht, who jumped from sixty-second to twelfth.

On Sunday night, the teams all left the Chateau and headed for Calgary's airport. On Monday they would arrive in Beaver Creek, the only US stop on the men's World Cup tour and a far more challenging course than Lake Louise. After that, there would be two more downhills in December, both of them in Italy: the Saslong downhill in Val Gardena, and then, right after Christmas, the Stelvio downhill in Bormio.

Those were all treacherous races in their own way, but the real danger would follow in January—the big classics that gave the downhillers their gonzo camaraderie and macho pride. These were the Lauberhorn downhill at Wengen and the Hahnenkamm at Kitzbühel. Those two prestigious events were at the heart of the downhillers' season, looming over the calendar all year long.

Kitzbühel in particular had an outsized significance, having created so many legends and destroyed so many careers. Olympic gold medals might make a downhiller a worldwide legend, but winning Kitzbühel was the surest way to win the undying respect of one's peers.

After the 2010 Olympics in February, there were two more downhills on the World Cup calendar before the season's title was awarded: Kvitfjell and Garmisch. There were ten or more racers who were in contention for the championship, but none of them was T. J. Lanning. After his helicopter ride to the base, an ambulance took him to Banff. The clinic there was not equipped to treat a broken neck, and the roads out of town were a snowy disaster zone. Lanning waited five hours to get transport. When he finally arrived in Calgary, it was the middle of the night. He endured a series of MRIs and CT scans before being deposited in a hospital room alongside a patient who had been injured in a hit-and-run accident. Finally, a medical evacuation service USSA had partnered with, Global Rescue, came to pick him up in a private jet and take him to Vail for surgery.

In Vail, doctors would cut open the front of Lanning's neck, move his esophagus to the side, and insert a metal plate with four screws, which united the pieces of the broken vertebrae. Later they would turn to Lanning's demolished knee, rebuilding the joint so that he could start out again down the road to converting his talent and bravery into overdue recognition and glory.

CHAPTER 14

Rivals

Alpine ski racing is primarily a man-versus-nature contest. This is one reason the top skiers often struggle when questioned about their rivals. Every racer grapples with a similar course and conditions, and can exercise virtually no control over his or her competitors; their fixation is on the mountain itself.

On December 4, 2009, the mountain was giving Lindsey Vonn a spirited fight. Midway through the Lake Louise course, she could feel the blood gushing from her tongue where she'd bitten it. Vonn was going more than 60 miles per hour. The cold Canadian wind caught the pooling blood at the corner of her mouth and sent a rivulet of it back toward her helmet strap, tracking a crooked, crimson path across her skin.

The air itself was an opponent, playing devilish little tricks on those who passed through it at high speeds. Skiing in a tuck at 70 miles per hour, for instance, the air could fold your lower lip down against your chin. At 80, it could wiggle its way behind your goggles and pull the tears off your eyeballs, freezing them against your temples. And don't even ask about contact lenses.

Racers train for the demonic wind because it can hurt them, especially on jumps. A racer who goes off a jump in a merely neutral stance invites the wind to find the tiny upward curls of their ski tips. The result is not unlike what happens when the wind gets underneath an umbrella and turns it inside out; skis become sails, and the racers attached to them, unanchored in flight, soon tip backward, powerless to stop the rotation. In a cruel instant, they are looking straight up into the sky.

Racers avoid this by forcefully plunging their upper bodies forward and down as the earth falls away—a technique known as "pressing" the jump. There is other specialized vocabulary associated with getting air. That thing racers do when they fail to press the jump, spinning their arms pointlessly, trying to counteract the backward rotation—they call it "rolling down the windows." And when such a racer touches down, often ass first, and has every piece of their equipment ripped forcefully from their bodies by the impact—there is a term for that too: a "yard sale."

But Vonn wasn't that badly off. She had a respect for the wind and a penetrating tuck that moved her through the air on terms it found fairly agreeable. Bloody face and all, she was piercing the air at Lake Louise on December 4 on her way to victory at the first women's downhill race of the year. It was always a relief for her to get back to this slope, where she had won at least one race in each of the previous five years. People had started calling the place "Lake Lindsey."

The tongue injury was a result of the snowfall, which made it hard to read the surface of the course. There was a patch of slippery ice about 20 seconds into the run, but Vonn didn't see it and went into a high-speed slide. As she tried to dig her edge in, shifting all her weight to her downhill ski, the icy patch ended, giving way to the grippy, dry snow the mountains around Banff were known for. Her ski edge suddenly caught and started tracking, throwing Vonn's whole upper body forward and whipping her chin into her knee. Her jaw snapped shut on her tongue, lacerating it despite the plastic mouthguard she held between her teeth. Drifting into the next turn on a sort of dazed autopilot after the impact, Vonn realized that she was off her intended line.

But with just a little extra pressure on her next turns, she was able to maneuver her way back on line without losing much speed.

There wasn't a big margin for error, though. Wind and snowfall on the top of the mountain that morning had forced the jury to lower the start, shortening the course by about 2,000 feet in length and 500 feet in vertical drop. The run now took only 86 seconds to finish, as opposed to the 110 it had required in the previous three days of training. That amplified mistakes like Vonn's, forcing her to ski aggressively and flawlessly for the next minute. To win, she had to charge ahead. She couldn't wonder if she'd lost a tooth, or think about the metallic taste of blood in her mouth, or let her mind drift to a similar experience, a swing-set accident she'd once endured.

Vonn plunged into the course she knew so well, blood streaming out of her mouth. She led at every interval and crossed the finish line in first place. At the bottom of the race course, she held a snowball to the blood on her face and accepted a trophy for her twenty-third career World Cup win.

"When I got to the bottom, I could feel the blood streaming down my face," she later told journalists with a small chuckle. "I was just a little bit confused, didn't know what happened, I was hoping that I didn't lose any teeth or anything like that. I'm happy that it wasn't anything major, just a cut. It's still bleeding just a little bit."

The soundbites and pictures were good, and with the Winter Olympics only months away, Lindsey Vonn was great. Over the next two days, she would win another downhill and finish second in the super G. NBC was already building its broadcast plans around her, and clearly Head had given her fast skis. This was her moment.

But even now, she was vulnerable. Skiing was a fickle sport, and it was nearly impossible to dominate in every discipline. Lindsey had to compete with one-event specialists like Marlies Schild, Austria's slalom queen, and also the experienced and versatile downhillers like Anja Pärson of Sweden and Elisabeth Görgl of Austria. No matter how unstoppable she may have seemed in Lake Louise, Lindsey Vonn had plenty of rivals.

Nearly six feet tall, with dark eyes and blonde hair that she kept stylishly short, Maria Riesch of Germany was by far her nation's best skier. Like her best friend, Vonn, the twenty-four-year-old Bavarian was an all-rounder. On November 14, Riesch had won the season's first World Cup slalom at Levi, Finland, and she finished third in the December 4 downhill where Vonn bit her tongue.

Riesch was from the historic town of Garmisch-Partenkirchen, which had played host to the swastika-themed 1936 Winter Olympics—the first to include alpine skiing. A US Army garrison established there after World War Two had evolved into a popular rest-and-relaxation haven for American servicemen, and the main ski area had hosted more than seventy World Cup races.

On the World Cup tour Riesch was all business, carrying herself with Teutonic seriousness through every race on the calendar in pursuit of the overall title. A veteran with the surgical scars to prove it, she was advancing her nation's long tradition of great female racers. Her Levi win was Germany's 182nd victory on the World Cup, but only thirty of those had come from the men. The Levi race had been essentially a two-skier duel between Vonn and Riesch; the American was only 0.08 seconds slower. The third-place finisher, Sölden victor and fan favorite Tanja Poutiainen of Finland, was 1.08 seconds behind Vonn.

Lindsey and Maria had been pals since 2000, when they were nervous fifteen-year-olds at the FIS Junior World Ski Championships in Quebec. When people asked Vonn to explain the basis of their friendship, she would point out that the two of them basically led the same life. They both were born in 1984, joined the World Cup at the age of sixteen, and chose all-around proficiency over specialization. Both of them were in romantic relationships with the men who managed their careers. Both skiers were now using Head skis. And both of them were determined to come away from Vancouver in February with at least one Olympic gold medal.

What went unsaid was that each deeply understood the sacrifices the other had made to get to the top of the sport, starting with an alienation from more carefree World Cup peers who worried less about duties and expectations. Confiding in their teammates about that kind of thing was out of the question; it was a by-product of speed and marketing potential, two coveted gifts. But when they were together, Maria and Lindsey could commiserate in two languages, share business and travel strategies, or simply relax, as they had done in Mexico that past spring.

Riesch had broken through on the World Cup sooner than Vonn, winning three World Cup races in three different disciplines in 2004. She was just nineteen years old and she finished third in the standings. But Riesch's comeuppance came the next year, when she blew out her right knee in January 2005 at Cortina, fought her way back to the World Cup in time for Sölden that October, and then destroyed her left knee a couple months later in Aspen.

When Riesch finally returned—having missed both the 2005 world championships and the 2006 Olympics—Vonn was waiting for her, a far more formidable adversary than before. Since then, more of their elders had moved on, and the two of them had emerged at the top, competing for podiums, prize money, and sponsorship contracts.

Riesch hadn't exactly welcomed Vonn's summertime switch from Rossignol to Head. Riesch had been on Head skis her entire career, and for much of that period had been far and away the top athlete in the company's World Cup stable. But with the recent stampede of great skiers to the Head brand, Riesch was now one of a half dozen potential champions, and she had to wonder if the company still rated her its highest priority. Would she still get the best skis to come out of the factory in Kennelbach? Would her suggestions still influence the design?

Maria's uncertainty bubbled into public view in the fall, when she complained to a journalist about being forced to fund her serviceman's month-long trip to New Zealand to help her test and prepare her skis for the winter. Apparently unaware of the specifics of Vonn's contract, Riesch observed that while Head could afford to sign Vonn, for her it was "*Sparmassnahmen ohne Ende*"—austerity without end.

Another challenger to Vonn's throne in 2009–10 was Tina Maze of Slovenia, a headstrong twenty-six-year-old from an impoverished mining town near the Austrian border. Maze had risen to the top of the sport without the kind of institutional support network Vonn and Riesch had enjoyed.

In addition to her diverse skills, Maze had perhaps the most striking looks of anyone on the women's World Cup tour, her dark brown eyebrows rising ever so slightly upward and tapering to points high on her temples, contributing to an overall impression of speed. You had to be standing up close to her to notice these features, and by then you might have learned that in addition to her native tongue, Maze spoke perfect German, Italian, and English in a monotone that suggested she was somehow bored with ski racing (indeed, she had pop music aspirations).

In her native Slovenian, her name was pronounced "Mahs," but quite a few people on the tour pronounced it "Mah-zay." No one dreamed of saying "Mays," as in "amazing," which made it confusing that after breaking away from the Slovenian ski team in the summer of 2008, she had named her newly formed independent program the Team to aMaze.

She came from a place called Črna na Koroškem, a town of about 2,300 inhabitants in a land of steep ravines and waterfalls. "Črna" means black, and it seemed fitting on winter afternoons, when it got dark early and a gloom pervaded the town. That might be the first time a visitor noticed what looked like a concentration of streetlights in a clearing next to town, only 100 feet above the rooftops. Climbing up a winding footpath and a staircase, you might expect to find a hockey rink before you stepped onto a gentle little ski slope that had turned out a half dozen Olympians.

It was primitive—no hotels or spas, just a small restaurant and a T-bar, a simple kind of lift where the seats are hooks shaped like upside-down Ts. The floodlights were the critical thing; kids in the ski club who came for after-school instruction could ski deep into the evening, as Tina did as a girl, taking so many laps on the T-bar that she would lose count. She and her friends would build jumps, or ski off down trails into the woods, all the way to their homes.

Lindsey Vonn would never forget the first time she laid eyes on Maze. It was 1998, when they raced at the Whistler Cup, an annual international children's race in Canada. Maze, then fourteen, won every event. The next year, the Slovenian ski federation started sending Maze to FIS races, and in January 1999 entered her in her first World Cup. She was fifteen.

By the time she got her first World Cup victory in 2002 (in a three-way tie for first at the Sölden opener that year), Maze was a very grown-up twenty-year-old. While almost every World Cup ski racer must leave home when they are young, those affiliated with larger teams, such as the US or Austria, are at least brought together with racers their age. Maze, on the other hand, was surrounded by adults— coaches, equipment people, and older athletes. She was navigating on her own and had to grow up fast. It wasn't easy, but it paid off later in her career, when independence became an asset.

By 2008, having grown tired of endless disputes with the Slovenian ski team, Maze and her boyfriend formed the Team to aMaze. She also switched from Rossignol to Stöckli, a tiny Swiss company where she could be certain she was the number one priority. She finished the 2009 season in sixth place in the standings. In the 2009–10 season, Maze's goal was to win the overall title and some Olympic gold medals.

And yet still she wasn't Vonn's most important rival.

By 2009, the most productive rivalry in the history of US skiing had been going on for at least a decade, and maybe more if you count the times that Julia Mancuso and Lindsey Kildow, at age eleven or twelve, heard some fragmentary legend about the other from halfway across the country.

Both were born in 1984, and were thrown together in 1998 as the impossibly young future stars on what was still Picabo Street's team. Over the decade that followed, they went from friends to enemies to friends a few times before settling into a sometimes tense coexistence. They downplayed their rivalry in the media, but there was no question they lit fires under each other. After Torino, Vonn was generally faster than Mancuso. But Mancuso had the Olympic gold, the one trophy Vonn lacked—and the credential that mattered to Americans.

They were kids in 1998 when they arrived on the US Ski Team's new development team, a project that coach Aldo Radamus had convinced Bill Marolt to fund. Coaches and teammates remember them generally as respectful girls with different personalities, Lindsey dutiful and ambitious and Julia more playful, but still a little private. That year, they shared a main coach: an even-keeled former math teacher named Todd Brickson, who immediately saw Minnesota and California in their technique. While Lindsey was edgy and aggressive, Julia had a lighter touch.

Lindsey was in the middle of a growth spurt and so had inconsistent control of her limbs, but she had a huge base of training from Buck Hill and Vail. Julia had lots of miles on her skis too, most of it skiing all over the mountain in different conditions. Neither of them skied anything like Street, who had learned to race on longer, straighter skis that only the best World Cup skiers knew how to coax into a carved turn; Julia and Lindsey had acquired the new-school shaped skis at age twelve and were already taking for granted the ability to slice from arc to arc before they even reached the World Cup. The bigger question for them was whether they could moderate this skill, and not let it take them too far out of the fall line.

They were both fifteen when they started on the tour. For the next four or five years they learned the ropes, toiling in the shadow of World Cup stars from Croatia, Sweden, and Austria. In another era of the US Ski Team, a coach might have pushed them to specialize in one event and start collecting wins, but alpine director Jesse Hunt was committed to the idea of being patient and letting "Jules" and "Linds" evolve into well-rounded skiers who could threaten for the overall title. By 2009, they were the US women's team's biggest stars.

The old personality differences remained. Mancuso was laid-back; Vonn was high-strung. While Vonn would spend her summer lifting weights in Salzburg or Vail, Mancuso would go kite surfing in Maui, doing Pilates on the side. If a race were postponed because of a snowstorm, Vonn and Mancuso might sit together in the lodge with the rest of their teammates until word came that the race was canceled. Then Vonn would remove her ski boots and head back to the hotel, while Mancuso would likely set off for the chairlift to go skiing outside the designated runs—off-piste, as it is known.

Mancuso was closer to being the leader of the US women's team, if such a thing existed. For one thing, she spent a lot more time with her teammates. Vonn was usually off with her husband, or staying in a different hotel with Red Bull picking up the tab. But mainly Mancuso had alpha status because she had the attitude, the experience, and the talent.

Over the 2009 summer, Mancuso had focused on rehabilitating her injured back and was feeling good. Her results in late 2009 weren't strong, but Vonn knew that was no indication of where things would stand come Vancouver. Mancuso was a big-event skier; the rarer the trophy on the line, the faster she went. She won eight medals at the world junior championships in 2002, 2003, and 2004. In 2005, at the world championships in Italy, she won two bronze medals (Vonn was fourth twice). And then came Torino, where Mancuso won both runs of the giant slalom, her joyous teammates tackling her in the middle of the finish area in the kind of celebration that every little girl who grew up skiing in America would envy—especially Lindsey Vonn.

CHAPTER 15

Almost Famous

Going east on Interstate 70 toward Vail, there is a place where if a motorist driving through during the first week of December happens to glance over at the right second, he might pick out a dark object in freefall against a white backdrop. This is the upper section of the Birds of Prey downhill course at Beaver Creek, Colorado—a plunge known as the Headwall, a geological term for the most imposing cliff faces.

Renowned course designer Bernhard Russi built the course for the 1999 world championships, slashing a new trail through a forested flank of the ultramodern resort. Russi used the steepest mountainside available, creating a downhill that only the world's very best skiers could handle. Though he called the course his masterpiece, he consistently credited the Almighty for providing such dramatic terrain.

Beginning 11,427 feet above sea level, the course opens with an easy 30-second traverse, where the racers tuck over gentle rolls and build up their speed while the announcers introduce them to viewers. Then the racers plunge off the edge of the world, crossing over a dropoff called the Brink and into the Talon Turn, the first big challenge of the Headwall, one of the most harrowing descents on the World Cup.

Below the Brink is a 45-degree pitch, warped by ledges and declivities that rush up to meet the racers at 70–80 miles per hour. In less
than a minute and a half, racers drop more than 2,400 feet in elevation.
The Vail Valley Foundation, which organizes the event, maintains more
than seven miles of safety netting, and the 17,000-pound snowcats
course workers use to till the surface into hardness have to be lowered
by powerful cable winches lest they roll into the woods.

There are a few flat spots, but they terminate in sharp dropoff
jumps. The jumps have names like Harrier, Peregrine, Screech Owl,
Golden Eagle, and Red Tail. The raptor motif fits perfectly; the racers
look like hawks folding their wings up and diving for prey down Russi's
course. It is a purposeful freefall; you wouldn't do it unless you are hungry for something.

Without exception, the world's fastest racers loved it, and the Birds
of Prey downhill became a mainstay of the World Cup calendar. Bode
Miller won there in 2004 and again in 2006. On December 5, 2009, he
gave it another shot. It was his 341st World Cup start, and it came seventy days before the opening ceremonies in Vancouver.

Miller kicked out of the start house, skated and pushed with his
poles, then dropped into his tuck. Fifteen seconds later, crossing the
sixth little roll in the course, he nearly lost his footing, but recovered. As he gained speed, contrails of powdery snow lifted from the
ground in his wake and drifted like vapor before settling back onto
the track.

This was a course where Miller usually performed at his best. He
had been down it dozens of times and knew how to handle the complex
terrain, which rewarded one of his greatest innate talents: his ability to
maintain contact with the snow. This year, his instincts were bound to
be dulled—he'd only had a few days of downhill training.

As Miller came into the Pumphouse section, he made a long turn
to the right, with all his weight on the left ski. Now it was time to transfer his weight and initiate the new turn. Letting his skis pass underneath him as his upper body drifted down the fall line, Miller went to
put pressure on his right ski just as a piece of the rolling terrain rushed

up to meet him. As he crested it, the ground dropped away and he was airborne, almost lying prone, like a base-stealing ballplayer sliding to beat a throw.

At more than 60 miles per hour, Miller floated sideways across the mountain a few feet above the snow. His hand dragged on the surface for a moment, but then he lost even that contact. The tips of his skis were pointing straight down the fall line, but he was drifting sideways across the mountain. His legs were fully extended, and his arms were behind him. He drifted 30 feet, 50 feet, 80 feet to the right of his intended line. When Miller finally felt his feet touch down, they were on a drift of ice shavings, dry as sawdust, that previous racers had peeled off the surface of the race line. It offered no solidity. The whole flight had lasted less than a second, but that was ample time for Miller's instincts and experience to inform him that when his edges sank through the soft layer and engaged the ice underneath, their orientation would make them start running back down the hill and to the left, while all his momentum wanted to go right.

This was what strength conditioning was for. In a tenth of a second or less, Miller's legs would go from the relaxation of pure flight to resisting extreme g-force—the equivalent of three or four times his weight under gravity, and with no mechanical foundation reinforcing his body's strength except his skis and boots. It was the ultimate athletic test—a pure reaction to a powerful stimulus, requiring agility, strength, and subtlety.

The edges of Miller's skis pushed through the duff, found purchase on the ice below, and caught. Miller squatted against the centrifugal forces. The edges held, the skis flexed, and Miller rebounded back to the left as if fired from a slingshot. As he swung into the next turn, he worked himself back onto the proper line, and a few gates later he was gunning for victory.

When Miller crossed the finish line, he was in first place, but he knew it wouldn't last. He moved into the little corral by the finish line, passed his equipment to the FIS representative for testing, and stripped off his helmet and bib. While he caught his breath, three racers came down and beat his time: Carlo Janka of Switzerland, Aksel Lund Svindal, and Didier Cuche.

Miller was elated by his performance. The mistake on the pitch wasn't the thing that cost him the half-second that gave Janka the victory. What slowed him down was the bottom section, where fatigue forced him to stand high out of his tuck and get bounced around a lot on the snow. It was high altitude, and his stamina wasn't what it might have been, but the recovery he'd made was sensational—something that proved his most precious skills were still at hand.

The save was reminiscent of one of Miller's most famous performances, the 2005 world championship combined event at Bormio, Italy, home of the relentless Stelvio downhill. Miller was the defending world champion in the event and a favorite for gold when he started the downhill portion of the race on February 3, 2005. Landing a jump about 15 seconds into the 110-second course, Miller felt one of his skis detach from his boot. He was traveling close to 80 miles per hour at the time and the long ski shot out from under him like a rocket booster popping off the space shuttle. Miller stood up from his tuck, teetering to maintain his balance over one ski, and then continued down the course. There was a long, wide runway up there where he could have steered himself into a big turn and stopped, but Bode just kept going, arms out to his sides for balance, on one ski. Before long he was knifing serious turns, traversing a ripply sidehill and even catching air. The approach to the daunting San Pietro jump would have been a good place to stop the show, but there Miller actually dropped into a parody of a tuck as he shot past the coaches and race officials, went off the jump, and kept going. He completed almost all of the course, only stopping when he was in view of the crowd. Few people remember that Benjamin Raich had won that race; Miller's Chaplinesque DNF was the highlight.

Almost five years later, Miller's latest balletic recovery at Beaver Creek was similar, as thrilling to those who saw it as anything Janka had done. It was the kind of thing Miller could have spent the rest of the day reliving, laughing with his teammates as he anatomized the whole episode in detail.

But he couldn't, because right then and there, across a small fence from the corral where he was catching his breath, stood a huge cluster of reporters and cameramen waiting to ask him questions. The group was larger than usual, reflecting America's increased interest in skiing during an Olympic year. It was time for Miller to be respectful, and patient, and sometimes that seemed to be harder for him than carving turns down an icy headwall.

———

To understand Miller's churlish attitude toward the media in the months before Vancouver, it is necessary to recall how intensely he'd been scalded by the spotlight during his star turn in the months leading up to the Torino Games.

The trouble had started at the World Cup finals in March 2005, where Miller won the overall World Cup title, becoming the first American to win the crystal globe since 1983. The finals were in Lenzerheide, Switzerland, where Miller clinched the title in the season's penultimate race, the giant slalom, on March 12. Because the next day's slalom held no import for him, and because everyone would leave town when it was over, Miller decided to raise a glass or two that night, finding a cozy lodge where he ended up surrounded by family, friends, sponsors, agents, coaches, ski team administrators, and teammates. There was a lot to celebrate, and it took most of the night.

It's impossible to know how much unmetabolized alcohol was coursing through Miller's bloodstream the next morning, as he gamely pulled on bib sixteen and participated in the last World Cup race of the 2004–05 season. Wherever he was on the spectrum of drunk to hungover when the first run of slalom started at 10 a.m., he raced well, winning the second run outright and finishing the day's race in sixth place.

The whole episode was a fuzzy, funny memory a few months later, when Miller agreed to participate in a *60 Minutes* profile that would run just before the 2006 Games. The CBS crew came to Franconia that summer and shot footage of Miller working out in the 120-year-old barn at Tamarack. They interviewed his parents, outlined his unusual career path, and took note of his expressed ambivalence about fame, fortune, and Olympic medals.

The segment's producers explored Miller's well-deserved reputation as one of the World Cup's party boys, and his coaches were quoted saying it worried them. But Miller was unapologetic. He wanted to have fun, and there was clearly a sympathetic lightheartedness to the on-camera exchange between correspondent Bob Simon and Miller in which they revisited the memory of his queasy slalom outing at Lenzerheide.

"Talk about a hard challenge right there," Miller said. "I mean, if you ever tried to ski when you're wasted, it's not easy."

It was all in good fun—not a confession so much as telling a funny story on himself. Bode grinned as he pantomimed the motion of clearing the gates out of the way in a slalom course.

"You're putting your life at risk there," he said. "It's like driving drunk only there's no rules about it in ski racing."

Was he saying he wouldn't do it again, Simon asked?

"No," Miller said, "I'm not saying that."

Half a year passed, and Miller was in the thick of his World Cup season on January 5, 2006, when *60 Minutes* began promoting its Bode Miller piece, slated to air four days later. The news release CBS sent out was headlined "World Cup Ski Champ Admits to Being Drunk on the Slopes," and told viewers they could count on Miller to be sober in Torino because "skiing drunk is too hard."

"He ought to know," said the release. "He says he's done it before and won't promise not to do it again."

It was a slow news day, and the 245-word Associated Press story that hit the wire was instantly picked up by websites and newspapers across the country. ("Brew-ski" was the headline in the *Boston Herald*.) Miller's agent put out a statement blasting CBS's "out of context and salacious" release, but it was too late to stop a media frenzy. The segment aired, angry phone calls flooded the USSA offices, and Bill Marolt issued a statement calling Miller's remarks "unacceptable" and "irresponsible." Promising to work with Miller to "recognize the seriousness of his comments," Marolt got on a flight to Switzerland, where Miller was racing at Wengen. (Miller maintains Marolt's trip was unrelated.)

Miller addressed the issue with a first-person piece published in the *Denver Post*, where he suggested he had shared the drunken skiing anecdote with the most "reputable and prestigious" news program in the US "to test their integrity"—a portrayal of events undermined by a profile in the January edition of *Maxim*, which hit stands a day later and quoted Miller speaking of arriving at races "just sobering up" by the first run. (Accompanying the article online was video of Miller soaking in a hot tub with the story's bikini-clad author.)

While Marolt made his way to Wengen, the US team's staff had been forbidden to speak to the media, but men's head coach Phil McNichol had to vent. In comments that were broadcast worldwide within hours, he spoke freely about his frustrations, and even mused that it was time to consider whether Miller and the US Ski Team were right for each other. "Can we still do this together?" he asked.

The comments, which exposed the deeper tensions between Miller and the team shortly before the Olympic Games were set to begin, infuriated McNichol's superiors. Meanwhile, it was determined that Miller would publicly atone. After the training run on the Lauberhorn course on January 12, Miller delivered his apology to a room full of journalists and television cameras. To anyone familiar with Miller's upbringing, the cruelest touch might have been the venue itself: a grade-school classroom.

The whole episode cemented Miller's conviction that the media hype surrounding the Olympics offered him few benefits and lots of trouble and pain. Instead of censoring himself, he simply retreated, declining hundreds of interview requests. America's mainstream sports media, which had bashed him so severely at Torino, happily ignored his extraordinary independent project.

Now here they were again, four years later, at the bottom of the downhill at Beaver Creek, waiting to ask him questions that would require diplomacy and tact. They wanted words, and they wanted the image of him speaking, his face framed by the camera lens, for their evening news sports segment. Miller wished that what he had done on the Birds of Prey that day was sufficient. It was precisely what he meant when he said that skiing was his way of expressing himself. You could call it a fourth-place finish, but to him it was really a piece of performance art.

But he knew that a verbal self-interpretation was due. He knew he would have to talk. These people had been waiting all week to hear what would be his first public statements since his press conference at the Staples Center two months earlier. Some of them remembered the old Bode, the one who could issue enthusiastic bursts of detailed theory about his sport.

By the standard of professional athletes, or really by any standard, he was articulate and analytical, and while he was still that way with his peers, he'd learned to withold himself from the press.

Now a shade fell over his face as he came to the fence. The questions came, and Miller did his best to be cheerful and answer them. He talked about his experimentation with equipment over the previous week. He talked about his mistake on the headwall. He was asked about the course at Vancouver, and his fitness, and about being a role model, and if he was more at ease in 2009. And of course he was asked about his goals for the Olympics.

"I don't really think about it yet," he said. "You can make something up if you want to."

The media's attention found a more comfortable resting place on the shoulders of Lindsey Vonn, who after completing her three races in Lake Louise—two downhill wins and a close second-place in the super G—flew to Europe, where she would remain until the Vancouver Games.

On December 8, she and Thomas landed at Frankfurt to discover they had missed their connection to Stockholm, which itself was only a transfer point. From there they planned to catch another flight, this one to Östersund, Sweden, for the ninety-minute drive to their destination, Åre, a familiar World Cup site on the edge of a frozen lake.

While the airlines rescheduled the Vonns for a later flight, Lindsey took the opportunity to update her public social network profiles. On Facebook she had just crossed the threshold of 10,000 fans. Every post she made there and on Twitter was met with an instant flurry of replies: encouragement, suggestions, and marriage proposals. It all would have seemed wildly easy and useful to Lindsey's best coach on the subjects of brand exposure and self-promotion: Picabo Street.

Their relationship went back to 1994. That winter, as nine-year-old Lindsey Kildow had watched the Lillehammer Games on television, her imagination latched onto the twenty-two-year-old from Idaho who won the downhill silver medal. With her cool name, fearless competitive drive, and seemingly bottomless confidence, Street was like a superhero to Lindsey. That spring, when Street went on a publicity tour with her new medal, she passed through a ski shop in the Twin Cities area and Lindsey's parents took her to meet Street, who engaged Lindsey in a conversation about ski racing.

She might have been just another starstruck young racer to Street, but the meeting was a life-changing event for Lindsey, who hung her autographed poster up in her room and announced her determination to be an Olympian. Seven years later, a sixteen-year-old Lindsey was standing next to a twenty-nine-year-old Picabo on the podium of a FIS downhill at Big Mountain, Montana, after finishing second to her. Street, near the end of her career, had come back from a series of injuries to find the US Ski Team stocked with much younger racers.

Picabo took Lindsey under her wing, and Lindsey studied everything the older skier could teach her, from course inspection to techniques for avoiding overzealous fans. Picabo mentored Lindsey on how to present herself around other people, how to win the mental side of the sport, how to use the crowds at big races to her advantage.

On the World Cup tour, Lindsey also watched the strategic way Picabo interacted with the media and sponsors. She was impressed with the way she had parlayed her name recognition into endorsement deals with Nike and Chapstick. Lindsey's father arranged to build a website that they hoped would help Lindsey find a headgear sponsor. She signed on with Picabo's people, agents affiliated with the sports marketing firm IMG.

Now the Vancouver Olympics were two months away, and Lindsey was seizing every bit of attention she could get. As part of her endorsement deal with Vail Resorts, she was chronicling her travels in a series of twenty-seven online video vignettes called "Lindsey is Epic; Vail to Vancouver." She had also started a contest in which fans submitted bids to design her helmet for the Olympics (the Red Bull logo and paint scheme weren't going to fly with the IOC or its soft drink sponsor, Coca-Cola).

What Lindsey seemed to have learned best from Picabo was how to manage her fame—how to negotiate the inevitable erosion of privacy that American Olympic stars must withstand. Because so much of the Olympic coverage was driven by biographical narratives, stars like Picabo and Lindsey were expected to be an open book; family affairs, illnesses, fights with friends—if Lindsey was going to succeed, all of it would be laid bare. The trick, Picabo showed her, was to do it on your own terms, and use it to create a recognizable, profitable brand.

One of Picabo's best lessons held that it wasn't easy to balance sponsor campaigns with ski racing. A typical endorsement contract spelled out a specific number of days that the athlete had to make herself available to the company. The company would use those days for photo shoots, meet-and-greets, and press conferences. But for each day you gave up, Picabo had pointed out, you had to add another two for travel, which might include jet lag. It was a deceptively heavy burden.

The landscape was different in 2009. When Lindsey was growing up in Minnesota, she had had to struggle to follow Picabo's career; World Cup races were rarely televised, and the *Star Tribune* carried only a few results. Now, unadulterated footage of every World Cup race was available online. With a few thumbstrokes on her phone, Lindsey could tell thousands of devotees what was happening on the tour that instant. She didn't have to rely on journalists or cameramen to capture her thoughts on her latest run and relay them to the world.

Yet the same forces that were enabling her to burnish her image could also sully it. Anything she said in any setting could be published in minutes without context or accountability. Anyone could snap a picture of her at any time and broadcast it around the world—as swimming star Michael Phelps had learned early that year, when a British newspaper published photos of him smoking from what appeared to be a bong.

And as Lindsey, Thomas, and everyone at the US Ski Team knew from watching Bode Miller combust in 2006, the media spotlight could be especially dangerous for an Olympic athlete. When the attention of mainstream America drifted away, the label you'd gotten by the closing ceremonies would be yours for at least another four years.

—

Bode Miller had no idols, no Picabo to show him the way, but when it came to handling fame on the World Cup tour, he did once say something revealing about the example he had seen in 1992 overall champion Paul Accola of Switzerland.

It was 2005, and Miller was at Kitzbühel. By that time, Accola was an active but washed-up thirty-seven-year-old who hadn't won a race in five years. Accola had enjoyed a fine career, but thirteen years had passed since his battle with Alberto Tomba was the tour's weekly drama. Now Accola rarely cracked the top twenty and had no chance of competing with the new generation. But he knew the downhill courses better than anyone, and so he survived. Watching him, Bode realized that Accola had it pretty good: he didn't have to do any interviews.

"If you watch Accola, he gets to walk right through the crowd after a training run," Miller said that year at Kitzbühel. "I watched him this morning. I was going up for my run, and he was on his way down. He walks right through and people say 'hi' or 'good job' or 'good luck.' He walks straight through with his skis on his shoulder. I can't even carry my own skis. I have to ditch my skis and my boots so that I can sign things all the time. The crowd doesn't get any smaller. I can sign for an hour if I want to, and one leaves, and three more come."

Miller liked the money and prestige that came with success, but he resented the attendant obligations. When he was young and relatively unknown on the World Cup in the late 1990s, he'd partaken freely of the tour's nightlife. Every place the circuit went there was someone— maybe a retired racer from that part of the world or an older teammate— who knew all the best places to go. But when he started winning World Cups at a steady clip, he found he couldn't go out and party without strangers besieging him, thrusting pens or business cards at him, or throwing an arm around his shoulders while a friend fiddled with a camera for "just one" quick photo. When he walked through the streets of a town like Val d'Isère or Bormio, a comet tail of children followed, chanting "Bo-deee, Bo-deee, Bo-deee." It pained him to turn down their autograph requests, but he had to conserve his energy. Ski towns were small, and everyone in them wanted a piece of him. This helped explain the importance of the motor home, a private space where he could avoid the tidal crush of admirers.

In 2006, his critics had called Miller a jerk for accepting the perks of Olympic fame and complaining about the responsibilities. They had a point: attention was an inescapable cost of earning millions of dollars by selling your name and likeness. But there was more to it than that. Miller's art as a skier was idiosyncratic and untutored. The pressure to be all things to all people—anodyne, in a word—involved a dangerous inner compromise. Tailoring his conduct and speech for new constituencies of curious strangers put at risk the stubborn originality that had gotten him to the top. Diplomacy was antithetical to his nature.

People who'd watched Miller's struggle up close knew he'd started to find the balance between Picabo Street and Paul Accola. After Torino, his actions made it clear that he wasn't interested in stockpiling a fortune if it eroded his peace of mind. Some contractual appearances had been necessary to fund Team America, but his late reentry to the sport in 2009 had closed most of the endorsement windows for him.

An exception was Hublot, the Swiss luxury watch brand. Lowell Taub had inked Miller to a deal with the company that required Miller to stop off in New York on December 7 on his way from Beaver Creek to Europe. Hublot was unveiling a limited-edition, $20,000 watch called the Bode Bang. Proceeds from its sale would benefit the Turtle Ridge Foundation, Miller's nonprofit organization devoted to supporting adaptive and youth sports programs. An event marking the launch would be held at the Sutton East Tennis Club in New York City.

There, in an air-conditioned bubble under the Queensboro Bridge, Miller played exhibition tennis with some minor celebrities and then stood by as Hublot's president introduced the watch and handed over a giant cardboard check for $10,000 made out to the Harlem Junior Tennis and Education Program, a youth group that Miller's nonprofit was sponsoring. Miller held a short tennis clinic for kids from the group before finally meeting with the small number of invited journalists and speaking about his prospects in the Alps.

One reporter's question noted that NBC, which had paid $5.7 billion for Vancouver broadcast rights, was behaving as if Lindsey Vonn was the only American ski racer headed to the Games—that Miller was conspicuously absent from the network's promotional spots. Miller nodded, a sly smile indicating that it was perfectly fine with him. One step closer to Accola.

"Lindsey's great," Miller said. "She's well sorted out for that stuff. She's just got a great attitude about the sport and Olympics in general. I think that's ideal. As we know, going into the Olympics, I was conflicted. I wasn't feeling great about where I was. That's not the kind of person you want to have as your poster boy for that. I believe what I believe. It just didn't match up with what everyone else believed. That was frustrating to have everyone trying to put words in my mouth all the time about how I should be feeling, what I should be doing, what my goals should be. That's frustrating for anyone. But I think Lindsey's the perfect person for that. She's skiing at the top of her game. I don't think there's ever been an American skier as dominant, and I look forward to seeing what she can do."

CHAPTER 16

Blood and Guts

B ode Miller had a well-established disregard for medals and trophies, but he was more mindful of records, and one of the most splendid records in the history of alpine ski racing belonged to him: in late 2004, in the span of just sixteen days, he had won a World Cup race in each of the sport's four core disciplines.

Only six other skiers had previously done it, and only two in the span of a single season—Marc Girardelli and Petra Kronberger. Wins in four events in sixteen days seemed as durable a record as Joe DiMaggio's fifty-six-game hitting streak. It was all the more remarkable considering the punishing trek it had involved; Miller's four victories came in Alberta, Colorado, France, and Italy.

Five years later, the relentless travel schedule demanded of the top alpine skiers had not eased up. These trips weren't hops between arenas in metropolitan areas. When Miller's flight from New York landed at the Zürich airport on December 8, 2009, he immediately set out on the five-hour drive to Val d'Isère, scene of the previous winter's world championships, where three World Cup races—a super combined, a super G, and a giant slalom—were scheduled for December 11–13.

After that, he planned to make an eight-hour drive across the top of Italy to the tour's next stop, a super G and downhill on December 18–19 in Val Gardena, Italy. From there it was a short trip over a mountain pass to new accommodations in Alta Badia, hosting a GS and slalom December 20–21. This was a typical mid-December schedule for the tour: seven races in ten days, plus training runs and driving.

Miller had some help along with him for the trip, a family friend named David Brantley. When Miller suddenly decided to return to the sport in September, Brantley had jumped at Miller's invitation to come on tour and do the on-the-ground tasks Miller's agents couldn't accomplish from the States.

As Miller's newly appointed business manager, Brantley was already exhausted by the pace of the tour by the time they got to Val d'Isère. Between all the travel and the skiing, ceremonies and sponsor gatherings, Miller was cramming in a whole summer's worth of conditioning. And when little gaps appeared in the schedule, it seemed to Brantley that Bode just wanted to play games—basketball or squash or volleyball.

On December 12, after Miller finished ninth in the super G at Val d'Isère, Brantley had wanted to rest in the plush hotel, maybe pack for Val Gardena, but Bode was bugging him to come join a game of volleyball at a nearby gym. Brantley went along grudgingly, and got a closeup view of the accident that would throw Miller's delicate plan for the 2010 Olympics into jeopardy.

It was a three-on-three game, and Brantley was Miller's teammate. They went up together to block a shot and came down in the same place, with Miller landing on Brantley's left ankle. Miller's right foot tipped over on its side just as his full weight came down on it. All 215 pounds of him collapsed instantly to the floor. He clutched his right ankle with a grimace. Miller hadn't shouted or even said anything, but his face suggested he wasn't going to stand up soon. The others surrounded Miller. It was his right ankle that he'd rolled—not the one he'd cracked the year before. Brantley asked if it was bad and Miller told him yes. They got him to his feet and hobbled out of the gym into the cold. Bode was limping severely, but he wanted to walk it off. Back at the hotel, Bode took off his shoes and socks and his ankle, grossly discolored, swelled like a balloon.

The next day was a giant slalom. Miller wasn't able to get his foot into a ski boot. Instead, he and Brantley and Mike Kenney, Miller's uncle, made the seven-hour drive to Patsch, Austria, where the US Ski Team kept apartments. There they rested for a few days, with Bode icing the discolored joint, before making the short drive over the Brenner Pass and down into the Dolomites to Val Gardena, where it was Miller's intention to stuff his foot into a ski boot and try to ski the Saslong downhill.

It felt okay once he got his ankle into the boot, Miller said, but wedging it down into that hard plastic cuff was excruciatingly painful.

Aksel Lund Svindal of Norway was alpine skiing's Mr. Consistency, racking up fewer victories and crashes than Bode Miller, but seeming almost always to land in the top ten. In the three races at Val d'Isère in 2009, he finished ninth, seventh, and fifth. As clouds were darkening over Miller's Vancouver prospects, the gloom was lifting from Svindal's.

After Sölden, Svindal had made the most of the four-week hiatus his lower-leg injury forced upon him. When he heard that his Oslo physiologist was going to Miami, he decided to go along, spending his days there in the sun, reading and working out, sailing and updating his blog and social media accounts. John Branch of the *New York Times* found him there for a story that ran on November 24 under a photo of Svindal at the beach leaping through the air in pink shorts.

"At least one Norwegian living in Miami, a South Beach real-estate agent named Roy Hansen, traced Svindal's movements and contacted him," Branch wrote. "Hansen and his friends took Svindal dancing and to a party that had Svindal shaking his head days later."

Svindal had returned to the tour at Lake Louise, with his upper shin taped up to help stabilize the loose bone. He was slow in Canada but had strong finishes in the three World Cup races in Beaver Creek, including a third-place finish in the Birds of Prey downhill. That was always a special race for Svindal; in 2007, he'd endured a gruesome season-ending crash there, but returned to the course a year later to win.

Things had gone well for him at Val d'Isère, too, but there was a problem named Carlo Janka. The Swiss twenty-three-year-old was on a streak, having racked up three consecutive wins at Beaver Creek and two other third-place finishes. Janka was a quiet kid from Obersaxen who'd picked up the nickname "Iceman," and was capable of winning races in downhill, super G, giant slalom, and combined.

It was impossible to forecast in mid-December, but to Svindal it already looked like Janka was going to run away with the overall title Svindal had hoped to defend. After ten races, Janka had 460 points. Next in the standings was Janka's older teammate, Didier Cuche, with 384 points. Svindal had 288.

He wasn't giving up on the World Cup, but Svindal's focus was shifting over to the Olympics. For Svindal, the remainder of the races in December and January were going to feel a bit like training for Whistler. He was twenty-six years old, one of the greatest ski racers of his era, and he still didn't have an Olympic medal.

Svindal was born on the day after Christmas in 1982. His parents were alpine skiers who imparted their love for the sport to Aksel and his little brother by taking the boys to Geilo, a ski area a few hours from their hometown near Oslo. Years later, Aksel still owned the pair of 40-inch skis that he had learned to ski on. His mother was gone, though, having died in childbirth when Aksel was eight.

When Svindal was young, alpine skiing was undergoing a revival in Norway, where cross-country skiing and jumping were national obsessions. In the early 1990s, a group of powerful alpine racers from Norway had made a major impact on the World Cup tour. Chief among them were Kjetil André Aamodt and Lasse Kjus, a hard-nosed duo who between them won three overall titles and thirty-six medals at the Olympics and world championships. Throughout the 1990s, they were role models for young Aksel, who at fifteen enrolled in a ski academy in Oppdal, an isolated town 260 miles to the north of his home. In four years there, Aksel studied and trained and qualified for the Norwegian junior team. He soon became the top junior alpine skier in the world, and by age eighteen he was racing World Cups, sponging up knowledge from Aamodt and Kjus, now his teammates.

The two "Attacking Vikings" taught Svindal a lot about the best lines on the World Cup downhills and how to handle a big crash (wave to the camera if you're okay after a crash, Kjus said, so your father won't worry too much if he's watching at home). But the main thing they taught Svindal was the virtue of not specializing, in keeping one's abilities well-rounded even if it makes the climb to the top a little slower.

Svindal was twenty-two when he won his first World Cup race, the super G at Lake Louise in 2005. When Aamodt and Kjus retired not long after that, Svindal took up the red and blue flag, winning races in multiple disciplines and gaining popularity with his peers and in the media. In the 2006–07 season, he won two world championship gold medals and the overall World Cup title. Indisputably the number one alpine skier in the world, he was twenty-four years old.

Svindal was surfing a wave of confidence in late 2007. With fast skis from Atomic, lucrative sponsorships, and a budding romance with Julia Mancuso, Svindal appeared unstoppable until the Beaver Creek catastrophe. He started the 2007–08 season with wins at Sölden and Lake Louise before arriving in Beaver Creek at the end of that November. He had a reasonable shot at sweeping the four races there, he thought. The downhill was a monster, yes, but Svindal had learned a lot racing there in the four previous seasons.

Svindal didn't see anything too worrisome on the morning of Tuesday, November 27, when he and the other racers inspected the downhill slope for the first training run. The surface was the chalky stuff you sometimes got in the high Rockies, where the arid winds could wick the moisture out of the snow. It was what Svindal and other racers sometimes called "hero snow" because it was responsive to the finest adjustments the racers made to technique and line.

Svindal started fourteenth that day, right behind American Steven Nyman, an old friend from the 2002 junior world championships. When his turn came, he tucked across the flats at the top of the course and then took an aggressive line through the gates on the Headwall, enjoying himself. Coming out of the long, fast corridor called the Pumphouse, Svindal sensed he was carrying more speed than usual. He was right; as he came onto the short, flat runway that led to the Golden Eagle jump, he crossed the beam of the third timing interval in the lead.

Svindal can't recall why he approached the Golden Eagle jump the way he did, drifting far to the right and staying low in his tuck at a place where racers always stand up to recenter their weight before takeoff. Svindal hit the edge of the jump off balance and his chest caught the wind like a sail. In an instant he was rotating backward 20 feet off the ground, going perhaps 70 miles per hour with his skis up over his head.

When Svindal looked at the footage later, it was obvious to him that he was doomed, but in the air he recalls thinking he could recover his balance and land on his feet. His confidence was so high that he thought his frantic reorganization of body parts would make a difference, but all it amounted to was a thrashing of limbs.

Svindal landed on his upper back with a sickening crunch. The tails of his skis hit the snow and detached from his feet, flying high into the air. As Svindal's body slid toward the safety netting, one of the skis returned to earth and somehow speared his backside, severely lascerating him there. Something else—his knee? the ground?—smashed him in the face, crushing bones and blacking out the world.

Svindal remembers waking up to the voices of his rescuers climbing through the tangled nets to reach him. He recalls doing a quick assessment of his limbs to determine the damage, and thinking his knees felt fine. Opening his eyes, he saw blood on the snow in front of him. "That's strange," he thought, and then passed out again. When he woke up again, he was in the ambulance. The next few hours were hazy, but as Svindal drifted in and out of consciousness, he registered an ambulance ride, a CT scan machine, dizziness, and feverish fluctuations of his body temperature. At one waking moment, a doctor knelt by him and told him a long list of injuries they had discovered. The last thing on the list was five facial fractures, the majority just below his right eye.

At the Vail Valley Medical Center, an unusually diverse group of medical specialists converged on Svindal to examine the deep, long gash where the ski had punctured his gluteus maximus and sliced major blood vessels. There was concern that it had damaged his bowels too. Back at the race venue, a rumor spread that Svindal's ski had partly castrated him. In the end, Svindal spent two weeks in the hospital, unable to get out of bed. Many of his peers on the World Cup tour came to visit him—Miller was the first, Svindal later recalled—and then they moved on to the season's next races at Val d'Isère while Svindal spent two weeks in a hospital room with a fine view of Vail's ski slopes. Finally he flew home to Norway, where he stayed at his father's house, recuperating.

A few months after the accident, Svindal began working out, but he was easily exhausted. If he went to the gym, even to do something easy, he would get so dizzy that he didn't dare drive home. But he healed, worked hard to get his strength back, and rejoined the World Cup for the start of the 2008–09 season. One year after his grisly accident, Svindal returned to Beaver Creek and won both the downhill and the super G. That was the prelude to the world championship combined gold and the overall title that put him on an equal footing with Aamodt and Kjus. In 2009–10, he was looking for some Olympic hardware to round out the trophy case.

***

Though exceptional in its particulars, Svindal's cannonball crash off the Golden Eagle was only one incident among a spate of life-threatening injuries that afflicted the sport in the years between 2006 and 2009. Ski racing had always been dangerous, but the downhillers at the top of the sport in the lead-up to Vancouver had good reason to feel extra vulnerable.

In February 2006, twenty-eight-year-old US Ski Team racer Dane Spencer crashed on a downhill course at Big Mountain, Montana, breaking his neck and pelvis. He shattered the C2 vertebra—the second one down from the skull—but the bone fragments spread outward, away from his spinal cord, saving him from paralysis. After a long rehabilitation, Spencer returned to racing, then became a coach.

More violence followed at Kitzbühel in 2008, a few months after Svindal's near-exsanguination at Beaver Creek. Racing the Hahnenkamm on his thirtieth birthday, American downhiller Scott Macartney went off the Streif course's final jump at 87 miles per hour, got twisted sideways in the air, and slammed into the snow so hard that his helmet came off. Macartney convulsed even as he slid, limp and unconscious, across the finish line. Airlifted to Innsbruck, he spent the rest of the day in a medically induced coma.

Later that year, the victim was twenty-seven-year-old Austrian racer Matthias Lanzinger. The scene was Kvitfjell, Norway—a World Cup super G. Lanzinger came over a blind jump, touched down on a collision path with a gate and slammed into it, breaking his left leg. His binding did not release, and as he cartwheeled to a stop, his still-attached ski became a powerful lever that caused his broken leg to twist violently. Two days after the accident, doctors were forced to amputate his leg below the knee.

Then, in January 2009 at Kitzbühel, Daniel Albrecht of Switzerland crashed in the same place where Macartney had been hurt, hitting the final jump going more than 85 miles per hour and tipping backward in the air as he flew an estimated 230 feet before landing on his back. His bindings and skis exploded, and his goggles shot up into the Austrian sky. The impact flung him onto his face and the lights went out—a three-week coma. The trauma caused severe lung and brain injuries, and though he tried to return, he was never competitive again.

These recent catastrophes formed the backdrop for the bloodbath the 2009–10 season had become by mid-December. In addition to T. J. Lanning breaking his neck and Nicole Hosp blowing out her knee, Canada's world champion downhiller John Kucera broke his leg at Lake

Louise, and the French team lost two racers for the season, downhiller Pierre-Emmanuel Dalcin and slalom ace Jean-Baptiste Grange. That didn't even count the training injuries, which weren't limited to Marcus Sandell's flight into the boulders at Pitztal. Lara Gut of Switzerland and Peter Fill of Italy—both leading Olympic medal prospects for their respective countries—had suffered serious injuries in pre-season training, and in November Resi Stiegler of the United States broke two bones in her left leg in a training crash at Copper Mountain.

Even by the standards of alpine skiing, the carnage was extreme. The trend had caught the attention of reporters, their numbers bolstered by the approaching Olympics. The impact on the home team for Vancouver underlined the problem; Kucera was one of six top Canadian skiers injured before the Games. The injury rates had athletes and coaches venting their worries in the press, putting pressure on the sport's leaders to address the issue. But what could be done? From the outset, it appeared that there were no common themes to the incidents.

The FIS nevertheless announced, late in December, that it would form a blue-ribbon commission to review the spate of injuries, and reexamine the equipment rules once again. The sport's purists groaned; the regulations were already getting expensive and obnoxious, with officials standing in the finish with calipers to measure boot-sole thickness, or running speed suits through a porisometer to make sure they met permeability standards.

Many skiers worried that downhill racing would regulate itself to death, for at the root of its appeal to athletes and fans alike was the concept of pure freedom to seek the fastest way from the top of the mountain to the bottom. And as with baseball, it was an old sport, and any proposed change to a rule or a venue fell under immediate suspicion. A racer tended to push the rules right up to the edge of the tolerance of those enforcing them.

On Wednesday, December 16, two days before the first race at Val Gardena, the FIS convened a summit meeting where senior tour officials would discuss reforms with top athletes. There, the people running the circuit would open themselves up to questions (and, most likely, recriminations) from the athletes. The FIS official guiding the meeting was race director Günter Hujara. Flanking him were two other FIS officials who helped run the men's tour. One was downhill course-setter Helmut Schmalzl, who was chiefly responsible for ensuring that speed venues met FIS standards, and the other was Mike Kertesz, a friendly Canadian who enforced the equipment rules at every race.

The meeting took place behind closed doors, but the participants emerged with tentatively optimistic accounts of the conversation. The athletes suggested greater attention be paid to the shape of jumps, the technology of bindings, and the setting of courses. Making courses more turny by spreading the gates across the hill, some athletes claimed, didn't make them safer but rather made them more fatigued, less able to react quickly to correct a mistake. The flags on downhill gates needed to be loose enough to come off if a racer caught a tip on them. Inspection was too crowded with people, and it was hard to see the race lines. These problems should be easy to fix, the athletes said.

Two days after the meeting, the racers went up for the super G on the Val Gardena race hill, and Svindal won—his first World Cup victory of the season and the thirteenth of his career. He covered the course in 1 minute, 38.35 seconds, edging runner-up Carlo Janka by 0.12 seconds.

Bode Miller was in agony getting his injured ankle into his ski boot, but once it was in there, clamped tight by the hard plastic, the pain was manageable. He finished fifth, 0.69 seconds behind Svindal. As was standard for every World Cup telecast, their speeds through electronic time traps were displayed on the screen so viewers at home could feel a little of the windy thrill from afar.

The Saslong downhill in Val Gardena, where the world's best have been racing since 1969, is named for the giant limestone monolith looming over it, casting a blanket of shade over a 11,306-foot-long track that slices through a forest down to the center of town. It's not uncommon for a racer to leave the ground twenty-five times or more on the relentless two-minute descent, The critical section is the Ciaslat, a farmers' pasture near the bottom of the course that presents a merciless series of small jumps and rolling terrain right when the muscles in the skiers' legs can least afford to be called to work as shock absorbers.

But the course's most notorious features come before that: the Camel Jumps, one of the sport's scariest tests, where racers leap from the crest of one bump to the backside of another, moving at more than 70 miles per hour as they fly over the deep saddle in between the two knolls.

On December 19, 2009, Günter Hujara of the FIS took his usual position on a vantage point off to the side of the Camel Jumps, where he could watch the skiers take flight. In 2003, he had personally marked the spot where Michael Walchhofer of Austria had landed to set the record for the longest flight ever off these jumps: 88 meters, or 289 feet—nearly the distance of a football field.

Hujara, a former coach from Neuenbürg, in the Black Forest region of southwestern Germany, had joined the FIS in 1991 and had been running the men's tour since 1994. In those fifteen years, Hujara had overseen nearly a thousand races, traveling with the World Cup all winter long, presiding over team captains' meetings at night, spending long days on the mountain, and driving or flying to the next stop. He didn't have absolute control over the tour, but he had the upper hand over everyone from coaches to photographers. Committed to an elusive ideal of fairness, he worked hard to show no weakness in an arena where everyone was searching for an advantage.

There had been no need for someone in Hujara's role in the tour's early years. When the tour was founded in 1966, its rules and standards were controlled almost exclusively by the will and whim of its chief founder, sports journalist Serge Lang. For at least the first decade, the former *L'Equipe* writer from Basel decided exactly which resorts begging to play host to World Cup races would have the honor of doing so. A technical delegate from the FIS saw to it that the courses conformed to basic rules, but that was all.

Throughout the late 1970s and 1980s, the FIS extended its control over the tour through its World Cup committee, and from the 1990s onward every race was overseen by a FIS race director. These officials reported to the FIS secretary general and took the lead position on the race jury, the small group that decided such things as when to cancel a race because of bad weather or sanction an athlete for misbehavior.

Hujara served as a perfect foil to Bode Miller during early stretches of Miller's career on the World Cup. Miller's anarchist spirit led him into countless showdowns with Hujara, some of which culminated in fines and reprimands. There was more than simple anti-authoritarianism to Miller's skirmishes with the FIS. Miller hated the stifling equipment regulations and spoke wistfully about his earliest days on the tour, when no one cared what kind of bindings he used or how thick his boot soles were.

"That whole *genre* of guy is a new thing," he would say, referring to the growing number of FIS officials on the tour. But their proliferation had started in the 1990s for a good reason. Of all the different factors that had intensified the FIS's control over the way World Cup downhills were run, few were as important as a pair of tragedies that occurred in the early 1990s, when the deaths of two Austrian racers rocked the World Cup to its foundations, leading to dramatic changes in how the tour was organized.

The first came on January 18, 1991, when a twenty-year-old rookie from Pitztal named Gernot Reinstadler died after a training-run crash near the finish of the Lauberhorn downhill, when his ski caught the netting and didn't detach. Three years later, super G world champion Ulrike Maier perished in the Garmisch-Partenkirchen downhill in Germany. Maier, in top form again after pausing her career to have a child, was tucking at 65 miles per hour when she lost control of her skis and barreled headfirst into an obstacle on the side of the course, breaking her neck.

Each of these episodes prompted searing accusations of negligence against organizers and the FIS, and in fact Maier's case led to litigation. An investigation zeroed in on a piece of timing equipment that was mounted on a wooden stake and surrounded by bags of straw, but eventually a prosecutor from Munich declared that Maier died when she collided with an icy mound of snow on which the timing equipment was mounted. Two top FIS officials were charged with manslaughter, and at their 1996 trial they blamed Maier's skis. The trial abruptly ended when a settlement was reached in which the FIS promised to compensate Maier's family with a fund that was equivalent to $496,000, and the FIS officials were required to make small payments to the mountain patrol service.

In the wake of these incidents, the FIS moved to centralize its control over safety standards at World Cup races. In what amounted to a lasting monument to Reinstadler and Maier, organizers were required to install miles of intricate netting on slopes where for years only picket fencing and hay bales had held spectators back. Some of these were virtual walls of nylon, hanging from cables strung on permanent steel arms. These were the A nets, 20 feet high and more taut than any trampoline. There were B nets too, rollable nylon fencing often placed to knock a skier off his feet before he hit the A nets.

An additional kind of barrier was produced after the December 8, 2001, crash at Val d'Isère where Silvano Beltrametti, a promising and kind-hearted twenty-two-year-old skier from Switzerland, veered off course at 70 miles per hour and sliced through a safety net, his speed seemingly undiminished, tumbling into a pile of rocks and paralyzing himself from the chest down. After that, the lower part of the netting was reinforced with plastic slip screens, making the World Cup downhill courses feel ever more walled off from courseside spectators.

In the years that followed those tragedies, the FIS and organizers have become ever more vigilant about any immovable objects placed in the race arena. Finish line installations are particularly sophisticated in their breakaway properties; occasionally, a crashing racer will slide into the posts holding up the banner above the finish line. Fans soon learn that those posts are nothing but wispy plastic, designed to explode in a scattering of broken signage and bungee cords.

The vigilance extends to the most common obstacle along the

course: people. At any World Cup, those who stay within the arena during the race—coaches, photographers, course workers—are expected to stand in predetermined zones, with their skis off; on the rare occasion that a skier slides into those people, the standing bodies scatter like bowling pins.

Günter Hujara personally controlled the distribution of course access passes at every World Cup downhill, so as he stood on the edge of the Camel Jumps on December 19, he could be reasonably certain that whatever danger the racers put themselves in, they wouldn't collide with anyone. Hujara watched sixty racers come down the Saslong that day and fly over the Camels. The fastest, in the end, was Manny Osborne-Paradis of Canada. Bode Miller, with his injured ankle, finished ninth.

"Each year they take away some of the teeth of these downhills," Bode Miller says, mourning the modernization of the historic World Cup races. It makes a lot of people in the sport uncomfortable, but that doesn't keep Miller from bringing it up often. In the name of increased safety, turns had been added and jumps had been shaved down. When Miller started out on the tour in 1996, he believed, the courses had been true tests of skill and bravery, and the racers had risen to the challenge.

The Saslong downhill was a noted example. First built for the 1970 world championships, it had played host to nearly fifty World Cup downhill races. The start and the finish hadn't moved, but the layout of the course had gradually evolved to contain more turns and fewer straightaways. It had always taken roughly two minutes to descend the Saslong, but modern racers were covering far more distance at a much higher rate of speed.

Technology was the primary accelerant. Well into the 1970s, speed suits had been made of wool, and were far more wind-resistant than the tight synthetic blends that the racers use today. Advances in ski construction conferred more stability, enhanced by plastic and metal shock-absorbing plates mounted between the ski and boot, so athletes could take a tighter line and carve more smoothly. Ski manufacturers had devised machines to grind sophisticated texture into the plastic bases of the skis—tiny grooves arranged in a geometric pattern that dispersed the snow and reduced friction. On top of the standard waxes applied to the bases, technicians could now smear on expensive powders—fluorocarbon additives that dispelled moisture.

Then there was the deliberate hardening of the snow, which assured not only a fairer race but also firmer guarantees for television broadcasters, who wanted races to start on schedule regardless of conditions. The artificial snowmaking systems that World Cup host sites installed in the 1980s had settings that allowed the production of wet slop that froze into ice as dense and hard as concrete. The snowcats used to groom race hills were fitted with tillers that churned the snow to make it even more compact and uniform.

In the 1990s, the age-old practice of spraying slopes with water was updated by the invention of water injection bars. Hoses were fitted to these long metal attachments, sprouting hundreds of tiny nozzles; coaches would grab hold of each end of the bar and move slowly down the slope, pressing the nozzles into the snow and spraying water deep into the surface.

The consequences of the increased speed were reflected in alterations to the classic Lauberhorn course at Wengen. One of its highlights was the Haneggschuss, a long straightaway near the bottom of the course that up until the 1970s had sent racers flying off a jump called the Silberhornsprung and into a treacherous section named the Österreicherloch—the Austrian Hole, in honor of three Austrians who crashed there in 1954.

By the 1980s, racers were coming off the Haneggschuss at close to 90 miles per hour—too fast for them to negotiate the Silberhornsprung and the treacherous terrain that followed. Organizers introduced a new right-footed turn below the Haneggschuss, designed to take racers out of the fall line and reduce their speed. Over the years, the gate marking the apex of this turn had moved out toward the fences until the racers were traveling 700 feet further than before, according to Hujara's estimation.

As a safety measure this was an imperfect solution, chiefly because making the racers turn more promised to exacerbate their fatigue, leaving them less able to absorb terrain and make recoveries. But the main problem was that by 2009 there wasn't much room on the tour's classic downhills to widen the turns without cutting down trees or altering the character of the slope. The next logical step was to reduce the jumps, fill in the compressions, and make the courses smoother.

The Camel Jumps were a prime example. Over the course of Miller's career, he had watched their profile slowly change. The distance between the two high points had shrunk—not by much, but enough so that a racer rarely needed to spring into the air anymore to clear the gap. Fearful of the catastrophic injuries that befell racers who fell short and slammed into a wall of hard snow, organizers had begun using snowcats to reshape the humps, pushing snow onto the back side of the takeoff and the front side of the landing.

Miller was as concerned about the outbreak of catastrophic injuries as any of his peers, but the fear he voiced more often was that the FIS and local organizing committees, in response to the accidents and the looming fear of another on-snow death, were going to rob the world's great downhills of their distinctive features. If Miller was more vocal about these worries than his peers, it may have been because his longevity gave him a view of more evidence. He remembered the debut of Russi's fearsome Birds of Prey downhill. In the decade since, the course had slowly been altered in places in the name of reducing speed. By 2009, it was still a world-class downhill and one of the most difficult on the tour, but it contained much wider turns than it had when Hermann Maier conquered it in his heyday.

Miller wasn't merely glorifying the good old days like so many sportsmen do. The changes were real. But such perspectives are always limited; Miller's first trip to Val Gardena came in 2002, and, according to Franz Klammer, who won there a record four times, Val Gardena had by then long since been defanged.

"I think they destroyed it," Klammer says today. "They widened the whole thing. It's not the same Val Gardena anymore . . . It's not scary."

And so it goes, back through the decades, with every generation of downhiller telling the newest generation that the race courses have been homogenized, that the risks aren't quite as meaningful, and that the *real* downhill is not available anymore. The logical conclusion is that the last downhillers passed by long ago. This theme goes all the way back to Arnold Lunn, the Englishman who organized the first Crans-Montana downhill in 1911. Lunn was a prolific writer who in his later years penned vivid histories of the sport from the hotel his family owned in Mürren, Switzerland. New-school racers, Lunn wrote in 1948, didn't even have to hike over glaciers to earn their descent, as he had done forty years earlier.

"In those days the climb was not regarded as a tedious prelude to a downhill run," Lunn wrote. "The austere spell of the remote and lonely snows meant as much to us as the actual run."

"Ausgeschieden, Aus der Traum" was what they said in Austria— roughly translated as "eliminated, out of the dream," with a pun on "skied out." It was one of the race announcers' catchphrases, uttered to salute the skiers who went off course. It could extend to an aborted season, or even to a whole career.

Bode Miller's dream of returning to the Olympics in Vancouver on pure terms of his own devising had been disrupted by his rolled ankle. After the Val Gardena races, it remained puffy and bruised despite ice and elevation, and it had not helped that one day later he raced a World Cup giant slalom at Alta Badia, one of the world's most difficult giant slalom hills. It was a sentimental favorite of tech racers, and Miller had won it back in 2002. But now, on his damaged ankle and with his GS abilities rusty to begin with, he couldn't even crack the top thirty to make the second run on December 20.

That's when Miller finally stepped back and made a realistic accounting of his Olympic ambitions. If he stopped racing for a few weeks to let the ankle heal, he would miss out on four or five World Cup races. The points weren't important this season, but the races offered opportunities to get back into form, and also to clinch start spots at Vancouver. The coaches had some discretion in choosing which four racers to enter in each Olympic discipline, but Miller wanted to secure his start rights on the objective criteria.

An ankle injury was especially problematic for Miller, who since the early days of his career had enlisted his ankles for precision steering of his carved turns. To that end, Miller made radical modfications to his ski boots, hollowing out spaces on their insides so he could roll inward his medial malleolus (the protrusion of bone at the base of the tibia). Over a decade of hard racing Miller had put so much torque on the ligaments—his official weight in 1998 was 191 pounds and had drifted upward toward 220—that the long-term effects were starting to show.

He did some new calculations. If he kept going and reaggravating the injury, the pain might still be a problem in February. The whole plan was to be ready for peak performance by late January—the downhills at Wengen and Kitzbühel, and then on to the Olympics. If he went home now he could still do some conditioning work, but he'd be cutting it close.

Bode chose the conservative route; he would step back from the World Cup immediately. There was a slalom at Alta Badia on December 21, but he would skip it, along with the tour's next stops at Bormio and Zagreb. He conferred with Sasha Rearick, and they targeted January 9–10 for his return, a weekend with GS and slalom at Adelboden, Switzerland. For the first time in years, Miller would spend Christmas and New Year's Eve in the United States—in California, with Dace, by now almost two years old.

CHAPTER 17

Coming and Going

The World Cup took a short break for the Christmas holiday, but there wasn't enough time for the all-rounders from North America to head home, so Lindsey and Thomas Vonn spent their Christmas where they usually did, as guests of Maria Riesch's family in Garmisch-Partenkirchen, Germany. The men's tech racers left Alta Badia and flew home to the US, while the speed team, minus Bode Miller, settled in at its traditional Christmas home of Bormio, Italy, where training runs for the downhill usually commenced right after the holiday.

The US women's tech team stayed in Austria for Christmas to prepare for GS and slalom races on December 28–29 at Lienz. All of them missed their families, except perhaps for Sarah Schleper, who brought hers with her. A fourteen-year veteran of the team, Schleper was approaching her fourth Olympics with her two-year-old son, Lasse, in tow.

Schleper was the longest-tenured member of the US women's team, and it had been a wild ride for her since her tenth-place slalom finish at the 2006 Winter Olympics. A few weeks after those Games, Schleper tore her left ACL; surgery for that injury, coupled with chronic back pain, persuaded her to take a full year off from skiing to recover. During that year she met a Mexican national named Federico Gaxiola de la Lama, and fell in love with him while they surfed in Baja.

By the spring of 2007, Schleper's knee was healed and she thought she was ready to race again. She went to Mount Hood, Oregon, a volcano with summer snowfields that was a mecca for young ski racers and snowboarders. There she learned she was pregnant, and suddenly the 2007–08 season was scratched too. That October, she and Federico got married. Lasse was born on January 30, 2008.

When the Vail snow melted months later, Schleper was two years removed from competitive skiing but eager to return. Federico was supportive, as was the US Ski Team, so that spring Schleper set out for the team's camp at Mammoth Mountain, with a contingent of friends and family tagging along to help with the childcare.

Allowing her entourage to join a training camp showed a major shift in the US Ski Team's policy, Schleper thought. She couldn't have imagined such flexibility back in the mid-1990s, when she joined the team. By 2009, the organization was far more adaptable, having learned to accommodate the individualized programs of assertive and well-represented stars like Bode Miller and Lindsey Vonn. They were treating Schleper like an adult, even when it was in uncharted territory.

It took a while for Schleper to find her groove in the 2008–09 season. At the world championships in Val d'Isère, she finished thirty-first and twenty-eighth in her events. At the end of the winter her feel for the skis started to return, but her World Cup results weren't strong, and in the spring of 2009 the team brass in Park City informed her that it couldn't justify giving her a fully-funded slot for the Olympic season. She could be part of the team, they said, but she would be responsible for her own airfare, lodging, lift tickets, food, and gas.

This was a common if unpopular arrangement in the Marolt era, and other national ski teams had made similar compromises with their fading or struggling athletes. Schleper decided it was worth it to push for one more Olympics. She figured she would need about $40,000 to finance the season. She and Federico gathered some sponsors and built a website to advertise their campaign. They took donations from all over. Dan Leever, a Denver businessman, contributed $5,000. So did the Vail Valley Foundation, passionate supporters of ski racing. Her father, Buzz Schleper, organized a ski swap fundraiser at Buzz's Boards, his ski shop in Vail.

Schleper's training in the summer and fall of 2009 was unlike that of any of her teammates or peers. While they could all follow a rigorous schedule that revolved entirely around their own needs, Schleper could never really count on rest; Lasse was much loved by his mother's teammates and coaches, but he wasn't always on a clock.

When the season got underway, her goal was simple: to qualify for the Olympic slalom event. The US team's four slalom start positions would be easier to secure than any of the four downhill slots. World Cup performance was the key criterion, and by the Christmas break Lindsey Vonn had secured one entry, but no one else seemed close.

On December 29, in the World Cup women's slalom at Lienz, Austria, Schleper started thirty-seventh and finished the race in fifth. It was an almost certain lock for the Vancouver event; unless three other women on the US team got top-four results in the upcoming slalom races, Schleper had proven herself the second-best slalom skier on the team.

Earning a trip to Vancouver was a thrill, but it was cause for rejoicing for a wider group too. By now, the whole women's tour felt a connection to Lasse. There had been times in the past year when the boy had fallen asleep in the lodge and his mom had nested him under a table, enlisted a teammate as a babysitter and gone out for inspection or her second run. Lasse was learning German to go with his mother's English and his father's Spanish. He was already skiing, and visiting some of the world's most beautiful mountain ranges. And just after his second birthday, he was going to go to a new mountain and watch his mom race in the Olympics alongside his surrogate aunts.

Jeremy Transue's twenty-sixth Christmas wouldn't bring the battered Hunter Mountain downhiller the sentimental career extension that Sarah Schleper was able to enjoy. It turned out that the 2009 Val Gardena downhill, his first time on the Saslong track, was also his last race as a member of the US Ski Team. There was little mercy in the endgame of the score-or-quit ultimatum Sasha Rearick had made in the spring.

Transue finished forty-ninth in the run, four seconds off the pace. When he got to the finish line, he was touched to see that his teammates had stuck around to watch him. All of them, including Bode Miller, came over and said a few words. It meant a lot to him. The previous month had been a nightmare for Transue, but then his entire career was a case study in racing's ability to hack away at an athlete's body until his competitive spirit is finally damaged too.

Transue had been one of America's top ski racing prospects in 2001 when he graduated from the Green Mountain Valley School with an invitation to join the US Ski Team's development squad. That summer he turned eighteen and moved to Park City. Still growing at the time, Transue put on lots of muscle in training. The injuries began soon afterward: first patellar tendinitis, then torn-up tissue in his knees, shoulder, and thumb. His knees took the worst beating, ripping apart and getting stitched back together in a new cycle of pain, operations, and rehabilitation. When one knee surgery resulted in a screw breaking off inside his bone, he went through a twenty-three-month gap without a single race. By the spring of 2009, when Rearick issued his score-or-quit ultimatum, Transue had undergone ten surgeries, but he came into the 2009–10 season healthy in body and mind—right up until his run at the downhill at Lake Louise.

Transue was boarding the lift on his way to the start when he saw T. J. Lanning's horrific crash on a giant video screen installed at the finish line. From the sudden deceleration of his friend's body, Transue knew it was very bad. When the chairlift carried Transue near the spot where Lanning was lying in the snow, Transue could hear the screams through the trees that obscured his view.

Transue started losing it right then. First, he became convinced he was late for the start and would miss his run. He got goosebumps and started shaking. Though he started on time, it was a lousy run: fiftieth place. In the next day's super G he was forty-second. A week later, at Beaver Creek, he finished forty-first in the downhill.

Transue flew to Europe with hopes of turning things around at the Val d'Isère super G on December 12, but a volleyball game with his teammates the afternoon before the race scuttled those plans. Blocking a spike from Erik Fisher, Transue broke the pinkie finger of his right hand. A hospital x-ray showed the middle knuckle to be completely demolished, the myriad ligaments and tendons pulling it out of alignment. He was going to need surgery soon—no later than two weeks. That left only the next day's race, and the Val Gardena races a week later, for him to score points to keep his place on the team.

Back at the hotel that night, Transue got one of his mittens and turned it inside out. He used a pair of scissors to snip away the strip of mesh lining that made separate compartments for his pinkie and ring finger so that he could tape the two fingers together, splinting the broken one to the complete one.

The next day, Transue went up to start fortieth in the super G. Making a fist was excruciating, and Transue didn't think he could grip his pole, so he asked the team's physiotherapist for help at the start. As the thirty-eighth racer went out of the gate, the physiotherapist took Transue's mangled, mittened hand in her own and asked him if he was ready. When he said yes, she crushed his hand around the grip of his pole and quickly wrapped it around with tape. The bone fragments in his finger scraped painfully together, but the pole was secured.

Transue pushed out of the start in terrible conditions. Fourteen of the thirty-nine racers before him had crashed or skied out, pulling to a controlled stop. Sure enough, Transue ran into turbulence and dropped his wounded hand to the snow, jolting it again. He cursed loudly enough for all the coaches on that part of the mountain to hear him. Unable to concentrate because of the throbbing pain, he made it about six gates down the pitch before pulling out of the course.

The next day, he and the team left Val d'Isère for the long drive across northern Italy to Val Gardena. Transue finished thirty-fourth in the super G. The downhill would be his final chance to score points. There was a race at Bormio on December 29, but he needed to get home before that for surgery lest the bone fragments begin fusing.

After the Val Gardena downhill, Transue knew it was all over, and yet he tried to convince himself that "the talk" wasn't going to happen. He went back to the hotel wondering if maybe Rearick would say he'd get one last chance in January. When the knock on the door came, Rearick and the other US Ski Team coaches told Transue it was time to pursue new options. He was flooded with a strange mix of emotions— sadness and anger and the disorientation of a career's end, but also relief at the knowledge that he wouldn't have to get hurt again. It felt, Transue would later say, like a sumo wrestler that had been sitting on his chest had gotten up and walked away.

The difference, Transue could see, had been Lanning's crash at Lake Louise. From then on, Transue had known that his career as a downhiller was pretty much over. T. J.'s crash had shaken him mentally, and soon he discovered that he couldn't attack the hill with the same abandon. The fight was gone. He would never again seek out the fall line on every blind breakover pitch or grab his tuck even before landing the jumps.

The next day, as the rest of the team went to Bormio, coach Chris Brigham drove Transue over the Brenner Pass to the team's apartments in Patsch, just down the road from the mountain where Klammer won gold in 1976. That was December 20. On the 21st, Transue flew from Munich back to the United States, and on the 22nd he flew to Vail to get surgery on his pinkie. On Christmas Eve, Transue took the red-eye home to New York, then traveled up the Hudson River to his parents' house, showered, and went to church. The next day he drove to Burlington, Vermont, where an old friend had a room available for him in an apartment. Transue sat on the couch for a month.

CHAPTER 18

The Hills Are Alive

t is difficult to overstate the cultural importance of alpine skiing in Austria, a country where some television channels consist entirely of live webcam images showing the current conditions at ski areas—continuous live feeds of midmountain scenes, often set to accordion-heavy mountain music.

Ski racers are more popular in Austria than any sports star can hope to be in the United States. Teenage girls moon over ski idols. Former stars of the Austrian ski team go on to host television shows or serve in parliament. In the days leading up to the Hahnenkamm races at Kitzbühel, the national broadcaster, ORF, airs full coverage of the training runs. Even the Austrian team's coaches are famous, their names and reputations known to hausfraus in the farming hinterlands as well as the ski racing cognoscenti of Salzburg and Klagenfurt.

One measurement of the nation's veneration for its national ski team—the Österreichische Skiverband, or ÖSV—is the sheer number of Austrian publications that send a reporter, or reporters, on the road every winter to write about the team. Such intense journalistic competition produces a certain uniformity in stories across Austria's various daily newspapers, but it also gives Austrian readers a deeply penetrating view of the sport.

As each race winds down, the Austrian beat writers pull out their notebooks and pencils, cluster tightly together against the fence of the athletes' corral, and begin a gentle but firm interrogation of the Austrian racers and coaches. In turn, every athlete in the ÖSV uniform is expected to visit the fence and face probing questions about their performance or their equipment, about the course setting or the snow, about the standings, the injuries, and the team dynamics.

Day after day, all winter long, the Austrian people read up on the complex inner workings of the national team, and while the scrutiny is no doubt occasionally uncomfortable for the subjects, it has a healthy effect on the Austrian team itself. If there's a whiff of dysfunction within the ÖSV, the Austrian beat writers will quickly pick it up. Knowing this, the Austrians tend to work out their internal issues far more quickly than any other team, and have thicker skins when it comes to outside criticism. They are skiing's New York Yankees.

The US Ski Team, meanwhile, encounters far less journalistic scrutiny on the tour. The team is used to keeping internal conflicts private, and is known to get more defensive in response to questions about even the mildest of controversies. Both phenomena—the sensitivity of the Americans and the hyperanalytical attentions of the Austrian media—collided in the second week of January 2010, when Lindsey Vonn won three World Cup races in a row at Haus im Ennstal, a place in Austria where skiing equates with worship.

After Christmas in Germany, Lindsey Vonn spent most of the last week of December and the first week of January in Austria, where her wintertime base was an apartment in Kirchberg. There was a cluster of good training hills near there, and the countryside had become home to Vonn, who even had some livestock she kept there.

The last days of 2009 were pretty rough on Vonn. On December 28, a day before Sarah Schleper's exultant fifth-place finish at the Lienz slalom, Lindsey crashed in the giant slalom there, coming down so hard on the ice that for a few hours she was convinced she'd broken her wrist. After an x-ray ruled that out, she raced the slalom despite excruciating pain that radiated up her arm every time she punched a gate out of the way. She finished eighteenth to end the calendar year's last race with 594 World Cup points, a 45-point lead over Maria Riesch after thirteen races of the thirty-two-race season.

After taking a few days off at their base in Austria, Lindsey and Thomas set out on January 2 to drive to Zagreb, Croatia, the site of an annual World Cup night slalom. A snowstorm and holiday traffic turned what was usually a four-hour drive into an eight-hour ordeal. At the race, Vonn finished fourteenth in the first run and then missed a gate on the second, disqualifying herself.

These and other tech events had been a lot of work for small rewards, and Lindsey was ready for a change of fortune when she arrived on January 5 at the Austrian village of Haus im Ennstal. Two downhills and a super G awaited. It was a slope she knew, relatively flat but not unchallenging. When the women's tour last visited in 2004, the course had dealt a serious injury to Kirsten Clark, the US team's best downhiller at that time.

In the first downhill training run, Vonn finished fourth. That day, Austria's largest daily, *Kronen Zeitung*, published an article previewing the upcoming races. Because weight is generally a speed advantage for skiers on flat downhill courses, the story outlined the distinct advantage the World Cup tour's larger women would likely enjoy over their smaller rivals. The newspaper's expectations were low for the Austrian women's team, whose racers were smaller than in previous years. The article affectionately labeled them *Pistenflöhe*, or "ski fleas."

There was nothing particularly unchivalrous about the article's noting that the three women on the podium at Lake Louise a month earlier—Lindsey Vonn, Maria Riesch, and Emily Brydon—were three of the biggest women on the tour. Vonn, officially listed as 5 feet 10 inches and 154 pounds, had eight inches and 22 pounds over Austria's twenty-year-old hopeful Nicole Schmidhofer. The article stated ironically that the Austrian women were fighting a weight problem ("*Gewichtsproblem*"), but nobody called anyone fat.

"Obviously this is a drawback," said the ÖSV's speed coach, Jürgen Kriechbaum, politely calling it a sign of "big class" that Vonn was able to use her size to her advantage.

When the races got underway, the result sheets fulfilled the *Kronen Zeitung*'s prediction; the larger athletes generally clobbered the smaller competitors. The rest of the media jumped on the story, with one outlet quoting retired Austrian downhill star Renate Götschl as saying that women under 65 kilos (143 pounds) had no chance in the downhill, and another speculating that 10 kilos represented a half-second advantage at the finish line. Newton's laws of motion were cited, and race organizers probably wished for a steeper slope.

When an interviewer from an Austrian radio station asked Vonn about the advantage her size afforded her, something apparently got lost in translation. Vonn soon claimed she was offended that people were calling her "heavy." As the reporters circled, Austrian women's coach Herbert Mandl sought Vonn out for a conversation that she interpreted as an apology, but which Mandl insisted was merely clarification.

The whole distorted sideshow soon jumped across the Atlantic, where restless elements in the American media, ready for stories setting up the Vancouver Games, readily latched onto an enticing narrative in which Germanic chauvinists were picking on America's sweetheart. Vonn was savvy enough not to get in their way, and reacted in a way sure to rally people behind her.

On January 11, Vonn, the most dominant athlete in women's skiing, expressed a pluckish woundedness over the Austrians' treatment of her in a "World Cup Diary" she published in the *Denver Post*, recounting the story under the headline "Vonn: Overweight? You've got to be kidding me!"

"I use things like that to push myself harder," Vonn explained in the post, reasserting how physically fit she was. Alongside the piece, the *Denver Post* ran photos of Vonn working out in her sponsor's gear, and posted links to her workouts, again in her sponsor's clothing. It was a publicity home run. For weeks, American commentators previewing the Games would casually lambast the Austrian coaching staff, who, they determined, were clearly threatened and embittered by Vonn's talent. For many Americans, this was their first encounter with Lindsey Vonn, and how could they not start rooting for her to win?

The Austrian beat writers were utterly mystified. A storyline that was initially about the powerlessness of the ÖSV in the era of Vonn had somehow been converted into one in which Vonn was the underdog.

In Austria, Franz Klammer was known as the Kaiser. Austria's passion for ski racing predated him, but Klammer's 1976 Olympic run had produced a new national madness for the sport, inspiring a generation of young boys and girls to put aside every ambition other than ski racing glory. Ski clubs were flooded with youngsters willing to train year-round to compete for ski sponsorships, invitations to summer training camps, and entry into two state-funded ski academies that became hives of competition.

As the Klammer generation came of age in the early 1990s, Austria overtook Switzerland as the World Cup's leading team. By 1999, Austria had three times as many World Cup points as any other team, and twice, in 1998 and 2001, Austrian men won every available World Cup discipline title, as well as the overall. In the 1999–2000 season standings, eight of the top ten men were Austrian. Sometimes it seemed like every race's awards ceremony saw the red-white-red flag flying and heard the Austrian national anthem playing—their beloved Mozart's "Land der Berge, Land am Strome." Austrian racers could win World Cup races and still get sent down to the Europa Cup tour. Others sought citizenship in other countries in order to secure world championship start positions.

On December 21, 1998, Austria's utter domination of the sport reached absurd heights at a World Cup super G race in Patscherkofel, where the top nine finishers were Austrian. All the racers, including the winner Hermann Maier, had been born between 1967 and 1974.

When they reached the finish line of the sacred Olympic slope, the Kaiser was waiting there to congratulate them.

But every great empire carries the seeds of its own destruction, and some time around 2007 the Austrian team started to slip. As the Vancouver Games approached, nobody thought the ÖSV would be able to reprise its magnificent performance at Torino in 2006, where Austrians took fourteen out of thirty Olympic medals in alpine skiing. Since then, the Austrians had been winning fewer races, and while they still ruled the Nations Cup, thanks to their depth, their athletes were winning fewer titles.

There were plenty of theories as to why. The leading notion was that Austria had gotten so strong on the World Cup in the mid-2000s that the national federation lost focus on developing the next generation of racers. This was not in terms of allocation of resources so much as in distribution of race start positions: young Austrians had been locked out of the World Cup by Hermann Maier's cohort, and when that generation began to retire the younger one was insufficiently seasoned.

Meanwhile, the Austrian team's success was such that it had created an international diaspora of Austrian coaches, expats who wound up running teams in Canada, Finland, and Japan. Few organizations were as aggressive in this recruitment as the US Ski Team. Austrians filled out the coaching ranks of the US team, and the Americans lived in Austria. Some people traced the US Ski Team's revival to the team's training partnership with the Austrians, which began in the late 1990s and continued up through 2004. Coaches said it didn't involve learning secrets so much as being around that team, seeing the professional atmosphere, and dismissing some of the ÖSV mystique.

Lindsey Vonn wasn't part of that program, but she had a deep fondness for Austria and had embraced her life in that country. She lived and trained there, her husband had proposed to her there, and she spoke German well enough to appreciate the dialects and go on Austrian TV shows. She even owned cattle there, progeny of a cow she had won as a first-place prize at the Val d'Isère downhill in 2005.

Vonn was an honorary Austrian, it seemed, because as the Vancouver Games approached, something else was happening: supporters of the country's ski team were claiming Austrian credit for her success. Even the president of the Austrian ski federation pointed out that Vonn had Austrian coaches, Austrian servicemen, an Austrian trainer, and Austrian skis.

If Vonn won gold at Vancouver, the Österreichers intended to take a little bit of pride in the result.

Austrian Benjamin Raich led the men's World Cup standings on January 7, the day that Bode Miller returned from the US with his sprained ankle still swollen and achy but his mind firmly set on competing in the giant slalom at Adelboden, a classic Swiss race.

Raich, an old rival of Miller's, had overtaken Carlo Janka in the standings the night before in a slalom at the Croatian capital of Zagreb. Finishing eleventh there had been enough for Raich to pass Janka; he now had 589 points to Janka's 577. But it was the guy in third place, with 481 points, that everyone knew was going to be the most dangerous, as the tour moved onto courses where only the most seasoned veterans were likely to grab points.

Having begun his World Cup career in 1993, thirty-five-year-old Swiss racer Didier Cuche was nothing if not seasoned. The tour's downhill champion in 2007 and 2008 was now in top form for giant slalom too, and came to Adelboden hoping for his twelfth World Cup victory since his first one there in 1998.

When Cuche was growing up in the tiny village of Le Pâquier, nobody expected him or anyone else from the region to be a champion. The great Swiss ski racers typically hailed from the country's famously jagged, snowcapped peaks, but those were hours away. Le Pâquier was northeast of Geneva in a seam of the Jura Mountains, a range of squat, rounded hills best known for its white wine and watchmaking traditions. The highest Jura summits were only 5,000 feet above sea level. Technically they weren't even part of the Alps.

The Cuche family's forebears had arrived centuries earlier in a wave of religious refugees from France. Didier was the youngest of three sons of Françis and Marlise Cuche. In addition to raising livestock, the family owned the Bonne Auberge, a modest restaurant where villagers gathered to eat simply, play cards, and talk about the weather. The small ski area across the street was no one's idea of a destination resort—just a few short chairlifts that the town ran as a cooperative (in mild winters they didn't run the lifts at all). The primary clientele were families from the nearby small city of Neuchâtel. While it might have taken them three or four hours to get to any of the picturesque ski resorts that hosted World Cups, it was only a twenty-minute drive to Cuche's town, where a whole family could have an affordable day's skiing and then stop in at the Bonne Auberge for fondue.

When he was a young child, Didier liked to hike up and ski down the slopes around his house. A neighbor who was a ski instructor noticed his enthusiasm and suggested to Didier's parents that they let him ride the chairlifts. At age three Didier started skiing at the mountain, and sometimes he would spend all day there skiing with friends, from nine in the morning to four in the afternoon. As he got older, he became more useful to his parents and was obliged to return to the restaurant to help with the lunchtime rush. His chores completed, he went back to the slopes in the afternoons.

Didier was thirteen when he watched the broadcast of Switzerland's World Cup star Pirmin Zurbriggen winning the 1988 Olympic men's downhill at the Calgary Games. Didier felt the nation's heart swelling with pride, and thought, *c'est pour moi*. He vowed to become a ski racer.

But someone else thought he should be a butcher, and soon. Swiss butchers typically began their apprenticeships at age fifteen, completing them three or four years later. Stubbornly, Cuche tried to pursue both paths. At the end of a week spent carving up animals, he would put down the knife, jump in a teammate's car, and head for the hills to train or race. After a weekend race he sometimes got home late on Sunday night, and on Monday morning he would be up early and at the butcher's by 6 a.m.

When Didier was sixteen, he qualified for the interregional team—the best skiers from the French-speaking areas of Switzerland. Now he had more funding to travel for skiing, but he had only five weeks off each year from the butcher's apprenticeship. He used all of that time for skiing, attending training camps in Zermatt and Saas-Fee. Using Switzerland's immaculate train system, Cuche made five-hour journeys that involved multiple transfers, dragging with him several ski bags, a duffel bag of clothes, and a box of tuning equipment. His peers would be asleep in their chalets when he disembarked, already exhausted.

"But I wanted to go," Cuche recalled years later. "If you would have said to me then, 'No, you're not allowed to go,' I would have been sad."

A breakthrough in Didier's understanding of the sport came when he qualified to attend a ski camp run by the legendary Bernhard Russi at Laax, a ski resort town in the Graubünden region. The invitees would focus on the elements of downhill racing: how to glide, how to jump, how to turn a ski at speeds above 150 kilometers per hour. It was a Swiss schoolboy's dream.

When Cuche got there, he realized he had some advantages over his peers who had grown up amid the spectacular mountains. For them, steeps made speed cheap. But success in downhill, Russi advised them, meant conserving speed when a steep course spilled onto the flats. For Didier, this was a given. Skiing on a flat little hill like Le Pâquier, the only way for him to ski fast was to preserve every bit of speed he could find; by necessity he had learned how to hold an aerodynamic tuck, to glide lightly on his edges, and to closely read the terrain.

On the last day of the camp, they had a race, and Didier Cuche, the butcher from the Jura, was the fastest. A few years later, he was the best Swiss downhiller at the world junior championships. In 1993, at age nineteen, he raced his first World Cup. He suffered a series of major injuries, but he persevered, adjusting to all the technological changes and outlasting many of his peers.

When Cuche arrived at Adelboden for the January 9 giant slalom, he was coming off a solid week of training. There were a record 32,000 fans on hand to see him and Janka race on the famed Chuenisbärgli course. Cuche had won it back in 2002, when Janka was fifteen (a twelve-year age gap separated the two Swiss racers). Now a fog bank settled around the mountain, delaying the race, and the organizers moved the start lower on the hill.

Cuche went sixth, and the crowd roared when he came onto the steep final pitch carrying so much speed into the tight turns that he had to throw in a tactical skid. It worked, but as he went into the next turn his outside edge caught and down he went. He slid into a course worker, knocking the man over, but both of them were unhurt.

The fog got so thick after that that the race was repeatedly delayed until the jury finally called it off. Of the fifty-eight skiers who took their run, Davide Simoncelli of Italy was the fastest, in 56.08 seconds. Ted Ligety was fifth best, 77 hundredths behind. Bode Miller skied out before the halfway point. Aksel Lund Svindal wasn't even there; he was home with the flu.

CHAPTER 19

Ebersoluble

n Vancouver, the $1.8-billion Winter Olympics were in danger of melting away before they could begin. On January 12, the managers of Cypress Mountain, the ski area slated to host the Olympic snowboarding and freestyle skiing events, closed the slopes to the public because rain and warm temperatures had demolished the snowpack. With the Games only a month away, Cypress was in crisis mode.

For months, the Vancouver Organizing Committee (VANOC) had been using snowmaking equipment to turn millions of gallons of water into a huge stockpile of snow on a mountainside near to Cypress. Two events scheduled for the venue, skicross and snowboardcross, featured athletes racing in groups down a track beset with jumps, banked turns, and other obstacles. Fearing there wouldn't be adequate snow to shape the terrain features, organizers ordered more than 1,000 hay bales. They would be arranged on the mountain in stacks, and snowcats and volunteers would cover them up with the available snow.

While VANOC representatives assured the media of their confidence, long-range forecasts showed no temperature drops, and a drumbeat of news reports sketched out the worst possible scenarios— canceled Olympic events. Vancouver's iffy weather had been a concern for organizers since 2003, when the city outbid Salzburg, Austria, and Pyeongchang, South Korea, for hosting rights. Now the worst predictions seemed to be coming true. Comparisons were being made to the 1964 Innsbruck Games, where the downhills had taken place on a stripe of white snow trucked in from the Brenner Pass, the portal to Italy, about 18 miles away.

Slightly cooler air prevailed to the north at Whistler Mountain, the alpine skiing venue, deeper in the mountains, and taller, with a summit 7,160 feet above sea level (Cypress topped out at 4,724 feet). There was an abundance of snow at the higher elevations on the mountain, a zone of world-class scenery and interesting terrain; the only problem was that the Olympic alpine races weren't taking place there. The downhills started half way up and ended at 2,706 feet elevation, near the bottom of the mountain. Down there, the snow hadn't disappeared but it was soft and slushy, completely inappropriate for racing.

Another issue was Whistler's famously intemperate weather, caused by the Coast Range's proximity to the ocean. In the 1980s and 1990s, when the FIS had staged World Cup races at Whistler occasionally, so many events were canceled because of huge snowstorms, or rain, or fog, that the FIS had renounced the venue in 1998 in favor of Lake Louise.

Nevertheless, given the challenges at Cypress, some members of the media wondered if the solution might not be to relocate some of the snowboarding and freestyle skiing events to the top of Whistler—but this was out of the question. Cypress, like Whistler, had held its IOC-mandated test events in the preceeding winters; the infrastructure was in place and the volunteers trained. VANOC insisted that the Cypress events would not be moved to Whistler under any conditions and set about saving the Cypress course.

For people who loved skiing, the news that the Winter Olympics would be right on the edge of snowless was sad but familiar. Over the years since the 1990s there had been winters with scarce snowfall. So had there been throughout recorded history (1963–64 was famously dry), but there had been nothing quite like the winter of 2006–07, a season of record-setting warmth that crippled much of the ski industry across the Alps and wreaked havoc on the World Cup circuit.

According to the National Oceanic and Atmospheric Administration (NOAA), it was the warmest winter since record-keeping began in 1880. Hundreds of FIS races were called off for lack of snow, and others proceeded in truncated form. Equipment factories eliminated jobs as inventory sat on shelves gathering dust. Snowmaking equipment sat idle, useless without freezing temperatures. Hotels slashed rates on their empty rooms, but people stayed away.

The World Cup tour was drastically altered as races were postponed, rescheduled, shortened, and canceled. For a moment, the strange plight of the world's best downhillers became an international story. Week after week, newspapers ran photos of idle racers in T-shirts sipping espresso on terraces of mountain hotels. There was plenty of time for interviews as the racers sat waiting for the inevitable word that the course was too soft for racing. The high temperatures lingered deep into January that year. When organizers did manage to get races off, patches of mud showed through the surface. Spectators who turned out for the races took picnics on grassy hillsides, listening to birds chirping in the woods and taking in the pungent aroma of thawing cow manure.

The thinness of the snow cover had an immediate effect on the racers' experience too. A deep snow base tends to create a smooth ski trail surface, filling in the declivities on the underlying slope. In 2006–07, the thin snow cover left the mountain's natural topography exposed, further exhausting the racers.

The cancellations were an economic catastrophe for the villages that host the World Cup. Television and newspapers across Europe scared away would-be tourists with images of disappointed fans waiting on muddy hillsides. The snow returned the next season, but the warm winter was a sober warning.

Many ski areas, seeing economic peril ahead, got to work transforming themselves into year-round resorts, building more spas and other non-skiing attractions. They were banking on the expectation that as global temperatures rise, so will the demand for an escape to higher elevations, where temperatures will still be relatively cool. Still, they worry for their future and the future of alpine skiing—not just the industry it sustains, but the deep and distinctive culture it represents.

A startling discovery awaits an American on his or her first trip into the Alps. Switching trains or filling up on diesel in some town at the junction of two rivers, one inevitably looks up to encounter a single mountain facade rising as much as 10,000 feet from the valley floor. A diversity of climates and landscapes is on vertical display: forests, vineyards, pastures, rocky talus slopes, glaciers—stacked one upon another on a steep face. The weather, and even the season, can vary drastically from tier to tier.

The surprise comes when the visitor's eye, raking across a sunlit snowfield or pursuing the source of a waterfall, trips upon a cluster of dark specks three-quarters of the way up the wall. It seems impossible that a human settlement could exist in such a place, but there it is, betrayed by a curl of wood smoke, or a series of fences designed to protect the homes from an avalanche. In Colorado or California, one could safely assume these were trophy homes erected before zoning laws restricted them. But in the Alps such dwellings are more likely to be ancient, their inhabitants perhaps living lives not radically removed from peasant forebears who watched Napoleon's armies trudge through the valleys below.

The Alps are full of such villages, many of them accessible only by foot to this day. They are vestiges of a way of life called vertical transhumance, an agricultural model in which people drive their livestock to higher elevations every spring and summer as snow recedes upward, opening new grazing pastures. Over time the encampments became permanent, and eventually the human population was organized vertically, a series of communities stretching from valley to peak.

In many places, skiing has for centuries linked these towns together.

When skiing the Alps, it is easy to intuit that the trails were well known to the herdsmen pushing animals up and down them for centuries. In a way, the downhill courses were being skied long before the adjacent towns had a chance to reinvent themselves as ski resorts. That is more or less how classic races like Wengen and Val Gardena were born. This heritage also explains why so many ski racers through the decades have been farmers.

In the Alps, a sport built around a stopwatch feels frozen in time. If you're at all the wandering type, you can journey your way into back-eddy corners of Switzerland and Austria where the barnyards and accents bear witness to a way of life at least as old as the crumbling castles in the valleys below. The World Cup often takes people to these districts and celebrates these traditions. When you ask ski racers from the town how long their families have been there, the answer is often "forever."

And yet things are changing in the Alps. Biologists have shown that plants and animals that need cooler temperatures are being pushed up the mountains to higher elevations. This transition may be manageable for certain wildflowers and deer, but is less so for the fish in the streams. A study published in 2006 found that warming Alpine rivers and streams have caused problems for brown trout, which rely on thermal cues for migration and reproduction.

After the winter of 2007, it was clear that ski racers are a vulnerable species too, in their own way. The sport may continue unaffected at high altitude and in places where snowmaking systems can to some degree compensate, but the racers' habitat is shrinking, and in the low, poor foothills where so many future champions have started their careers, fewer and fewer young people will have access to the snow they need to make their way to higher elevations.

In January 2010, one Olympic constituency with an especially acute sense of Vancouver's unseasonable warmth was NBC, America's Olympic network and one of the International Olympic Committee's most important business partners. NBC hadn't paid a fortune for the broadcast rights in Vancouver to get a puddle in return.

After broadcasting every Winter Games since 2002 and every Summer Games since 1988, NBC had its coverage plan down to a lucrative science, taping most of the events instead of airing them live, then airing a heavily-edited version of the footage during prime time, when they could extract the greatest fees from advertisers.

For the whole thing to work, the network needed to vigorously police the Internet for pirated overseas clips. It needed to demolish the natural drama of an alpine ski race in favor of a shorter, sleeker narrative that portrayed each competition as a showdown between as few as five or six racers—the top Americans, the favorite, the actual medal winners, and maybe a few skiers who crashed. But what NBC needed most was snow; to sell ads against Shaun White, the red-haired snowboarding dynamo, the network needed White to have a halfpipe to perform in; and so January 2010 was the month when NBC executives at Rockefeller Center actively monitored the meteorological forecasts for Cypress Mountain.

The Olympics were critical business for the network, almost guaranteeing it a two-week span of prime-time ratings supremacy. It was a huge business; the $2.3 billion that NBC paid for a package of broadcast rights to the 2004, 2006, and 2008 Olympics was, at the time the deal was struck, the biggest broadcast rights contract in the history of television. Naturally, these sums gave the American network an invisible seat at the IOC's decision-making table in Lausanne, Switzerland. Prior to the 2008 Beijing Games, NBC succeeded in getting the finals of the gymnastics and swimming events scheduled for prime time in the United States, which was morning in China.

The Vancouver broadcast rights had been in NBC's grip since 2003, when programming mastermind Dick Ebersol aggressively outbid Fox and others to offer the IOC some $820 million for the 2010 Games (the host city hadn't yet been determined at the time). That sum was part of $2.2 billion NBC paid in a package deal for the rights to the 2010 and the 2012 Olympics together.

Now NBC had to convert. America's long recession had suppressed ad sales enough that the question wasn't whether the Olympic broadcast rights were worth their price tag, but rather how many tens of millions the network would lose. The thought of NBC's Olympic team—hundreds of accredited big shots and worker bees—arriving in Vancouver outfitted in nifty parkas only to discover that light sweaters were sufficient was not a welcome one.

But there was nobody Dick Ebersol could call about the weather.

CHAPTER 20

Varieties of Religious Experience

"Best in the World" would mean nothing if the US Ski Team's racers didn't make a strong showing at the most prestigious events on the World Cup calendar, a cluster of races that came every year in the second half of January. On the men's side it was mainly two back-to-back weeks of racing at a pair of fabled venues: the Lauberhorn at Wengen, Switzerland, and the Hahnenkamm at Kitzbühel, Austria. Between them, the two races captured most of the superlatives of alpine racing.

The Lauberhorn downhill is the oldest and longest ski race on the World Cup tour, starting on the shoulders of some of Europe's most fearsome peaks—the Eiger, the Mönch, and the 13,642-foot-high Jungfrau—and winding its way for 2.75 miles down to Wengen, a tiny Swiss village that has played host to the races every year since 1930. The whole poetic scene lies in view of Mürren, where the basic format of slalom racing was invented by Sir Arnold Lunn (some said precision skiing was an outgrowth of mountaineering, a way of calculating the prowess of those who could safely descend through the glacier fields after a climb).

The Hahnenkamm races feature the world's scariest downhill,

what World Cup founder Serge Lang called "the sport's greatest measure of excellence." The Streif is so difficult that cutting it in half would still yield two of the world's most dangerous courses. If you win there, you are a bona fide member of ski racing royalty. The Hahnenkamm races, which go back to 1931, also see the biggest crowds, with as many as 100,000 fans converging on the small medieval village over the course of the weekend. Inebriation is common.

Though they'd each begun holding their downhill races around the same time, only Wengen had kept their race going through World War Two; Kitzbühel had no races and was a scene of final surrender for the Nazis. Ian Fleming set Bond stories in each area.

Although the women's tour doesn't have anything to match the long history or adrenal rush of those two downhills, in late January Lindsey Vonn and her colleagues get to race on the world's most beautiful course—the Olympia delle Tofane track at Cortina d'Ampezzo, Italy, the site of the 1956 Winter Games. The magnificent downhill there, weaving between limestone towers and down into a forest, has been a mainstay of the women's tour since 1993.

These three fabled venues typically host a three-day weekend of races, with the Saturday downhill the biggest draw. Success on the downhill tracks had mostly eluded the US Ski Team through the years, but that changed during the ski team's twenty-first-century revival. At Wengen, no American man had won the Lauberhorn downhill until Bill Johnson's wild ride in 1984, and victory eluded the US Ski Team again until Kyle Rasmussen's triumph in 1995. Then Daron Rahlves won the 2006 edition, and Bode Miller followed in 2007 and 2008. Picabo Street won the Cortina downhill in 1995 and 1996, but that was an anomaly until, around 2004, the American women cracked the Tofane track's code. Between that year and 2009, Vonn and Mancuso combined for ten speed-event podiums there, with Mancuso winning the 2007 super G and Vonn the 2008 downhill.

The Kitzbühel downhill resisted the US team. After Buddy Werner won the eighteenth running of the race in 1959, no American man conquered the Streif again until 2003, when Daron Rahlves made his winning run on a shortened course. Though Rahlves won a super G the next year, and Miller the combined in 2004 and 2008, the downhill remained an elusive prize for the US team. The slalom did too.

In 2010, less than a month before the Vancouver Games, athletes in other Olympic sports were tapering their conditioning regimens and taking care not to injure themselves. But not the alpine skiers. Miller and Vonn and their peers on the World Cup were going to run a gauntlet first. Odds were heavy someone would get hurt.

Perched on a sloped shelf high above a glacier-carved valley, Wengen is a car-free village. The World Cup skiers who began arriving there on January 11, 2010, traveled the same way their fans would a few days later—via the old-fashioned train that climbs up out of the Lauterbrunnen Valley, stops in Wengen, and continues over the pass at Kleine Scheidegg and down to the town of Grindelwald.

The train had transformed the region from a poor farming community to one of Switzerland's biggest tourist destinations. In two decades at the start of the twentieth century, nearly thirty hotels were built in Wengen. They were solid old beauties, charmingly worn at the edges now but retaining their Edwardian charm.

The racers who loaded their skis onto the train for the 2010 edition of the race were arriving from several directions. The pure downhillers had been resting, training, and testing equipment since the last World Cup speed race, the December 29 downhill at Bormio, which had been won by Andrej Jerman of Slovenia. The all-rounders in the group were coming from Adelboden, where Julien Lizeroux of France won the slalom.

Bode Miller had been coming to Wengen since 1999 and, like everyone, he cherished the unique atmosphere, happily leaving his motor home in Lauterbrunnen. As he and the other racers spilled off the train, they were met by emissaries from the family-owned chalets and grand old hotels that would play host to them for the next week. The Beausite Park was the US team's hotel in Wengen. (It had always been so. Even in the 1950s, before Bob Beattie had formed the modern US team, and the American skiers at Wengen were often part of a US Army team based at Garmisch.) On their way there, the racers passed a plaque in the middle of town bearing the names of the winners—*Die Sieger*—of every race held on the Lauberhorn slope. Wengeners are particularly proud that they didn't suspend their race even for World War Two, when several of the competitors were war refugees.

Wengen is long on tradition. Every year for as long as anyone can remember, the start order is settled the night before the race in an upstairs classroom at the town's small schoolhouse. Local children then fan out in pairs to deliver printouts of the start order to the hotels. The whole town mobilizes itself for the race, which is really an elaborate infomercial, compelling untold numbers of vacationers to book visits to the area. Locals take roles in the organizing committee, knowing that a few days of shoveling snow and punching tickets will drum up a year's worth of financing for their schoolhouse and chairlifts. Their efforts are bolstered by manpower from the Swiss army and the canton of Bern's civil guard—about 250 men ready to build tents, move equipment, and spend cold nights on the slope removing any new snow from the track.

The 2010 races would take place on Friday, Saturday, and Sunday—a combined, the downhill, and a slalom. But first came the training runs for the downhill. The home crowd's favorite, Didier Cuche, won the first training run. Bad weather canceled the second run, and Andrej Jerman won the third.

The Lauberhorn has all the elements of a definitive downhill—big jumps, high speed, varied terrain, straight gliding sections, confounding undulations, and sudden sharp turns that require tactical moves at high speed. Its middle third is especially quirky, with strange obstacles and narrow passageways; racing it is not unlike speeding down a highway, exiting into the heart of a city and weaving wildly through the streets, then getting back on the highway again and driving even faster.

The slalom hill is a classic also, tripping down a series of steep tiers toward a finish area that the slalom shares with the downhill. Along the way, the course weaves among some ancient barns, their haylofts full and their dark wooden walls wrapped in padding in case a racer hits them.

Over the three-day weekend, more than 50,000 fans might attend the races, but a relatively small number of them congregate at the finish; while many people go to the Kitzbühel races to drink, the fans flocking to the Lauberhorn are there to hike, and during the downhill they climb from the train station and spread out on the mountain until they line most of the course.

On Friday, January 15, the combined event got underway. To give the slalom skiers a chance at the podium, the downhill portion of the combined was a shorter version of the Lauberhorn downhill. Miller won the downhill portion, and his time was respectable enough in the afternoon's slalom that he finished in first, edging out Switzerland's Carlo Janka and Silvan Zurbriggen for the win.

By tradition, the racers who finished on the podium were treated to a helicopter ride to the press conference in town. Miller seemed in good spirits when he walked into the room and sat in the same place where he'd been obliged to deliver his apology for the *60 Minutes* fiasco four years earlier. It was his first World Cup win in nearly two years, and it certified him as a legitimate threat for the Olympics.

"It's an easy hill to be excited about racing," Miller said, noting "all the great racers that have won here" and describing how the logistics of just getting around on such a big mountain—from inspection back up to the top—are a challenge.

The next day, Miller was within reach of a third career Lauberhorn downhill victory when he crashed in the course's final 10 seconds, going down on his hip and finding himself unable to summon the strength to stand up again. The victory went to Switzerland's Carlo Janka; and the best American finisher was Andrew Weibrecht in thirteenth. The result all but guaranteed Weibrecht a spot in the downhill at the Olympics. Twelfth at Lake Louise and eleventh at Beaver Creek, he was clearly the second-best downhiller on the team behind Miller, with only Kitzbühel remaining before the Vancouver picks were made.

Because the steepest and tallest spines of the Alps have so often served as the natural boundaries for nations and armies, the World Cup tour, which frequents those snowcapped frontiers, is often staged in towns of rare culture and dialect—dead-end valleys where they speak a fading language, or mountain regions that have been repeatedly annexed and reclaimed by now-defunct empires and carry a distinctive blend of identity and allegiance. Cortina d'Ampezzo, nominally Italian, is one such locale.

Years after Picabo Street's retirement, while she was living in Alabama and raising four boys, she would dream about Cortina d'Ampezzo.

"I can't tell you how many times I've woken up in the middle of the night and I'm rocking Cortina in my dreams," Street said. "It's got the turns, the straightaways, the jumps, the drops, the speed, the gliding, the flat light, the blind turns, it throws everything at you. I'm jealous. I am green with envy at the end of January every year when I know they're ripping Cortina."

Set amid the jagged peaks of the Dolomites in northern Italy, Cortina rivals the Lauberhorn for sheer beauty and stands tallest among the women's downhills as the most esteemed athletic challenge. No one gets lucky with fast skis or a good start position there; Cortina victories invariably go to great downhill champions like Renate Götschl, Katja Seizinger, and Street.

No course flows so naturally over terrain, funneling the racers over gentle knolls that can sometimes glow with the pink sunlight reflecting off the looming monoliths of the Tofane mountain group. The single best place from which to witness the race is the deck of a venerable midmountain restaurant, the Rifugio Duca d'Aosta, a few chairlift rides up the mountain and nearly 7,000 feet above sea level.

There, just before a race, you can find Lindsey Vonn, most likely sitting alone in a corner of the cozy little building, away from the distracting babel that ensues as representatives of every World Cup team crowd up to a small bar, order cappuccinos, and drink them while their walkie-talkies squawk with multilingual updates from various points on the race course.

When Vonn stands and heads out for the final chairlift ride to the start, as focused as a brain surgeon, you have about twenty minutes to get your second cappuccino, take it out to Rifugio's ample deck, and gaze out at one of the most splendid panoramas in all of Europe. And then perhaps you hear a shout, and you turn and look up and see Vonn appear in the notch beween two giant limestone towers before she drops into the Tofane Schuss. Already moving at high speed, she folds her body in upon itself like some oversized, candy-colored peregrine falcon.

The top of the Tofane Schuss is cast in a deep blue shade even on sunny mornings, but midway down the face of it she bursts into sunlight and starts bending her skis and guiding herself into the turns, the schuss giving way to a relatively flat runout as she passes the Rifugio. Next comes the ripping sound she makes as she splits the thin mountain air, her skis tracking parabolas in the snow at 70 miles per hour and depositing her within inches of where she wants to be. She zooms past the deck and over a jump, and the last thing you see as she drops out of sight is her ponytail sticking out behind her helmet, maybe wrapped several times in ribbons the way Picabo used to do hers.

If you saw Vonn on January 23, 2010, you would have seen her winning with her perfect technique, exceptional strength, finely calibrated equipment, and boundless confidence. She looked far more relaxed than any of her peers, even as she took a line few of them dared attempt. She wasn't flawless—she lost her composure in the air on two of the jumps, and dragged her hand once in an angulated turn—but she didn't overreact. She held her tuck all the way to the end, where she thrust one arm out to trip the beam of light that registered her finish.

Vonn's time of 1 minute, 37.70 seconds was 0.42 seconds faster than the runner-up, her friend Maria Riesch. In third was Anja Pärson of Sweden, 0.86 seconds back. The two of them could only watch and smile as Vonn pumped her fist and raised her skis—a pair of men's skis that she and Heinz Hämmerle called the 117s and were considering setting aside for the Olympics.

With Cortina, Vonn had now won all five of the winter's World Cup downhills plus the final one of the previous season. Six downhill wins in a row tied Picabo's American record, and left no doubt that Vonn was the best female downhiller on the planet twenty-five days ahead of the Olympic women's downhill.

To see the Hahnenkamm up close is to forever forgive downhillers for the cockiness they occasionally display; racing down such a course requires a mind adept at tricking itself into confidence, and sometimes overcompensation is inevitable. The first time 1994 Olympic downhill gold medalist Tommy Moe came to Kitzbühel, he wasn't totally sure it was raceable.

"I was like, oh my god, this is really—we're *racing* this thing?" he recalls. But after a few seasons, he grasped the mentality it required. "It's such a great course when you get in the rhythm of it, where you really hit the gas and you're looking for speed, rather than being on the defensive and waiting for things to happen. But it takes a while to get to that point."

The start alone is psychological torture. Racers wait there in full view of the first jump, a monstrous dropoff called the Mausfalle (Mousetrap) that arrives at their feet after eight seconds of steep acceleration. Upon landing, they are going 80 miles per hour, only 10 seconds into their race. At that speed, racers are moving close to 117 feet per second while making decisions about their critical next moves.

A bowl-like compression is followed closely by a sudden blind turn to the right and then a plunge into the Steilhang (Steep Slope), a vertiginous pitch that rolls away from the racer at a deceptive angle. It was said that Buddy Werner pioneered the brave, direct line at the entrance that set the standard for the higher speeds of the 1960s, but the Steilhang exit was the real crucible. Four-time Kitzbühel winner Franz

Klammer calls it the most difficult turn in all of ski racing, mainly because of the convexity that makes it impossible for the racer to see the upcoming terrain until it is underfoot. In 1989, Canadian racer Brian Stemmle nearly died after crashing into the safety netting at its exit. Litigation followed. A bigger, smoother wall of fencing was later put in, and at the 2008 downhill Bode Miller had skied right up onto it, sliding at 60 miles per hour over the hard plastic barrier before dropping back onto the snow in his tuck (he finished second).

After the Steilhang, the course spills onto a narrow road through the forest—the Brückenschuss—where close to 20 seconds of tucking connects them to the Alte Schneise (Old Scar). From there, the course opens up into a relatively straightforward series of pitches and flats that include the Seidlalmsprung and the Lärchenschuss. But that is all prelude to the final 20 seconds of the course—a graveyard of careers and the scene of downhill racing's ultimate initiation rite.

The final 2,000 feet of the Hahnenkamm begins with racers soaring off the Hausberg jump, where they first come into view of the huge crowds at the finish. Upon landing, the skiers build speed through a long, undulating right-footed turn and then drop off a ledge onto one of the world's most unforgiving tests of balance and courage—a long sideways traverse across a frozen pasture that is part of the farm of Familie Peter and Inge Feyersinger.

Racers crest 80 miles per hour on the traverse, but this is no surrender to gravity. The central drama of the Streif's final pitch consists in the racers' desperate fight against the fall line, which drops straight down to their right toward a menacing barrier of reinforced safety nets. The racers must brace against gravity's pull and travel on an angle to their left, maintaining enough elevation to reach the final turning gate above the finish line, the Zielschusskante. Undermining their efforts are icy corrugations of the surface that constantly jostle them into the air and the thigh-burning fatigue of the previous 90 seconds of racing.

Every year racers fail the test, losing their footing and dropping down the slope into the netting. Two great names in the sport—Patrick Ortlieb, Todd Brooker—crashed so hard there that they never returned to ski racing. But the vast majority of the competitors somehow manage to squeeze around that final gate, usually by only a few feet or even inches. Only then they can point their skis straight down the Zielschuss, the direct plunge to the finish line. They crouch low for aerodynamic efficiency, speed close to 90 miles per hour off a final jump and into that ecstatic congregation. The racers who make it down say there is no better feeling.

On January 21, 2010, Bode Miller completed the final training run at Kitzbühel with the fastest time of the day: 1 minute, 52.21 seconds. It was only a training run, but it was a tantalizing result. He'd been first in other prestigious downhills—Wengen, Beaver Creek, and Bormio— and he'd won the Kitzbühel combined twice (in 2004 and 2008) and had even finished second in the downhill in 2008, but in seven tries stretching back to 2001, he'd never gotten to the top step of the podium at the Super Bowl of downhills.

Because Daron Rahlves never won an Olympic medal, he lacked the name recognition Picabo Street and Tommy Moe enjoyed, but by the time Rahlves retired in 2006 he was arguably the greatest American downhiller of all time. A clean-cut Californian, small for a downhiller but tremendously surefooted, Rahlves performed best when conditions were ugly. Over six seasons he won twelve World Cup races, nine of them downhills, including the feared and respected ones at Bormio, Wengen, and Beaver Creek.

The Austrian ski team would never forget the day that Rahlves won the 2001 world championship super G, outskiing Hermann Maier in the legendary racer's best event at the peak of Maier's powers. But within the US Ski Team, Rahlves's landmark performance was his 2003 Kitzbühel downhill win, the first American victory on the Streif in forty-four years. Some people unfairly attached an asterisk to this result (bad weather forced a lowered start, so it wasn't the full Hahnenkamm—"a *mickeymaus* downhill," Maier called it). This was especially cruel given that Rahlves usually aced the steep and scary upper sections, and was at a disadvantage starting on the relatively flat Alte Schneise. His mastery of ski racing's most important venue was evident in his seven career podiums at Kitzbühel.

Rahlves was the US speed team's golden boy when Bode Miller began to venture in earnest beyond the tech events and started raiding the World Cup's downhill and super G podiums. When they joined forces in 2004, pooling the equipment and service support they got from Atomic, the combination was the most formidable duo the US Ski Team had seen in the twenty-nine years since Phil and Steve Mahre were at their best. Miller and Rahlves on the top of the podium together became a regular sight. On the days when Lindsey Vonn won her race too, the team had no trouble convincing sponsors to keep the momentum going; "Best in the World" seemed like a self-fulfilling prophesy.

Rahlves and Miller used their clout to demand more personalized support on the tour. They pointed out that the top racers from other countries never wasted energy slogging heavy bags in and out of hotels, but often had a muscle guy on staff who took care of that kind of thing. That was how Baby Huey became a member of the US men's speed team—Pete Lavin, a memorable fixture on the men's World Cup tour from 2003 onward. He drove, he oversaw workouts, he did some crowd control at the Londoner pub during Kitzbühel's famed post-downhill blowout party. Mainly he was the start coach; TV viewers saw and heard the mustachioed giant in the start house, bellowing encouragement to the American downhillers in the last minute before they set out on their perilous descents.

Six-foot-four and 275 pounds, Baby Huey was a landscape contractor from California who lifted weights with Rahlves in the summers. Taking the team doctor's spot at the start house of the Kitzbühel downhill in 2003, Huey fired Rahlves up so much with his shouts that the team hired him. He spent the winter months driving the skiers from one end of Europe to the other, loading a few thousand pounds of gear into a cargo van at one hotel and unloading it at the next. He was so effective at his main job, motivating and focusing the racers before they went out of the start house, that in time other teams began employing their own "hype man" at the start. But none had the presence of Baby Huey.

There he was again on the day of the 2010 Kitzbühel downhill, January 23, shouting Miller out of the start—"C'MON BODE! C'MON!"—clapping his enormous gloved hands together as Miller scrambled out onto the Streif wearing bib fifteen. The juxtaposition of Huey's amped-up imprecations and Miller's pre-race mellowness was jarring, but it worked; Miller was going 40 miles per hour within three seconds, dropping into his tuck and chasing his first victory on the Streif course.

At first he looked on track for it, nailing his lines through the Mausefalle and Steilhang. His feet appeared magnetized to the snow as he moderated perfectly the pressure he applied to his arcing skis. Gone was the wild-child flamboyance of his early downhill career; this was Miller the downhill ace, piercing the cold air with his indy-car tuck, low and shock-absorbent, flying off the Seidlalmsprung hugging his thighs to his chest, a face-first cannonball.

Miller remained the fastest through the first 46 seconds of the course, and lost only a little speed in the middle gliding sections, not an insurmountable problem with an inspired run on the final section. A huge cheer greeted Miller at the Hausberg, but as he landed and turned onto the famed traverse he was forced to put all of his weight on his sore right ankle. The pain was shocking, an electrical bolt that sizzled right through his determination and forced him to step gingerly where he needed to be stomping hard.

Miller held a good line, but it wasn't enough. When it was over, the victor was Didier Cuche, who started twentieth, came down the slope with his arms out to his sides like a tightrope walker, and won the race in 1 minute, 53.74 seconds. Miller finished ninth, 1.16 seconds behind.

CHAPTER 21

The Final Schuss

On Tuesday, January 26, after a final consultation with USSA's top alpine ski coaches and lawyer, Bill Marolt issued a press release announcing the US Ski Team's nominations for the 2010 Olympics—the twenty-two skiers who would represent the United States of America in the alpine events at the Vancouver Games.

There were ten women and twelve men: Stacey Cook, Hailey Duke, Julia Mancuso, Chelsea Marshall, Megan McJames, Alice McKennis, Kaylin Richardson, Sarah Schleper, Leanne Smith, Lindsey Vonn, Will Brandenburg, Jimmy Cochran, Erik Fisher, Tommy Ford, Tim Jitloff, Nolan Kasper, Ted Ligety, Bode Miller, Steven Nyman, Marco Sullivan, Andrew Weibrecht, and Jake Zamansky.

The selection process, based on a delicate combination of World Cup results and coaches' discretion, was not without heartbreak; veteran racers who had arguably skied as well as some of those named would be left at home—notably Keely Kelleher and Scott Macartney. And although thirteen of the nominees had never been to the Olympics, their celebrations were muted by an awareness that some of them, inevitably, wouldn't race. Only four Americans could start in each medal event, and although in some cases World Cup performances made the right to start unambiguous, in other events it would be up to the coaches to decide.

It was the strongest Olympic ski team the US had ever fielded, with the possible exception of 2006, and the 2010 squad had a distinct edge on the Torino team in that Vancouver was in the US team's backyard. The American skiers knew and loved Whistler. As kids, many had attended summer training camps there on the Horstman Glacier. It would be like racing at home, but without the pressure of being the host nation.

The World Cup's Olympic intermission was not yet at hand. After Kitzbühel, the men's tour went to Schladming, Austria, for a night slalom on January 26, and then to Kranjska Gora, Slovenia, for two GS races and a slalom on January 29–31. While the men were racing there, the women would have their own final pre-Olympic cluster of three World Cup races—super combined, downhill, and super G—at St. Moritz, Switzerland.

Lindsey Vonn was in Salzburg the day the Olympic team selections were announced. There she worked out with her Red Bull trainers at the soccer stadium near the airport before she and Thomas took one of the company's private jets to St. Moritz. They touched down near the posh Swiss resort less than an hour after takeoff and were settled into their hotel in time to watch the men's race at Schladming on television.

The Schladming night slalom drew nearly 50,000 fans—a *Glühwein*-swilling crowd that lined the spectacular race hill and lit road flares as their favorite skiers came down a steep pitch so icy it glistened under the blazing floodlights. With his mistakes, Miller finished DFL (dead fucking last), but was able to tinker with his slalom set-up between his runs and liked the way it felt. Instead of following the tour to Kranjska Gora, he opted for San Diego.

Miller would have a full week at home before joining his teammates in Park City for a final pre-Olympic training camp. From there, the first wave of them would depart for Vancouver on February 8. The plan for the US women's speed team was to train in Zell am See, Austria, after the St. Moritz races and get to Vancouver on February 9.

What they would all find in Canada, in terms of actual conditions, was a matter of hot debate. Officials from the FIS were already on the soggy ground in Vancouver, inspecting the competition sites. At Cypress Mountain, VANOC had deployed helicopters, dump trucks, and snowcats to save the snowboarding and freestyle skiing venues. More than 1,000 hay bales had been covered with 300 truckloads of snow.

Meanwhile, up at Whistler, a series of late January storms had deposited huge amounts of snow on the upper elevations. This was unwelcome for the alpine venue, which needed to have a solid, icy surface in place before the first training runs on February 9. Snowcats would either have to plow the fresh snow off the track or churn it into a suitably dense mixture that could solidify overnight, assuming the temperatures got below freezing.

In response to numerous news reports about the weather, IOC president Jacques Rogge held a conference call to assure reporters that the Olympic venues were "absolutely impeccable and ready for competition." Meanwhile, the organization Environment Canada told the *Salt Lake Tribune* that Vancouver had seen an average daily temperature of 44.8 degrees in January—the warmest January since record-keeping began in 1937.

On January 31, Lindsey Vonn won the St. Moritz super G, the last World Cup race before the Games. It was her ninth victory in the season's twenty-six races.

Just the day before, her downhill streak had come to an end when she hit a rut awkwardly, almost took out a gate and wound up 1.21 seconds off Maria Riesch's winning time. On any other day Vonn would have been disappointed, but she actually felt relief; had she won her seventh consecutive downhill, the Olympic expectations would have ratcheted even higher. Fans needed to know she was mortal.

Vonn herself needed no reminder. On the 29th, she had finished third in the St. Moritz combined behind Anja Pärson, the two-time overall World Cup winner whose forty-one race wins put her fourth on the tour's all-time victory list for women. Like Miller, the twenty-eight-year-old Swede had built her winter program around a late-January surge.

Another racer showing steady upward progress was Julia Mancuso. At the Cortina downhill she had finished eighth, and in the speed portion of the St. Moritz combined, a super G, she'd finished third. No one knew better than Vonn how much Mancuso was able to turn up the intensity for big events.

Vonn left St. Moritz feeling great. Her plan was to go to Zell am See with the rest of the speed team and train for a few days, if more snow didn't interfere. Either way, she planned to return to Park City on February 4. She would stay off skis, do a little weightlifting, and otherwise lie low in seclusion—no TV, and as few interviews as possible—before heading up to Vancouver on February 9.

Julia Mancuso went home to Squaw Valley, where the mountain managers closed a run for her to stage a private training camp. With her coach and technician on hand, she trained full-length courses down the middle of the mountain, looping around for each run on a snowmobile. She enjoyed home-cooked meals with her family and went freeskiing in the off-piste wilderness that had been the foundation of her groundbreaking career.

Every other national team had its own plan for the week before the Olympics—ceremonial sendoffs at royal palaces, training camps at locations not disclosed to the media. The Austrian team went to North America. While their men's team gathered in Sun Peaks, a British Columbia ski resort where they had a training base, the Austrian women took a three-day vacation in Fort Lauderdale—a trip that happened to coincide with the festive lead-up to Super Bowl XLIV in nearby Miami Gardens. Knowing nothing about the sport, the Austrian women resolved to watch "the football finals" in the lobby bar at their hotel, the Sheraton. The Indianapolis Colts were the oddsmakers' favorite, but Andrea Fischbacher took one look at the uniform of the New Orleans Saints and instantly knew which team Olympic medal hopefuls should be rooting for. *"Die goldenen Hosen gewinnen,"* Fischbacher told her teammates—"the gold pants will win"—and they did, 31 to 17.

Ted Ligety landed at Salt Lake City's international airport on February 1, three days after winning the World Cup giant slalom at Kranjska Gora, Slovenia, one of his favorite slopes. The victory, the fifth of his career on the tour, came 309 days after his knee injury at Alyeska and twenty-four days before the Olympic men's giant slalom was to be run.

In the same Kranjska Gora race, two other significant things happened. Marcus Sandell of Finland, who had recovered from the Pitztal crash that cost him a kidney, had forerun the event—skiing the course minutes before the official start. His time was good enough to convince his nation's Olympic authorities to send him to Vancouver. And Didier Cuche of Switzerland had crashed hard on the second-to-last gate, breaking his right thumb. He underwent surgery and announced plans to compete in the Games with a brace on his hand.

Ligety was in the mix for a medal at Vancouver, but after a long European tour he needed just a little time back at home. He was restored just to see the Wasatch Range as his plane came in. Utahans took pride in the convenience of their airport and its proximity to the best of ski country; Ligety could be home in Park City in less than forty minutes.

Instead of going straight there, he stopped at In-and-Out Burger in Salt Lake. Only after he got a cheeseburger did Ligety drive up Parley's Canyon to his house, where he got a night of sleep, then went up to join his teammates on the hill where he'd grown up racing: the Eagle Race Arena.

Sasha Rearick had chosen Park City for the men's team pre-Olympic camp mainly because it was home to the race arena, site of the alpine giant slalom for the 2002 Winter Games. A set of steep trails accessed by a high-speed chairlift, its main slope features sharp breakovers dropping onto steep pitches that spill onto relatively flat sections, then down to another tier. It opened years before the 2002 Games, and by the time Ligety was ten teams from all over the region came to race on the icy man-made snow there. A run with such a profile demanded smart tactics and solid form. Acclaimed coaches like Jesse Hunt and Olle Larsson coached their teams there.

Rearick thought the camp was already a big success, both as training and as a team-building session, especially considering that he had salvaged it in five days. Arriving on the 27th from Munich, he'd found the slopes in substandard condition. Deep ruts that local teams had left in the surface were overlaid by a few inches of fresh snow. Rearick made a distress call to the world's foremost race slope preparation expert, Tom Johnston of Pinedale, Wyoming. "Cowboy," a former coach whom the FIS sent all over the world for this kind of thing, drove down to Park City. During two full days of exhausting work and physical discomfort he, Rearick, and a group of other coaches and volunteers used snowcats to plow the surface into three-foot-high furrows, sprayed the trenches full of water and smoothed it all out again.

The reengineered hill had set up nicely by the time the athletes arrived, moving into slopeside condos where they cooked their own meals. They trained super G and giant slalom, with a few slalom sessions for the guys who needed it. To simulate race conditions, they put on racing bibs and took only a short number of high-intensity timed runs.

Ligety showed up on the first day of timed super G and smoked everybody, even beating Miller by almost two seconds. Rearick was pleased with the trash talk that followed, seeing it as a sign of team spirit. Miller decided to run the course on his downhill skis—which were longer, and meant for bigger turns. He liked what he felt, and told Rearick he might do that in the super G at Whistler.

Curious locals came to watch, including Jesse Hunt, the US team's former alpine director, now program director of the local ski team. Hunt brought along some of the kids he coached and stood with them on the side of the course, helping interpret what they saw their idols doing. This closed a circle; Hunt had been Milller's coach back at the 2002 Games, when he won a GS silver medal on the Park City slope, and

Ligety had been a junior racer on a volunteer crew tasked with side-slipping the race line between racers. Eight years later, Hunt was dispatching the next generation to do the same thing on the course for Ligety and Miller.

———

One of the most dreaded ailments in skiing, for recreational skiers as well as for racers, is shinbang, a deep, painful, often invisible bruise that develops midway up a skier's lower leg, where the padded cuff of the ski boot ends—a fulcrum point in which a skier's leg, or the attached ski, is the lever.

Shinbang can be debilitating. It prevents a racer from leaning forward and applying pressure to the front end of the ski, making it grip the snow and start to carve. Lindsey Vonn had suffered a bad case of it at the 2002 world junior championships in Italy, where she was able to race with a modified boot but didn't win any medals. That episode was nothing compared to the shinbang she got on February 3, during one of her last training runs before her planned trip home to the United States.

The Vonntourage was in full swing that Wednesday, as Lindsey, Thomas, and the rest of their crew set out from their apartments in Zell am See for an ambitious double training session—a morning of super G with the US Ski Team at Saalbach, followed by an afternoon of private slalom training at Hinterreit, a tiny ski area down the valley.

While Lindsey's speed skiing was in good shape, her slalom was rusty—she'd been only sixteenth fastest in the slalom portion of the St. Moritz combined—and she was counting on this session to get back on track. After a quick warm-up, Vonn started down the course for her first run.

As an all-rounder and a threat in the combined event, Vonn had made this transition thousands of times—going from long skis to short ones, and from a sleek downhill suit to bulky padding. More significant was the change in technique, the switch from long, swooping turns to snappy, rapid ones.

It had snowed heavily the previous few days at Hinterreit, so the surface was tricky—soft underfoot, but icy in patches where the fresh snow had been cleared away. You had to be forceful in some spots and subtle in others, and pretty soon Vonn made a mistake, pressuring her skis harder than she needed to and feeling them snap sideways while her momentum carried her forward. Like a cyclist going over the handlebars, her upper body lurched forward. For a brief, panicky moment she floated through the air, with her legs extended but disconnected from the snow. As gravity pulled her back to the earth, Lindsey was tilted radically forward, and when she came down on her skis she felt a sharp jolt of pain as the hard plastic cuff of her ski boot dug into her right shin. She crumpled and screamed.

At first, Thomas was certain that she'd broken her leg. His guts twisted in a knot; the first Olympic event was eleven days away, so their carefully planned journey would end here. But after a feverish evacuation from the mountain, they looked at Lindsey's shin and found no discoloration.

It was extremely painful, but Lindsey was able to stand up—a sign that there wasn't a complete fracture. There was either a small break or else they were looking at the worst case of shinbang either of them had ever seen. When the pain hadn't subsided the next day, they scrapped their Park City plans; they would stay in Austria, seek treatment there, and—most of all—not let anyone know what was happening.

Like any racer, Thomas had experienced shinbang before, but he was always able to walk without pain. Part of the annoyance of the condition was that it only hurt when you put on your ski boot and leaned forward. Lindsey's case was especially bad. For two days, she had difficulty walking at all. Running was out of the question. She refused to get an x-ray; if there was a fracture in her tibia or fibula, she didn't want to know about it. If it was just shinbang, then it might last for weeks. They stayed in Austria and did therapy around the clock.

The ideas began rolling in. Red Bull's therapist wanted to change the ski boot, lowering or raising the cuff so the damaged area would no longer receive the pressure. But Lindsey and Thomas thought that was impossible just days before the race; such a change would dramatically affect performance and require a cascading series of equipment changes.

The mood inside the Vonntourage was grim. Repeatedly Lindsey tried on her ski boots, but the pain was excruciating. It got to the point where she didn't want to try her boots on again because it was so upsetting. They tried everything: lymph drainage massage, electromagnetic pulses, laser therapy. Thomas's mother, who was Norwegian, swore by castor oil, and they rubbed castor oil on Lindsey's shin, wrapped it in cloth, and let it sit overnight. The most outlandish experiment was contributed by her physio from Red Bull, Oliver Saringer, who came up with applying cheese to the injured area. Topfen cheese, also known as quark, a common ingredient in Germanic meals. It has the consistency of ricotta. It sounded laughable, but they were willing to try anything, and these folk remedies had been recommended for centuries.

As the days passed, Vonn avoided high-impact exercise—no agility drills or running. She did want to keep in shape, so she got on an arm-bike, spinning her arms until she worked up a sweat and was breathing hard. But this was not part of the plan.

Fate had it that the US team's departure for the 2010 Winter Games coincided with the death of one of the most beloved figures in the US skiing family. American ski racing pioneer Jimmie Heuga passed away on February 8, forty-six years to the day after he won bronze in the slalom at the 1964 Games. The cause of his death was health complications of multiple sclerosis, a disease he'd been fighting for four decades.

Before 1964, no American man had ever won an Olympic medal in alpine ski racing. The slalom event had been the country's last chance for a men's medal at the Innsbruck Games, and Stateside expectations were high, thanks to promises Bob Beattie had made during his vigorous fundraising campaigns. The team's ace, Buddy Werner, had missed the podium in every event so far. Heuga was the little guy on the team, a scrappy and fleet-footed son of Basque immigrants out of Squaw Valley.

Pepi Stiegler of Austria won that slalom, but they might as well have given the gold to Beattie, because just ahead of Heuga in second place was another of the coach's protégés: Billy Kidd of Vermont. *Sports Illustrated* immortalized the historic finish in a photograph centered on Beattie's megawatt grin as he threw his arms around the necks of his two recruits. The three men remained friends, each of them settling in Colorado and keeping a paternal watch on the doings of the US Ski Team.

Bill Marolt had been Heuga's teammate at the University of Colorado, on the national team, and at the 1964 Games, but their friendship went back to the early 1950s, when the fourteen-year-old Heuga and his mother had lived in Aspen. Heuga had gone to school with Marolt and trained and raced with him in the Aspen club. Later, when Marolt's older brother, Max, qualified for the 1960 Olympics in Squaw Valley, Marolt and his friends drove a borrowed car 1,000 miles to cheer him on, and stayed with the Heuga family.

Now, fifty years later, Marolt wouldn't have a chance to talk over the Olympic results with his old friend. Heuga died in Boulder in the afternoon with his wife, Debbie, at his side. She had flown straight home from Los Angeles three days earlier, where she had been visiting one of their three sons, when she got word that Jimmie had gone to the hospital. Finding him nonresponsive there, she kept her vigil. At one point, when the doctors and visitors had all left the room, she took her husband's hand and said his name. He opened his eyes, looked at her, and said, "I love you and the boys." She said they all loved him back, and then Heuga closed his eyes and never opened them again.

Kidd had driven down from his home in Steamboat that day to mark the anniversary of their glorious Innsbruck race. He arrived about ten minutes after his old friend passed away. He and Debbie sat on opposite sides of the deathbed, each holding one of Jimmie's hands, and for nearly an hour they told stories from Jimmie's life. Then Debbie called family members while Kidd got on the phone to notifiy Beattie.

When Beattie received the word, the man they called Coach cried and cried. He was at his home near Aspen, up Woody Creek. His old vitality had diminished somewhat, but he was following the US Ski Team's progress toward the 2010 Olympics as closely as he could. After he collected himself, he called Marolt and told him what had happened. Marolt was already on his way to Vancouver.

PART 4

Gold Rush:
The 2010 Winter Olympics

February 2010

CHAPTER 22

Faster, Higher, Wetter

MONDAY, FEBRUARY 8, 2010

For years Bode Miller had resisted pressure to drop slalom from his repertoire. "There are times when you gotta listen to people and times when you gotta listen to yourself," Miller told his teammate Will Brandenburg as they drove up to Whistler from Vancouver. It was a stunning 80-mile journey, the road clinging to the steep side of a tidal inlet, then snaking up a river valley that drains the snowy Coast Range mountains.

Miller was sitting shotgun while US men's team coach Sasha Rearick drove. Brandenburg, a twenty-three-year-old from Walla Walla, Washington, was sitting in the back seat. He was the discretionary pick the US team coaches had made for the Olympic men's combined race. He had raced in four World Cup races; Miller had started more than 350. Rearick had foreseen a learning opportunity for Brandenburg, but now he wished he had brought a tape recorder for himself as Miller launched into one of his patented soliloquies, an animated mix of anecdotes, theories, grievances, and jokes that lasted nearly the entire trip.

It had been shockingly warm when the first group of athletes from

the US men's team arrived in Vancouver the day before. After temperatures that had exceeded 50 degrees the day before, media outlets were
starting to call these the "Brown Games," because of the muddy hillsides outside the competition slopes at Cypress Mountain.

Miller, Brandenburg, and a few other racers had spent the previous
day in Vancouver, moving through the US Olympic Committee's "pro-
cessing" routine. In the ballroom of a Vancouver hotel, they were plied
with heaps of gifts from the team's sponsors and fitted for the Ralph
Lauren outfits they would wear at the opening ceremonies on Friday.
They were also compelled to attend a quick seminar on etiquette and
self-presentation known as "ambassador training." The USOC had
established the program in 2008, in reaction, most believed, to several
highly publicized embarrassments the US Olympic team had endured
in Torino, including Miller's unhappy flameout.

Finally, they arrived in Whistler. They wouldn't go back down to
Vancouver until the opening ceremony, four days away. In the mean-
time, the men's downhill training runs were scheduled to start two
days later, on February 10, provided some cold weather arrived to
freeze the snow into something more solid than slush.

Any town hosting the Olympics feels like the center of the universe
for three weeks. As Miller, Brandenburg, and their teammates settled
into their accommodations, there was no question that Miller was
there to stalk his first Olympic medals since 2002 and perhaps even his
first Olympic gold medal ever. At Whistler he had come home, and the
trials he'd endured to arrive there would give a medal the kind of emotional heft he needed it to have in order for him to respect it.

TUESDAY, FEBRUARY 9, 2010

It was still abnormally warm in Vancouver when Lindsey Vonn stepped
off the plane at Vancouver's airport wearing a knee-length black coat
over a beige sweater with a big collar.

She immediately began signing autographs and posing for photos
with a phalanx of fans that had gathered in the terminal, perhaps

alerted by the television cameras. With her long blonde hair and elegant attire, it would have been easy to take her for a movie star if not for the ski boots hanging by a strap over her shoulder—ski boots she couldn't wear because of the pain in her shin. While the American skier worked the barricades, Thomas stood patiently a few steps away in a red shirt and jeans, carrying her bag. Like his wife, he smiled despite secret worries.

Lindsey hadn't skied since the crash in Austria on February 3. The night before their flight to Vancouver, at their home in Park City, Lindsey had grown distraught over the condition of her shin. She tried on her ski boot for the third time since the accident, and the pain was still severe. Fighting the urge to cry, she had sent out a Facebook message saying how nice it was to be home in the United States, to sleep in her own bed and see her friends.

"Tomorrow I'm heading up to Vancouver and I can't wait," she wrote.

Now here she was, and the Games were beginning whether she was ready or not. In a few hours, Lindsey was going to explain her injury publicly for the first time in a taped interview with NBC's Matt Lauer. By then, another little secret she had been carrying around would be revealed—her appearance in the *Sports Illustrated* swimsuit issue. The shoot had taken place in late June the previous summer, in Whistler, but she had kept it confidential to ensure maximum publicity effect.

After arriving in Vancouver, Vonn met with one of the US Ski Team's doctors, Bill Sterett of the Steadman Clinic in Vail. There had been some talk within the Vonntourage of icing Vonn's leg to the point of numbness, but Sterett thought of something better: a topical cream containing lidocaine, a local anesthetic that would numb the injured area and wouldn't violate any anti-doping rules. They would have to be careful not to apply so much that it numbed more than the target area and left her completely unable to ski.

That night, as Vonn went to bed at a hotel in Vancouver, the swimsuit issue hit newsstands with Vonn featured in a pictorial dubbed "Best in Snow." Shot by photographer Warwick Saint, the pictures showed Vonn standing on the balcony of her slopeside hotel, lying on the snow in ski boots and a red bikini, lounging in a sauna, and leaning up against a red helicopter at the top of a mountain.

"Last summer we went prospecting for Olympic hopefuls who would melt the mountains where this month's winter games will be held," the spread declared. "What we mined was pure gold."

Lindsey had managed to get her sponsors represented in the shots—she wore an Under Armour top in one, Uvex glasses in another, and a knitted Red Bull hat in another. One photo depicted her in a bathtub full of bubbles, apparently nude but for a necklace, its silver pendant carrying the Red Bull logo. The one sponsor to miss out on the incomparable advertising bonanza was Head; the company had not yet locked up Lindsey's contract in time for the shoot, and now had to endure the viral spread of images in which their biggest star posed alongside gear produced by Rossignol.

WEDNESDAY, FEBRUARY 10, 2010

Early on Wednesday morning, Americans who tuned in to NBC's *Today* show over breakfast were greeted by Matt Lauer broadcasting live from the predawn darkness of Vancouver, a scarf around his neck and the city's downtown convention center glowing blue behind him.

"The Olympic Winter Games haven't even begun and already there is a major drama to report today," said Lauer, as video showed Vonn getting off the airplane the day before, signing autographs. "Just hours after she arrived here in Vancouver, skier Lindsey Vonn, one of Team USA's brightest stars, revealed that she has injured her right shin in a training run one week ago."

For NBC, the presentation was a perfect mix of news and enter-tainment: a breaking story, a network exclusive, and the start of a sus-penseful narrative that viewers could follow in the coming week. It was precisely the kind of content that NBC needed, and it worked in Vonn's favor too, as it slightly lowered expectations.

There was no video of the training crash in Austria, but that hardly mattered; as Lauer described the injury, viewers saw the clip of Vonn's hideous wreck in the downhill training run at the 2006 Games. Now her medal hopes might be dashed again, Lauer said, as producers cut to the taped interview.

"I don't honestly know if I'll be able to do it," Vonn told Lauer, whose face mirrored her concern.

While Vonn's interview aired, the men's team was up at Whistler Mountain, inspecting the men's downhill course for the first time. The first of three scheduled training runs was slated for that morning, but no one expected things to follow the schedule. It was snowing on the course and the forecast showed storms all the way through the weekend.

All ten of the Alpine skiing events were to be contested on a pair of trails that snaked crookedly through the forest at Whistler—one trail for men and one for women. The two trails converged as a sort of V on the mountainside, intersecting right above a shared finish area. The logistical elegance of this layout was that none of the finish-line infrastructure needed to be duplicated at any point. As the Games proceeded from speed events to slalom, each event would require less trail; workers could simply move the start house down the mountain.

For now, the men's venue started at 5,510 feet above sea level, at the top of the Dave Murray downhill, named after one of the Crazy Canucks. For most of the non-Canadians in the race, it was their first encounter with a course that had not hosted a World Cup downhill since 1995. It was a challenging slope, dropping like a crooked staircase down a narrow path through the forest. Sections had names like the Sewer and the Toilet Bowl. The Olympic organizing committee had felled some trees to widen the trail, but the course was mostly the same.

This was a great relief to the racers, who knew that Olympic downhills weren't usually staged on the world's most rugged courses. One reason was the need to accommodate relatively inexperienced racers who showed up to represent their country. A more significant factor was the mercenary politics of the IOC, where voting members weighed a wide range of considerations before granting host status to places like Sarajevo, home to a downhill venue so short that the course began on the rooftop of a restaurant.

The Dave Murray downhill course had a lot of varied terrain, with big turns that demanded perfect timing. As the trail wound through the woods, racers would go from a steep pitch onto flats, making tactics important; they would need to set themselves up to go as straight as possible and build up speed before the course leveled out, then prepare for compressions. In one section called the Fallaway turn, the course dropped off a steep pitch onto a long flat that actually had the racers going uphill at one point. There was no 80-mile-per-hour straightaway, but racers would be staying active throughout, turning in their high tucks.

The American racers wore their new red-white-and-blue Spyder race suits, which conformed to the Olympic rules by being free of sponsor logos. While other racers had acquired new helmets that didn't bear the logos of their headgear sponsors, Miller simply opted for a strip of black duct tape over the Superfund logo on the front of his helmet.

Training runs had a special significance at the Olympics, because the best national teams used them as unofficial inter-squad races to select their starters. For decades, the Swiss and Austrian teams had practiced this ritual at both the Olympics and the world championships, calling the training runs the "qualies," and it always created an interesting subplot; the majority of the starters got to experiment on the course while a few racers were putting everything on the line, even to the point of exhausting themselves ahead of the race itself.

At this Olympics, the US Ski Team was following this protocol. Three American racers—Bode Miller, Marco Sullivan, and Andrew Weibrecht—had qualified outright for downhill start positions, but the team's final slot would go to either Steven Nyman or Erik Fisher. Officially, the decision would be based on "coaches' discretion," but both men had been told that their training run performance would be a factor.

In addition to those five racers, there were two more Americans on the start list for the training run: Ted Ligety and Will Brandenburg. They were not going to be in the downhill on Saturday but were slated to start the downhill segment of the men's super combined the following Tuesday.

The training run got underway in a snowstorm, but instead of sending racers out of the start at the usual intervals, the jury repeatedly ordered last-second delays, pausing the run until visibility improved. Racers waiting nervously at the start received radio reports from teammates who had finished, telling them the course was in good condition, but that the surface got softer at the bottom of the run, where the air was warmer and the wet snow hadn't completely frozen.

By the time the first ten racers had started, the lower parts of the course were starting to break down. All those heavy racers pressuring their skis in the same spots, run after run, had created holes in the course. Racers would ski into the divots and get jostled off their intended line. Succeeding in such conditions required a radical approach. Racers who used a powerful style of skiing would suffer as the snow gave way underfoot, throwing them off line or causing them to crash. They would have to lengthen their turns and be subtle and soft on their edges. It was a change in technique, but more than that it was a change in mind-set—the kind of thing that tended to favor the experienced.

Sure enough, after thirty racers came down, the leader was Didier Cuche of Switzerland, who completed the course in 1 minute, 53.22 seconds, despite skiing with a brace on his broken thumb. The next fastest skier was hometown hero Robbie Dixon of Canada, who was 0.29 seconds behind.

The whole training run should have taken no more than two hours, but three hours after the first racer went out of the start, only forty of the eighty-seven racers on the start list had come down the course. The weather worsened and the jury canceled the run after forty-two racers. Bode Miller, who had started seventeenth, finished seventh. Andrew Weibrecht was tenth.

When Ted Ligety came down, he was surprised by how turny the course was—it ran a little faster than he'd thought it would during inspection. At times it almost seemed to have the faster tempo of a giant slalom, which was fine by him. He thought the race victory on Saturday would go to someone like Cuche or Janka—guys with good GS technique who also know how to let the skis run down the fall line. The fastest part, it seemed, was the straight shot to the finish, where racers came down a steep pitch in their tucks at nearly 80 miles per hour.

As soon as he finished the course, Miller was notified that he had been picked for anti-doping tests. A doping control officer would be at his side until he donated the sample. Several other skiers, including Austria's Benjamin Raich, were also taken aside for testing.

The racer left stranded in the start blocks when the run got called off was number forty-three, Erik Fisher, who had been on an emotional yo-yo all morning as he prepared for the run, determined to risk everything and secure a start position.

A twenty-four-year-old Idahoan with the shaggy locks and laconic voice of a surfer, Fisher had been dreaming of this moment for at least half of his life. He had learned to ski at Bogus Basin, a mom-and-pop resort outside Boise. In his first lesson there, he got so bored waiting for the other kids in his group that he made tracks for the bottom of the mountain, prompting an all-mountain search. After a scolding, he was introduced to the mountain's ski team, where he excelled. In 2004, he made his way onto the US development team.

Two weeks earlier, on January 26, Fisher had caught a tip during a Europa Cup downhill training run at the remote French ski area of Les Orres. He went down hard enough to crack his helmet and break the third metacarpal bone in his right hand. After that crash, he had gotten up and skied down to the finish on his own, but didn't remember doing so afterward.

Now, in this head-to-head race for the last American start spot, Fisher was chasing Steven Nyman, his old friend and World Cup roommate. Nyman had gone out of the gate thirty-seventh and had finished thirty-eighth after forty-two racers. All Fisher had to do was ski well and he might finally be able to answer all those friends and family members wondering if he was going to race the Olympic downhill.

It takes a certain amount of preparation to go out of the start gate at a ski race—stripping down to one's speed suit, clicking into one's skis, adjusting one's goggles just so. You also want to get your heart rate up a little, if for no other reason than to supplement the thin layer of porous fabric separating you from the wintry conditions. But if you get too warm and start sweating, and then there's a course delay, your sweat will freeze.

The whole routine was made more complicated by Fisher's broken hand. The brace meant he couldn't effectively grip his pole, so he had taken his coat off and duct-taped the pole to his hand. That meant he couldn't snake his hand back into the sleeve of his coat. Nor could he buckle his own boots. That had to be done for him by his technician, Matt Schiller.

Fisher got himself fired up several times for the run. At one point, he was told that he would start in ten seconds, prompting him to plant his poles on the far side of the wand and focus on the course below, but then a cloud passed over the course and the run was on hold again, this time for good.

————

For Miller's teammates, sitting beside him at a team press conference was like attending a dinner party with a tipsy aunt—she was likely to say something politically incorrect, to get grumpy or hostile, but she was family. You couldn't act embarrassed, and you might be entertained.

That uncertainty prevailed on Tuesday afternoon, a few hours after the training run, in the press center at Whistler. The US men's alpine speed team sat at a dais for a news conference. Sitting alongside Miller before a group of international journalists and a bank of cameras were Marco Sullivan, Ted Ligety, Steve Nyman, Erik Fisher, and Will Brandenburg.

For quite a few in the audience, it was the first they'd seen of Miller since his disgrace in Torino. Doug Haney, the team's press officer, welcomed everyone and introduced the racers. When it was Miller's turn to talk, and he began speaking in his poker-face way, a fusillade of camera shutters went off.

"I'm psyched," he said sleepily. "I'm ready to win."

The racers talked about the weather forecast, about getting the free gear the day before, the wind tunnel testing they had done on the suits, the course terrain. While guiding the questioning for Ted Ligety, Haney mentioned that Ligety had come in "under the radar" to win the combined event in 2006. Gary Kingston, a writer from the *Vancouver Sun,* then used the term while posing a question to Miller.

"Do you think that by coming in here under the radar you can perform a little better, or perform the way you want to, without all that attention on you?" Kingston asked.

"I feel like people think coming in under the radar is like being a fighter pilot, and actually coming in under the radar, where that actually means something—it's a completely ridiculous idea, to come in under the radar at the Olympics," Miller said. "Everyone's on the radar here. If one of you guys were to come out to race, that might be under the radar."

There were nervous laughs. Miller had used the radar analogy himself, but now he seemed offended by it. "You guys" was one of Miller's tics when he spoke to the media, along with answers starting with "no."

"No I'm ready to race," Miller said. "I was ready to race in Torino. I didn't have a great Olympics, but I've had lots of races that have gone much worse than that. I come in here prepared and fired up, so hopefully it pops up on the radar here and there."

Buried deep in his answer was Miller's argument that Torino hadn't been as bad as everyone said it was.

When a journalist asked for the men's thoughts on Vonn's injury, there was dead silence. How could they say she wasn't really their teammate? They competed separately and hardly ever saw her. Finally, before the tension got thicker, Steven Nyman leaned forward and said, "She'll compete."

"Nobody else wants to venture in?" the writer asked.

"I don't think any of us know anything about it," Miller said. "What we've heard is from you guys, and that's usually not the best source of information for stuff like that. No offense."

A Norwegian television reporter asked about the US team's suits, and rumors that they were a second faster than anyone else's.

"I think Ted's the only one that has the wonder suit," Miller said, joking about the lime-green suit Ligety had worn in that day's training run. "I don't know. I haven't been informed about anything wondrous about our suits. I wore the suit that I intend to race in today, so if that was a second faster then I'm in trouble."

That afternoon, Lindsey and Thomas Vonn made their way up to Whistler. Her injury was international news, its revelation prompting a stream of messages on Facebook and Twitter, hundreds of replies and comments offering support and suggestions for homemade remedies. The first training run for the women's downhill was scheduled for the next day, and Lindsey knew it was going to hurt no matter what she did; she hoped she could ski through the pain.

Lindsey had been anticipating this experience her entire life, but she never would have guessed that in the seven days leading up to her first training run at the 2010 Olympics she would have struggled merely to put her ski boots on. Testing skis, giving television interviews, getting lots of sleep—these were the things she'd been visualizing and planning. Most of her thoughts had been focused on Franz's Run, the women's Olympic downhill course, which was 9,642 feet long and dropped 2,526 feet in elevation. It was a very challenging track, with several big jumps and tricky sidehills.

This was a rarity. Throughout Olympic history, female downhillers had been handed some real duds—gentle runways that tested wax and aerodynamics almost as much as technical ability. The very best female racers, eager to showcase their skills before an international audience, found it infuriating, and controversy had followed. In 1994, the originally planned site for the women's downhill was so dull that the racers had staged a boycott. The racers were similarly underwhelmed by the 2006 venue at San Sicario, and sent organizers a letter ahead of the Games outlining their critique, after which organizers responded by adding terrain.

Franz's Run, by contrast, boasted big jumps and a higher average speed than the women's Olympic courses in 2002 and 2006. Four years before the Games, VANOC had hired US Ski Team coach Pete Bosinger to oversee the venue preparation; using bulldozers and explosives, he and his colleagues had contoured the mountain to create marvelously varied piste that denied the racers any chance to rest between challenges. The women had been able to test it out during a visit in February 2008 and gave it rave reviews.

The 1.82-mile-long course linked together parts of three trails, the longest of which was a wide slash through the woods named for Franz Wilhelmsen, the Norwegian who had founded the resort in the 1960s with an eye to the possibility of staging the Olympics there. Only the upper parts of the course were steep, but what the lower half lacked in pitch it made up for with airtime. There were five jumps, and at least a dozen places where the racers would "get light" as the ground shifted beneath their feet.

In one section, the racers would speed into a feature called Frog's Bank, an imposing sidehill that curved around to the right like the banked oval of a NASCAR track. A rock bluff had stood there originally. Blasting it apart, organizers discovered a high concentration of iron in the rock. Fearful that it would leach into groundwater, they left the rubble in place, contouring it into a smooth wall that the racers would ski up onto and back down. (It owed its name to *Ascaphus truei*, also known as the coastal tailed frog, a vulnerable species that lives in the adjacent creek; organizers bent the course in several places to protect the frog's habitat.)

Best of all, perhaps, was what the organizers had done at the bottom of the course, where Franz's and the Dave Murray track spilled into the same wide ravine. The two mountain trails zippered themselves together in a wide trail that had a few clusters of evergreen trees standing in the middle—tree islands, in ski resort lingo. The men's and women's courses could have taken any route through this area, which comprised about 30 seconds of racing toward a common finish line.

The most dramatic feature in that area was a big dropoff called the Hot Air jump, always a formidable challenge on the Dave Murray track back when the men's World Cup had visited in the 1980s and 1990s. For the Olympics, the organizers had taken it away from the men, rerouting the men's course around a tree island and over two smaller bumps into the finish. This alteration allowed organizers to send the Franz's Run track right over this spectacular launching pad. It was big and scary and it came at the end of the race, in full view of the stadium and broadcast booths.

Vonn knew that by the time she and her rivals reached the Hot Air jump, they would be tired. Perhaps they would have made some mistake above, and would be desperate to make up time. They would be taking risks, digging deep, and looking for speed. On trail maps, the upper sections had names like Wild Card and Jimmy's Joker, and the first two big turns were Ace and Deuce, in keeping with the poker theme. But it was here at the Hot Air jump that the big-stakes gambling would happen.

Wednesday night, the US men's team spent hours in their condominium studying video that their coaches had shot of the potential medalists during the day's training run.

One of the Olympic traditions cherished by so many athletes is staying in the Olympic Village, a block of athlete housing at every Games notorious for strict security and ample condom stockpiles. But at Whistler, the US Ski Team had paid a small fortune to house its athletes elsewhere, in a cluster of units at the Northern Lights condominiums, a secluded set of luxury homes midway between the base areas of Whistler and Blackcomb. The condos, which the coaches had found on a 2008 scouting mission, were part of the team's plan to correct some of the problems that had afflicted American racers at Torino. The team suspected that bad food at Sestriere's Olympic Village had depleted its skiers.

The location was perfect. From their doors, the athletes could hike up a short slope to a ski run that took them down to the gondola that would transport them to the race venue. They could get there without the hassle of taking a bus to the mountain and going through security. When they were done, they could do their interviews at the finish line and then load into the lift and ski right back to their accommodations without pushing through the hordes in the town square below.

The condos were meant strictly for the men's and women's teams— athletes, coaches, physios, doctors, and the team psychologist. In principle that meant no agents, no media, no friends and family, no ski team administrators. The garages would be converted into gyms. The team would eat dinner together, and watch the other Olympic events unfold on huge televisions. The coaches were no less devoted to the ideal of team spirit than Bob Beattie had been. Sasha Rearick was prepared to kick out any outsiders who showed up, though he was not enthused about telling the racers they couldn't have their girlfriends sleep over.

Tonight they watched video of the training runs, paying special attention to the Canadians, who had trained on the slope more than anyone else in the world. In recent years, their national championships had taken place there, giving them races and training runs on the slope for a week at the end of the season. They'd skied in all conditions there—sunny days and flat light, snowstorms and rain.

What tricks they had learned, if any, would be easily identified through comparison of video clips. Several coaches had climbed trees alongside those sections to get better vantage points with their video-cameras. This footage was uploaded to laptops, the digital files labeled and sorted for quick access. The US team slowed down the film, diagnosing the issues in every competitor's line. By comparing the time it took the Canadians and other top racers to move through critical sections, the Americans were able to identify which approaches were the fastest and why, dialing in their tactics for the next day, making a particularly close study of how tightly a racer could hew to the fall line in the Weasel and Fallaway sections.

For all the technological sophistication of the process, the subject was timeless and simple: choosing the best line. Some of the skiers were going "straight and late," diving into the fall line so directly that their momentum built and they had trouble getting the next turn started on time, forcing them to pressure their skis in a sudden correction. They weren't being careful enough. Others appeared to be skiing perfectly, and yet they were slow. Their line was "too round," and although their skis were making clean arcs, evenly distributing the pressure they put on the surface, they were covering too much distance. These racers were being too careful.

The shorter route, or the cleaner one? Which would it be? Which was faster? The pull of gravity or the mastery of its effects? Ultimately there was no clear answer, and anyway, when the day of the Olympic downhill race finally arrived, a mix of emotion and luck would take over, as it had in 1972 for that year's gold medal winner, Bernhard Russi of Switzerland. Had Russi been there with the Americans, watching them study video, he would have told them that while there was theoretically a perfect equilibrium between going not straight enough and too straight, they weren't going to find it until the critical moment of the race.

"You see probably an ideal line, but it's very theoretical what you are doing," Russi would say. "The real limit, you can only achieve the real limit while you are racing. It comes out that you have, for example, the idea that I have to go 10 meters to the right and then make the turn. And then your instinct tells you, straight on, this is also a possibility. Or you tell yourself that this jump, I'm gonna stand up maybe 20 meters before the lip, and when you are racing you know okay, now that's 20, but I stay down, I wait. That's the limit, that instinct. That's why this sport is not controllable. It will always be full of surprises."

CHAPTER 23

The Waiting Game

THURSDAY, FEBRUARY 11, 2010

Before dawn on Thursday morning, Greg Johnson was out on the mountain at Whistler, surveying the troubling condition of the Olympic men's downhill course. For more than a decade, Johnson had been responsible for the annual Birds of Prey downhill at Beaver Creek, and the FIS had chosen him as its technical delegate to sit on the jury for the Olympic men's races at Whistler. Of course Günter Hujara outranked him, but that was more than acceptable to Johnson.

Johnson's home race had its own challenges—it came early in the season, and the crew usually had only a few weeks to put everything together—but excess moisture wasn't one of them. The air at the start of that downhill was so dry it wicked the water right out of the artificial snow. The top of the Olympic men's downhill at Whistler, meanwhile, was only about 40 miles from the ocean and often damp.

Given all that, Johnson had known from the beginning that the weather in Whistler was going to be trouble, and what he found on the course on Thursday morning confirmed his fears. In the previous days, warm temperatures had settled over the Pacific near Vancouver, sending humid air into the valley toward Whistler, where, upon meeting the mountains, it moved upward. About halfway up the downhill course, that moisture was blocked by some high pressure and was trapped in place, leaving a band of fog.

Fog was one thing; snowfall was another. For the course to meet FIS standards, it would need to freeze solid at night. The temperatures on the upper part were suitably low, but if even an inch of snow covered the course it would insulate the surface and prevent it from freezing. Keeping the race hills free of snow during a snowstorm meant sending volunteers down it repeatedly, sideslipping the top layer of fresh snow out of the way to allow the hard surface to stay naked and freeze.

A further complication was the shared finish area for the men's and women's courses. It was a fine plan under the original schedule for training runs and races, but what would happen if bad weather forced organizers to stage men's and women's runs simultaneously? Johnson had worried for months about such a conflict, and his fears appeared to be coming true on Thursday morning. The meteorologists advising the jury were forecasting about ninety minutes of unobstructed visibility starting around 9:30 a.m. After that, a major storm was coming in.

Johnson and the other jury members got together with their counterparts on the jury for the women's races, and came up with an imperfect but chivalrous solution. It was decided that the men's training run would end short, with racers skipping the last 20 seconds of the course. Their training run would end about 550 feet up the hill, giving the women the chance to use the finish area.

It was noted that the bottom of the men's course wasn't ready for skiers, but even if a training run stopped above that section, the racers would still get experience with the rolls up above. That would actually work out well because the women had priority to get a full training run anyway. The men had gotten a chance the day before.

The trick was to act fast. The jury put the word out to coaches that the training runs were on, and the racers should be ready to inspect as soon as it was light enough to see. The run would have to start at 9:30, which meant everybody had to be in place and hope for the best.

At 5:20 a.m., Lindsey Vonn awoke, made her way to the kitchen of her condominium, and had breakfast. She was intent on treating this day as if it wasn't extraordinary; she was going to set a plan and stick to it, as she had throughout her career. Thomas got up twenty minutes later, and helped her apply the lidocaine cream to her shin. They left the condos and headed for the lift. Soon they were rising through the forests in the purple light of morning.

The night before, Lindsey had tried her boot on for only the fourth time since the injury a week earlier and it had felt better. The analgesic cream and the Tylenol and Aleve were helping, and Lindsey thought her shin might be in good enough shape to sideslip. In that fashion she could at least inspect the downhill course. Now, as she inspected, she was careful not to put any strain on the injury. At the bottom she told Thomas that she felt good enough to go on a freeski run to see if she was ready to try the training run.

Together, they rode the gondola back up to the top and came to an open trail that was closed to the public and reserved for racers warming up. Thomas looked down the slope and didn't like what he saw. The snow was choppy, and he feared that as his wife rode out those long arcs, the jolting of her skis on the bumps and ripples would be transferred through her boot to her shin. Then again, this was the test they needed. Lindsey wanted to make sure that she could ski safely down, which meant attacking aggressively.

"If you're skiing defensively," she would say later, "it's always dangerous."

With Thomas following close behind, Lindsey made real turns, trying to push forward against her shin to make the skis arc. It was painful, but as she descended the slope, she could grit her teeth and endure it. Thomas thought she looked okay. She never pulled up in pain or stopped, but made the efficient, beautiful turns that only a few women in the world could make. When they got to the bottom, Thomas pulled up and saw his wife was smiling.

"I think we can do this," she said.

As the men made their way to the course, the Canadians got a taste of the special pressure placed upon the home team at the Olympics, fielding ovations, high fives, and good luck wishes from fans at every step of the commute. While other racers could concentrate while moving through the village and up the chairlifts, the Canadian racers were constantly reminded of the hopes riding on their performances.

Perhaps no one felt this more acutely than Robbie Dixon, who had grown up in the White Gold Estates, a neighborhood in Whistler with streets named for skiing legends (Nancy Greene Drive, Toni Sailer Lane). He had begun skiing on the Olympic mountain when he was twenty-two months old.

Dixon was one of eighty-nine racers representing twenty-nine different countries on the start list. Just as the second men's training run began at 9:30, a fog bank came drifting up the mountain, making it hard for the racers to identify the dimensions of the snow—a condition known as flat light. This compounded the trouble the surface gave them, as the soft snow began to deteriorate under their skis. Again, as the racers came down the course, they noticed that the lower they got on the mountain, the worse the snow felt underfoot. Up top there was nice winter snow, but toward the bottom it got warmer and wetter. Ruts and holes developed, increasing the likelihood of injuries.

When it was over, Cuche was again the fastest racer of the day, with a time of 1 minute, 34.41 seconds. But he was disqualified for missing a gate, and the fastest official time went to Michael Walchhofer of Austria—1 minute, 34.46 seconds. Dixon was second best, and Bode Miller finished seventh, 0.74 seconds off the pace. Weibrecht was right behind in tenth.

One thing was certain: now that the men's field had taken an official training run, it was possible within the rules to have a race. If the weather cleared up on Saturday, the men's downhill race could take place as scheduled.

While removing their boots and putting on their coats, then moving through the maze of fencing and stopping to talk to journalists, roommates Steven Nyman and Erik Fisher barely spoke to each other, knowing that the decision about which of them would race was likely already made. Nyman had finished twenty-seventh, and Fisher had been far slower at the final interval before he missed a gate near the bottom of the course, drawing a disqualification.

From where Stacey Cook stood in the start house of the women's downhill course for the first training run, it looked like she was about to jump out of an airplane into the middle of a cloud.

Cook wore bib number two and was the first American to ski the run. She had stood in her skis and watched as the racer in front of her, Lucia Recchia of Italy, pushed out and disappeared into that fog. Recchia, Cook would later find out, saw no sense in racing if she couldn't see from one gate to the next, so she had stood up tall through most of the course instead of tucking. As soon as Recchia crossed the line, she was asked to give a report to the officials; she said the visibility was good enough up top, and the snow was good the whole way down, but the lower part was so foggy that she hadn't known where she was going. By the time the jury considered this, Cook was on the course, feeling her way down.

About 30 seconds into the women's downhill course was a blind dropoff the US women called the Tunnel Jump (a tunnel underneath it gave skiers passage beneath the race hill). Its potential for big air was clear, but the racers couldn't know from inspection how fast they would approach it. Cook, it turned out, was carrying plenty of speed, moving much faster than Recchia or any of the forerunners. She also had the wrong orientation when she got to the edge of the Tunnel Jump, her skis pointing farther left than she had intended. The next thing she knew, she was airborne and completely out of control, flying for what seemed like an eternity, and unable to correct her trajectory.

"Oh shit," she thought. "I'm way too far left."

Cook landed feet first, her skis slapping the snow, but the impact was so severe she had no chance to assert control. Instead of holding a squat position, she crumpled, her butt driving straight to the ground. Locked in that position, going at least 50 miles per hour, she slammed straight into the fences. A gasp went up from the small crowd watching on monitors at the finish.

Cook, in pain but conscious, stood up and then thought better of it, sitting back down. A helicopter took off with a rescue team, and pretty soon Cook was in a spine-stabilizing brace, strapped to a backboard, and being ferried to a hospital. The jury called off the run. That night, the coaches would visit Cook. Her quad and hip flexor were hurt, and her neck and her back—but it was all muscle. Everything else was okay.

That evening, a new snowstorm hit Whistler, and it was pretty clear to everyone in town that there would be no training runs on the downhill courses the next day. Up to four inches of snow was expected overnight, and forecasts didn't call for a possible clearing of the skies on Friday before late afternoon.

This all came as a blessing for Lindsey Vonn, whose shin was now the primary Olympic story for the American news media. When Cook fell, Lindsey was in a heated tent with her fellow Olympians, waiting nervously for her turn. When the run was called off, she went straight back to her hotel for more therapy. Her single freeskiing run had given her some confidence that she was healing. When she pushed her shin forward against her boot, the pain she felt was less debilitating, approaching something she could grit through. Taking the training run would have been painful, but it was doable. She just needed more time. The more snow that came, the better—it would give her more time to heal while depriving her rivals of an opportunity to take aggressive lines and figure out the secrets to Franz's Run before she could.

FRIDAY, FEBRUARY 12, 2010

It snowed all night on the upper elevations of Whistler. The course crews, wearing headlamps, went onto the mountain at 4 a.m. on Friday to start clearing new snow. About ninety minutes later, the race juries for both the men's and women's downhills went out for their early morning inspection. They found the upper part of the mountain frozen, but the lower half soft and soggy. Worse still, the middle section of each course was socked in by a band of thick fog.

The men's jury immediately called off the day's training run, opting to preserve the course for a possible race on Saturday. The women's jury decided to hold out hope for a potential midday clearing, and announced that the Friday training run would take place at 1 p.m. The women's jury also called for an adjustment to the Tunnel Jump, shaving down the lip that had sent Cook sailing.

While most of the men's team went out to ski powder on the upper elevations, and a few tried to train slalom, Erik Fisher stayed back at the condominiums to meet with Sasha Rearick and accept the bad news he knew was coming. Rearick told Fisher that he was the fifth guy. The American starters for the men's downhill would be Miller, Sullivan, Weibrecht, and Nyman. Sasha had decided that Nyman had put in greater effort and was in a better position to race. Fisher was disappointed, but realistic.

"I did not qualify for the Olympic downhill race tomorrow," he wrote in a Twitter dispatch. "The training run was canceled today and so I was not able to show what I can do."

When Lindsey Vonn woke up on Friday morning, her shin was feeling pretty much the same as it had the day before, which was pretty good considering how hard she'd pushed herself. It could have easily gotten worse, but it didn't. The key was the mental game; she had to keep the injury from disrupting her careful routines. She made her way to the mountain for inspection. The training run had been pushed back to 2 p.m. and was likely to be canceled. After inspection, Vonn sent out a tweet updating her followers on the delays, then a Facebook post.

"I just got done inspecting the DH course," she wrote. "The course is in pretty rough shape due to all the warm weather and rain. The course crews are doing the best they can but it's hard to overcome Mother Nature."

At 2 p.m., the jury called the run off. They also announced that they wouldn't try for a training run the following day. Even better for Vonn was the fact that Sunday's scheduled women's race was the combined event, which included a downhill; since the rules prohibited staging that race without a training run, that too would be postponed. The earliest possible day for a women's medal race was now Monday.

Just over the mountain from the alpine venue, less than a mile away from the Americans' condos, was the Whistler Sliding Centre, home to what had turned out to be an exceptionally fast new luge course. On Friday, the men competing in the Olympic luge event were getting their final training runs there. One of the athletes, a twenty-one-year-old luger from the Republic of Georgia named Nodar Kumaritashvili, was exiting the final turn of the course traveling close to 89 miles per hour when he lost control of his sled. He was thrown from the track into an unprotected steel support pole. He died instantly.

The death sent a shock wave through the Olympics. Gruesome digital images of the crash spread online, along with a rush to fault-finding and an outpouring of sympathy for the Georgian team. The memory of Ross Milne was invoked. He was the Australian ski racer who died in a downhill training run at the 1964 Innsbruck Games after tumbling off the course and smashing into a tree.

There were people at the alpine venue who remembered that, but many more who had been present at Gernot Reinstadler's death at

Wengen in 1991, including Reinstadler's coach, Hans Pum, who was now the alpine director of the Austrian ski team. In an interview that Friday afternoon, Pum spoke of what a death could do to a team of athletes. It was essential, Pum said, for ski racers to put fear of mortality beyond reach. The death of a fellow athlete could be disastrous for his teammates' mentality, and Pum believed he had seen such a chilling effect on the Austrian men's team in 2008, after Matthias Lanzinger's accident at Kvitfjell that led to the amputation of his leg. There was no question that the team's performance had dropped off.

Talk of the horror of Kumaritashvili's death was on the lips of all the coaches at five o'clock that evening as they arrived at the heated white tent where the team captains' meeting would be held. When Günter Hujara arrived, he was still in ski gear after spending most of the day on the waterlogged mountain. Hujara called for a moment of silence, then addressed the coaches about the condition of the mountain.

"If the slope remains the same as today, there will certainly be no downhill," Hujara announced. Hujara had examined the slope himself, studied the maps and projections of the meteorologists, and drew on his own hard-won judgment from running the World Cup for nearly two decades. He had spent part of the day in an emergency meeting with an international group of television executives eager to get a sense of when the Olympic races might happen.

"It all depends on the weather," Hujara said. "The slope has suffered a lot from today's temperatures and humidity, and we have rain. We will be up there in the night and will watch the situation. Right now there is only one thing that will help us out, if the temperatures drop."

For days, Hujara had been trying to save the Olympic men's downhill. At any given moment, his brain was full of ten different plans. He stood ready to lead the troops in any one of them without looking back, or appearing to look back, all the while being totally exhausted. Resources weren't a problem. If on his afternoon inspection he saw that a pitch needed work from snowcats, he could order a fleet of the $250,000 vehicles onto the course, some of them lowered by winches because they were so heavy. Back up the mountain Hujara would go again, and when he got there, the snow would have turned to heavy rainfall, and he'd order the snowcats off the slope.

Through most of these Olympics, Hujara had avoided dispatching the snowcats for fear they would damage the course. Instead, he had a total on-hill work force of 2,000 at the alpine venue, including about 1,400 volunteeers who had come from all over the continent in the hope they could get out on the downhill courses and help. Luckily for Hujara, he had an experienced core crew, made up mostly of experienced volunteers who had worked on World Cup venues and had come to the Olympics hoping for an extreme adventure. Hujara called them the Green Hats, and they were divided into teams assigned to different sections.

Through it all, there were windows of opportunity—half-hour or three-hour windows when the sky would clear and the temperatures were low enough that you could imagine the surface hardening. If you could time the races right, by looking at the detailed forecast and then having everyone in place at the key moment, you could conceivably get a race off.

Although Hujara had a hotel right near the bottom of Whistler, he hadn't been there in several days. He had been on an unbroken circuit of trips up the mountain to inspect the course, trips back down to the bottom to look at weather data and brief various people, and then trips back up again.

This was what the FIS paid him for, and he could hardly stop working when hundreds of volunteers were on the hill, sometimes around the clock. They would get a section ready, and then 10 centimeters of snow would fall or it would rain. Or one of the athletes could make a comment about the rugged conditions being unsafe that, once published, would undermine everyone's efforts. Hujara could see the volunteers losing heart over that.

Hujara had been through it all before—at the world championships in 1993 at Morioka, Japan, at the 1998 Olympics in Nagano, and at the 2007 world championships in Sweden. He'd seen plenty of meteorological nightmares; that was the nature of an outdoor sport. And safety wasn't his only priority; so was fairness. Hujara's job was to ensure that a race was viable for every athlete involved. Nobody wanted a situation where the winner's victory wasn't considered legitimate because he'd had a better surface than the other racers.

***

On Friday night, the town of Whistler was filling up with spectators. Among them were some of the great ski racers of years past, including Antoine Dénériaz, Kjetil André Aamodt, Günther Mader, Luc Alphand, and Carole Montillet. Crowds gathered in a central plaza in Whistler to watch a big screen airing a live broadcast of the opening ceremony down in Vancouver.

It was a lavish production, drawing on the participation of more than 60,000 spectators on hand at the BC Place Stadium. It culminated, as always, in the lighting of the Olympic cauldron. One of the Canadian athletes selected for that honor was fourteen-time World Cup race winner Nancy Greene. Lindsey Vonn watched on TV as her teammates paraded into the stadium in Vancouver. There went Chelsea Marshall, Alice McKennis, and Leanne Smith, emerging from the tunnel waving little flags. She wished she could be there with them, but there was no chance—she was back in Whistler, trying every therapy she could.

Most of the men's team stayed home too, watching the ceremony in their condo. It was Steven Nyman's twenty-eighth birthday, and according to the traditions of the team, he could expect to be hit in the face with a pie. Andrew Weibrecht did it. Unable to locate a pie, or even whipped cream, Weibrecht got a paper towel, heaped it with Greek yogurt, walked up behind Nyman and smashed the whole mess into his face.

The only starter in the men's downhill who made the trek to Vancouver for the ceremony was Bode Miller. He had been planning on it all winter. He told Sasha Rearick before the Games started that even if the downhill race was the next day, he would attend. And there he was, walking out into the stadium beside Ted Ligety and Will

Brandenburg—the latter would later recall Miller telling him that "this is the most powerful feeling in sport." Miller had come back to his fourth Olympics looking for inspiration, and he had found it. He felt the chills. He was nervous, and had been a little bit scared, but that was turning into positive energy. He was ready.

When the Georgian team entered the stadium, they wore black scarves and armbands in honor of Nodar Kumaritashvili, and kept a place open for him in the procession.

SATURDAY, FEBRUARY 13, 2010

On the morning of February 13, when the men's downhill was scheduled to take place, Hujara and the jury went up on the hill once again, took a look at the snow, and immediately called off the race. The lower course was what he called a *rohes Ei*—a raw egg. The jury postponed the race until 10:30 a.m. on Monday. The next week's calendar would be jammed with races—if the conditions ever improved.

As many had feared, the mountain had become a nightmare for racing. The downhill courses had been separated into three parts. The top, which was still in decent shape, had been receiving snow that had to be pushed off the surface. The middle was getting a mixture of snow and rain, making it difficult to move the snow out of the track. And on the bottom of the courses it was raining, which raised the possibility that all of it would melt away before the race could commence.

For the skiers, adaptability would be crucial. To succeed, racers would need to feel their way down, adjusting their approach to suit the different conditions. Up top there was going to be relatively normal snow, possibly softer than usual because of a layer of new snowfall. This would require a subtle touch. As they descended into a warmer climate, the snow was expected to be "peely" in the technical sections where they had to be aggressive. Then, at the bottom, it would be all about balance—staying balanced over the skis while letting them run. With all the rain, the surface would be so soft and rutted that the same racers who began with a delicate touch would need to stand hard on their edges or risk being jolted completely off line.

Once the men's race was canceled, Sasha Rearick immediately told the team to enjoy a day off. Some went powder skiing, others worked out and did media spots. A group of coaches played squash. Only Miller went out and trained, rising early to take runs on his super G skis. Vonn got therapy on her shin, baked banana bread, and watched the rain come down.

That night, at 7:30, the alpine skiers gathered in their condos and watched the finals of the first skiing event of the Games, the women's moguls, a freestyle event combining a quick run through mounds of snow with several aerial tricks. Two American athletes finished in the medals: Hannah Kearney won gold, and Shannon Bahrke bronze. For the skiers, the Olympics were underway, and for USSA, the organization that had yoked its identity to Olympic excellence, there were points on the scoreboard.

SUNDAY, FEBRUARY 14, 2010

On Sunday morning, with the women's downhill training postponed yet again, Lindsey Vonn went out and skied, even doing a little slalom training. Her shin was definitely improving, but within her little world it was creating a quiet tension that caused people to act abnormally casual. The conspicuous effort to appear un-nervous became an invisible gorilla that followed Lindsey everywhere. When she and Thomas finally got some privacy, they'd talk about the gorilla.

"Everyone's so damn nervous, I wish they'd just chill out," Lindsey told Thomas.

People meant well. But there was a greater abundance of ski team staffers than normal, and everyone wanted to do their part. People were constantly asking Lindsey if she needed anything or wanted anything. Thomas could tell that his wife was getting nervous, and the eagerness of the people around her was contributing to it.

That afternoon blue skies appeared over Whistler, the temperature started to drop, and the satellite images showed no imminent major snowstorms. As the coaches filed in for the team captains' meeting, there was a fresh anticipation in the air. Hujara addressed them with a businesslike smile. He had just come from the race hill, which was still "fragile," but things were "developing quite well."

It was going to happen. Within a day, the first alpine skiing medal of 2014 would be awarded, and a certain immortality would be achieved. Only sixteen men had won Olympic downhill races: Antoine Dénériaz, Fritz Strobl, Jean-Luc Crétier, Tommy Moe, Patrick Ortlieb, Pirmin Zurbriggen, Bill Johnson, Leonhard Stock, Franz Klammer, Bernhard Russi, Jean-Claude Killy, Egon Zimmermann, Jean Vuarnet, Toni Sailer, Zeno Colò, and Henri Oreiller.

Among those sixteen names were some of the all-time greats of the sport. The seventeenth name to join that pantheon was somewhere on a big board that stood at the front of the room. It held the names of sixty-four men from twenty-eight nations, arranged by their ranking following recent World Cups. Their coaches had all inspected the names and rankings upon their arrival at the meeting, and there was only one thing left to do.

"Have you all checked the board," Hujara asked the coaches, as was the custom. The coaches responded with total silence, and the top thirty names on the list were rearranged before a room full of witnesses.

At Whistler there was no question that going early was advantageous, as the lower part of the course was likely to break down. As the start order took shape, the US team came out lucky. Miller, who was ranked eleventh, drew bib eight. Weibrecht drew number four, and Steven Nyman, who was ranked thirty-two but got moved up a tier because the number of Swiss and Austrian racers was capped at four each, scored bib six. Only Marco Sullivan pulled a crummy number. He would start twenty-seventh.

That night, Miller went to dinner with a group of friends at a Whistler sushi restaurant. When they emerged, the streets were packed and the temperature had dropped. For the first time since the racers had arrived a week earlier, stars were visible in the sky above the town. The Olympic men's downhill was going to happen the next day and nobody, not even Miller, knew what it was going to be like.

Four days would have passed since anyone had skied on the course. In that time, it had seen snow and rain, snowcats and injection bars, and the ministrations of hundreds of dedicated workers. It was a moody trail. No ski technician really knew what wax would work best. No coach could say how fast the skiers would be going as they entered the jumps.

In that way, it was the perfect Olympic race; it was as if nobody had ever seen the run before. Fortune would favor quick studies—the skiers who could attack with a plan that was two hours old, adapt to a changing environment. The medals, and the bragging rights, would go to racers with the mental tenacity to lean forward into rugged conditions.

———

The reigning Olympic men's downhill champion was on site, but he wasn't racing. Antoine Dénériaz of France, the surprise winner in 2006, was doing commentary for French television. A family man at thirty-three, he was enjoying his retirement from ski racing, a sport that had in the end become a prolonged form of psychological agony.

Just a month after he won gold at Torino, the sweet-natured Dénériaz was racing a World Cup downhill in Sweden when he crashed violently off a jump, his head whiplashing into the hard snow of the landing. He slid down the slope with a bag-of-potatoes limpness that only unconscious people exhibit as they fall, and his helmet came off as he smashed into the fences.

His career never recovered. In that month, Dénériaz had experienced the wildest extremes: a gold medal, near death. The accident came in the last downhill of the season, so Dénériaz had all summer to recover. When he came back the next year, he was ridiculously slow.

Scared of steep sections and jumps, he was unable to unleash the aggression needed to win. On race days he woke up feeling terrible, and he finished outside the top thirty in four of the five World Cup downhills he started.

Dénériaz ended the 2006–07 season with just nine points, fifty-fifth in the downhill standings after scoring in only one of six downhills he entered. The next summer he sought professional help, but he couldn't explain his invisible injury to therapists. The year before the Olympics he'd blown his knee out, but that could be fixed. This was totally different.

"I tried to see people who could help me mentally, but it was impossible to put it out of my mind," he said. "It's engraved on the hard disk in your head. It's part of you."

He had always been one of the tour's best gliders, but that uncommon magic was gone. In December 2007, after finishing eighty-third in a training run on the Birds of Prey downhill, Dénériaz pulled the plug, withdrawing from the race and flying home. In Annecy, he started a family, began doing television work, and was happy.

Two years after he quit, in Whistler, a *Canadian Press* reporter asked him for his picks to win the Olympic men's downhill. Dénériaz mentioned Bode Miller, but said he hoped it would be Michael Walchhofer, who'd been the runner-up to him in 2006.

CHAPTER 24

The Medal Table

It was still dark when the sixty-four racers left their accommodations in Whistler and headed to the mountain for course inspection. By noon, someone would be an Olympic downhill champion. That would be 9 p.m. in Innsbruck, Zürich, and Oslo. Riding up the lift together, Marco Sullivan and Bode Miller hardly exchanged a word, but Sullivan would later say he sensed that Miller wanted to do something special. It wasn't anything Miller said, exactly, but a feeling Sullivan had gotten that Miller was as fired up as he had been all week. Sullivan knew that focus had occasionally deserted Miller, but not now.

When they got to the top, hundreds of course workers were carrying out their assigned tasks in the crepuscular light. They could look out to see snowy peaks in every direction, white on top and dark green below, a distinct line marking where freezing temperatures had turned the rain to snow. Below them, Whistler glowed warmly under the dissipating fog that had settled into the valley. Severe floodlights traced the glistening white path of the deadly luge and bobsled track.

Workers who had spent the night on the slope warmed themselves in a local ski team's supply shed, some dozing among the piles of gates and fencing. Near the start house, the racers gathered to wait for inspection to open, quietly musing on the morning to come. Radios squawked. Television crews hovered nearby.

Bode Miller really felt like he was at the Olympics. They were going to race, and a race like this always brought out big performances. He actually felt nervous. That was no small thing. In 2006, he hadn't felt any of the butterflies he'd felt as an Olympic rookie in 1998 in Nagano. In Torino, he'd felt he was racing clinically, as though it was just his job and he had to execute. There, he was the best—he had the best skis, and all of the experience. Now he was the underdog, the pressure was back.

Inspection began at 7:30 a.m., and the racers spilled onto the mountainside in a stampede, shouting to one another, tapping the snow with their poles, and stopping to turn around and look back up the course. The snow on the upper section of the course was grippy and hard, but not glazed ice. The racers moved slowly down the hill—Miller out in front, preferring to get a sense of the course's flow rather than memorize every crucial turn.

They hadn't been on the course since the 12th, and the changes three days had wrought left everyone a bit shocked. The course crew had injected water into the first few turns, and also the whole steep pitch. The course was full of ripples and bumps, and the racers were going to be crossing them at speeds over 70 miles per hour. It was going to be old-school racing, a bouncy, rough ride.

To Miller, the anxiety was good. It helped everyone get excited, feeding off of each other's energy. But Didier Cuche's agitation during the inspection was too great. There were too many people on the course for his liking, and he couldn't make out his line. He was yelling at people to get out of the way so he could see the jumps.

Miller was the first racer to complete his inspection, reaching the finish line in less than fifteen minutes. This was typical for Miller. While other racers consulted their coaches about tiny imperfections in the snow surface, Miller often plunged down the course swiftly and silently and retreated to his hotel room or motor home to prepare in solitude. Over the years Günter Hujara and other officials had reprimanded him for going too fast through inspection. Once, at Wengen in 2005, Miller had even skipped inspection entirely and finished third.

Miller was long gone by the time Cuche arrived at the finish, the last man to complete his inspection. He lingered at the bottom, leaning forward on his poles with his eyes closed, visualizing the two-mile-long course. In ninety minutes the race would begin, and fans were starting to arrive at the finish stadium. It was almost eight degrees warmer there than it was at the top of the course, and much more humid. The wax technicians faced a huge challenge.

***

Marco Büchel didn't feel ready for the race. There was no reason for such a feeling. The thirty-eight-year-old downhiller from Liechtenstein was at his sixth Olympic Games; no one was more experienced. But the three-day break since the last training run hadn't helped. He had skied a little and worked out at the gym, but all the lying around had bored him and sapped his energy. Now he had to ramp up the intensity.

Just after inspection, he went to the restaurant near the top of the course. There he ran into Bode Miller and asked the American how he was doing. Miller, who often spent the hour before a race reading novels in the lodge, said he was nervous.

"What!? Nervous? You?" Büchel asked. "I've never seen you like this. I don't know you like this."

Büchel thought Miller had changed. He knew Miller as someone who loved to race, but didn't love what surrounded the racing.

"Well," Miller said, "I'm excited. I'm nervous."

***

The oldest competitor on the start list, Patrik Järbyn of Sweden, happened to get the first number in the start order. That seemed fitting, given that history's first downhill race, back in 1911, had begun, as Sir Arnold Lunn had noted, "when the oldest competitor gave the word go."

Järbyn was forty, the grizzled survivor of more than seventeen years on the World Cup, and had adapted to many changes and setbacks—not just injuries, though he'd had his fair share of those, but also team politics. Not once but twice the Swedish ski team had dumped him, steering its funding toward a surge of talented young slalom skiers. Sweden had lots of technical skiers but not many downhillers, and often Järbyn was the only Swede at the big races like Kitzbühel, where he'd competed thirteen times.

His team's first attempt to dismiss him came in 2003, but Järbyn paid his own way the next year and scored well, compelling the team to take him back. When his results slipped again in 2006, they cut his funding. He was nearly thirty-seven and hadn't ever finished higher than second in a World Cup race. It really looked like the end, but again Järbyn was steadfast. He found his speed and won a bronze medal at the 2007 world championships in his old hometown of Åre, Sweden.

And there he was at 10:30 sharp, pushing out of the Whistler start, downhill's ambassador to the world, because everyone would watch this run—not only Olympic fans around the world, but most of the racers, too. The training runs hadn't been televised, and there was much to learn from watching Järbyn run the course. It was the closest you could come in 2010 to a mass start.

Järbyn went all out, feeling his way down the course. He was a wily, daring, hardnosed old athlete. He didn't overpressure on the flats, and a crafty way of working with the terrain. His stance on his skis was reminiscent of Daron Rahlves, the great American downhiller who had come and gone within the span of Järbyn's career.

He'd been "overpsyched" the night before to learn he'd pulled bib one, thinking, "Oh man, this is my chance." But the iciness meant he was carrying more speed through the upper sections than he'd counted on and he made some mistakes adjusting to the quick pace of the turns. Then down below, it was soft—a full spectrum of snow surfaces. His legs were exhausted, but as he came into view of the finish he dropped low in his tuck amid a huge roar of applause from the fans.

Järbyn came into the finish and braked hard on the bumpy snow, but with his depleted muscles his hockey stop wasn't quite enough to arrest his momentum. Before he reached the end of the finish area, he stood up and let his body flop onto the soft airbags that lined the bottom of the finish corral. Old guys knew all the energy-saving tricks.

He quickly pulled himself up onto his feet and gave the world that familiar old smile. The oldest competitor had given the word go, and now the race could start.

Bode Miller stepped into the start gate wearing bib number eight. He had traded in his old helmet, the one with duct tape over the sponsor logo, for a new one that bore a large American flag. He stomped his skis on the snow a few times, rocking his body a bit before settling into his famous pre-race posture—standing still as a post and gazing blandly off into the distance. Then he pushed out of the gate, dropped into his tuck, and dove into the course with his hands straight out in front of his face.

One of the deepest held myths about Bode Miller is that his form was purely sui generis. Though Miller's technique and tactics were radically his own, there were those who saw traces in it of one of his earliest teachers, his mother's long deceased brother. Peter Kenney, whom everyone called Bubba, had raced professionally before dying in a kayaking accident near Franconia in 1981. Whether it was a genetic matter of body shape or a young child's instinct for mimicry, enough of Bubba's style was imprinted on Miller that people noted the resemblance decades later.

Among these was Steve Utter, a noted ski coach in Vermont who had been Bubba Kenney's teammate on the NCAA ski team at Middlebury College in the late 1970s and early 1980s. Utter was there in 1996 at the junior race at Sugarloaf when Miller used his K2 Fours to catapult himself onto the US Ski Team.

"I think my knees buckled when I learned they were related, because I was seeing Bubba so vividly in Bode's skiing—tactics, technique, general approach," Utter would later recall. Miller's uncle Mike Kenney would confirm the existence of this bond that united his brother and his nephew. And now Mike could see it again from his perch on the side of the Olympic downhill course.

The unduplicatable combination of skills that animated Miller's run couldn't be shown in a freeze-frame image because it was a pure movement, his weight rocking forward and backward in harmony with the land and gravity, his balance expressing itself in the stillness of his upper body as his legs jerked up and down like pistons.

"I think Bode Miller is even way harder to copy," Franz Klammer would say later, asked to compare their downhill styles. "Almost impossible. He sits on the backseat, his upper body fairly upright, but what's down here is incredible. He gets so much force on the skis, it's unbelievable."

Miller felt great. The skis were amazing in the turns. At the bottom, as the snow got soft, there were tracks from the previous racers. Each had left a deep groove in the surface of the course. Miller was very careful, feeling his way through the course. A few times he pushed too hard and felt the snow giving way. He stood up, sacrificing aerodynamics for balance.

The crowd came alive as Miller approached. He flew off the last jump and tucked toward the stadium. As he crossed the finish line, before he looked at his time on the scoreboard, he made himself do a quick assessment of his run, and he was pleased. He'd pushed hard and done everything he could do. Then he looked up and saw that he'd taken the lead by 0.42 seconds.

Aksel Lund Svindal started sixteenth. A big-event skier, he came down the course confidently, making some small mistakes but recovering. He knocked Miller out of first, beating him by two hundredths of a second. Calculated against the 3,105-meter length of the course, that was like a head-to-head race in which Svindal crossed the finish with Miller only 21 inches behind him.

Svindal came over to Miller, who greeted him warmly with a high five. Breathless, Svindal told him about seeing his run on the television at the start.

"I saw that you were leading, and that made me think my plan should be to go real straight," Svindal told Miller.

That was about as specific as anyone's plan could have been, Miller thought; you go out and race as hard as you can.

They stayed that way, first and second, after Austria's best down-hiller, Michael Walchhofer, finished his run with a time almost half a second slower than Miller's.

Didier Défago had been feeling good all morning.

Since qualifying for the final Swiss start position the week before, a weight had left his shoulders. He had done some nice freeskiing with his coaches at Blackcomb, and had used his laptop to link up with his wife, Sabine, and their kids, Alexane and Timéo. He'd felt relaxed in the morning during inspection, and while waiting out the early starters in the race. Wearing bib eighteen, he watched Miller's run on the television at the top, and saw that you had to fight the whole way from top to bottom.

Now Défago dove into the course and everything clicked. He found all the lines he wanted to take, and his skis felt perfect. When he came down and saw that he was in first, 0.07 seconds faster than Svindal, he threw his hands in the air with his index fingers pointing up.

Back in the Valais they went up too. The first Swiss Olympic downhill gold since 1988 seemed a fait accompli, because here came Didier Cuche, the gold-medal favorite before his thumb injury, running twenty-second, the last position in the top seed. He crossed the finish line and was stunned to find himself in sixth place. He thought he'd had a good run. But then he saw that he was only 0.36 seconds off the winner; four years earlier, that would have been enough for a silver, but in such a close race as this one it wasn't enough.

Now Canada's Robbie Dixon was on course, wearing bib twenty-three. Everyone turned to watch him, one of the last people on the start list who could disrupt the podium. Though he was only twenty-four, he had trained on the course more than any of the Europeans or Americans. The moment called for Klammerism.

But his run was a disaster. In one of the first turns on the course, he cut too close to a gate and blasted through a panel, which knocked him off balance. He settled back down into his tuck, but soon the snow became too soft, and at the Fallaway section he overpressured his skis. His ski responded too quickly, hooking up in the soft snow, throwing him to the ground. So ended the home team's chance at a downhill medal to honor the course's Crazy Canuck namesake.

Long before the sixty-fourth and final racer, Andrei Drygin of Tajikistan, came down the course, it was clear that the men's downhill podium would be Défago, Svindal, and Miller—three of the most experienced racers on the mountain. With the three medalists within a tenth of a second, it was the closest downhill in Olympic history.

This time, Miller was on what he called "the right side of the hundredths." The fourth-place finisher, Mario Scheiber of Austria, had finished 0.12 seconds behind Miller—a difference so small that most people couldn't depress the button of a stopwatch twice to reproduce it if they tried. And yet Miller was now sure to be treated as the superior racer of the two.

Miller had, of course, had his turn on the other side of the hundredths at the Torino Games four years earlier. In the 2006 downhill, where he finished fifth, he had been 11 hundredths from the podium. Over the length of that run, the time gap was the equivalent of being 10 feet 9 inches from the finish line when the bronze medalist reached it.

They were tiny margins, and yet after the 2006 race Miller's critics savaged him for being unready and overhyped, while now the narrative was sure to swerve back to themes of resurrection and canniness. There was an illusion at the bottom of this business.

But there was plenty of solidity to the bronze medal that slipped around his neck. His third Olympic medal gave him more than any other American skier ever, and the Games were just getting started.

<hr>

While Miller and the other medalists posed for photographers on a podium that had been quickly erected in the finish area (the real medal ceremony would follow in the evening), the three other American racers exited through a maze of fencing, each of them stopping before a crowd of American journalists on deadline.

Before peppering the Olympians with questions about Miller, the reporters dutifully asked each racer about his own experience on the mountain. Steven Nyman and Andrew Weibrecht had finished twentieth and twenty-first, and Marco Sullivan had been disqualified after crashing.

Sullivan said he'd been surprised, starting twenty-seventh, by how good the conditions were; the surface had begun to deteriorate, but the sun had emerged to illuminate the ruts and reveal the dimensions of the bumps, an advantage the earlier racers hadn't enjoyed. He'd felt balanced on his skis all the way to the Fallaway turn, but it started to get slushy after that. As he approached the finish line, he lost focus, looking too far ahead and flying farther off the last jump than he'd expected. Off balance in the air, he crashed, ending up on his back. After recounting all this, Sullivan waited gamely for the inevitable.

"Did you guys expect this of Bode?" asked Tim Layden of *Sports Illustrated*.

"Yeah, I thought he was going to win actually," Sullivan said. "He's fast man," he added, laughing. "You guys don't give him respect, but he is fast."

"We know that in general," Layden said, "but based on stuff you've seen in the last month or two, did you think?"

Sullivan pointed out that Miller had won the last training run in Kitzbühel despite problems in the race, and had won splits all year.

"Sometimes his focus wanders," Sullivan explained. "Obviously today he was very focused and almost came away with the win. I don't think anyone in the race was really surprised to see him on the podium."

Sullivan then moved along toward a group of fans, mostly friends from the Tahoe area, their matching knit hats emblazoned with the words "MARCO ROCKS." Sullivan didn't know it yet, but NBC would spare audiences at home from seeing his crash. Instead of showing Sullivan's Olympic downhill run, the network would air one of their tennis people's feature on Canadian polar bears.

Among the spectators at the men's downhill that Monday was John Ritzo, the man who had noticed Bode's raw talent decades earlier on Cannon Mountain and then later, as headmaster of Carrabassett Valley Academy, had arranged for his scholarship and log-cabin digs.

Ritzo had come from Maine to Vancouver to cheer on both Miller and another CVA alum, Seth Wescott, who was competing in the men's snowboardcross down at Cypress Mountain. But with the downhill's postponement, the two events had landed on the same day, forcing Ritzo to choose. Fearing a transportation snafu, he stayed in Whistler and witnessed Bode win his bronze medal.

It was bittersweet for Ritzo because his wife, Patty, wasn't there to share the moment. Circumstances had kept her back home in Kingfield, at the house that had been the way station on Bode's snowmobile-assisted commute up to the CVA campus.

For all Ritzo had done for Miller, and as much as he loved the Kenney family, he knew that he wasn't "included" the way Patty was. Patty had grown up with Bode's mother in Franconia. When the other girls in their elementary school wanted to watch *American Bandstand*, Patty and Jo had been into sports. Patty understood the whole Tamarack culture, and fit into it nicely. Whereas Bode was a little standoffish with John—"he guards his space," John would say—there was instant warmth between Bode and Patty.

That warmth was on John Ritzo's mind that evening, when a friend of his who was involved in USSA's fundraising efforts called him up and invited him to come over to the Four Seasons hotel at the base of Black-comb Mountain, where the team had arranged a reception to celebrate Miller's medal. Nothing major, just about fifty people at the Four Seasons, where Miller was going to make a quick cameo between the awards ceremony and a taping of an interview for the *Today* show.

This was something the US Ski Team did really well. The "toasts" that the team put together seemed like impromptu gatherings, but they were a crucial part of the team's fundraising, a chance to bring the donors and corporate sponsors close to the athletes and make them feel involved with the team's success.

When Ritzo arrived at the Four Seasons, the party was underway and people were standing about waiting for Bode. Ritzo saw a lot of familiar faces, including Woody Miller, whom he'd known for decades. Then Bode showed up with his bronze medal and the celebration commenced. While Bode signed autographs and posed for photos, John and Woody went over to a corner to chat. Then Bode joined them, and immediately asked John where Patty was. As John explained how disappointed she was not to have been able to come, Bode grabbed a big white linen napkin and wrote the words "we miss you Patty, love Bode."

"I think that downhill run was as close to perfect as I could have skied," Bode told John Ritzo. "I feel really good, and I think this is going to be a good week."

TUESDAY, FEBRUARY 16, 2010

While the men had raced their downhill Monday, the women had taken a two-part training run on their own course, running the first 90 seconds of it at 10 a.m. and testing out the last 15 seconds in the early afternoon. Lindsey Vonn had skied well, but aggravated her shin bruise on what she called "the bumpiest course I have ever skied."

That night, with 15 new inches of heavy snow having fallen on the course overnight, organizers were forced to cancel the events scheduled for Tuesday and draft an entirely new schedule: women's downhill on Wednesday, the women's super combined Thursday, and the men's super G on Friday.

Vonn took most of Tuesday off, resting her shin and hanging out with her mother and siblings, who were in town wearing "Vonncouver" hats. One of Lindsey's younger brothers shaved his head, leaving a Mohawk stripe on the top, an L on one side, and a V on the other.

At Tuesday night's team captains' meeting, the start order was determined. Stacey Cook, who appeard to have recovered from her spill well enough to race, would go fourth, Julia Mancuso tenth, Vonn sixteenth, and twenty-year-old Alice McKennis twenty-third. The race would begin at 11 a.m.

That night, Thomas and Lindsey watched video from the training runs, thoroughly analyzing Vonn's runs and those of her peers, with a special focus on a few sections. Two days would have passed between the training run and the next day's race, and they knew that the surface might be completely different by Wednesday morning, but they could assess that during inspection.

They discussed the plan for the race, and whether Thomas should be at the start, as he had been at the previous year's world championships. They both knew that Thomas preferred to watch from the side of the hill, and there had been races where he had waited too long at the start with her and then had to scramble through the woods to get into place.

If Lindsey was in the right frame of mind, she would want Thomas to be on the course, or at least in front of a television—somewhere where he could gather intelligence and share it with her. Only if her nerves were a problem would she ask him to be at the start. The decision would have to wait until tomorrow.

WEDNESDAY, FEBRUARY 17, 2010

Lindsey Vonn might have been pleased with the weather delays, but they hadn't been easy on Heinz Hämmerle. All week long, he had spent the days and nights tuning and retuning her skis for conditions that seemed to change by the minute, scrambling back and forth between the top of the soggy mountain and his makeshift workshop. Now race day was finally here. At 8 a.m., it was 17 degrees Fahrenheit at the top of the course and 34 degrees at the bottom. This presented more than a little challenge for a serviceman.

Vonn had brought more than forty pairs of skis to Vancouver, and Hämmerle pulled out the pair that she had used in her January 23 win at Cortina—the 117s. Lindsey and Thomas approved of the selection. There might have been something faster in her quiver, but these were the ones that were proven, and if you started winning on a ski you gained trust in it.

The night before, he had waxed them ten times, scraping and brushing them each time, then leaving a final layer on before going to bed at eleven. Now he scraped off the last layer of wax, brushed the skis, and applied an overlay of fluorocarbon powder, rubbing it in with a block of cork. Then he strapped the skis together, jotted down what he'd done in his notebook, and left. The skis would not touch snow again until Lindsey stepped into them.

⸻

It was cool and clear at dawn on Wednesday when Lindsey Vonn woke up, believing in herself as surely as she ever had. It was a strange feeling, this calmness.

She numbed her leg with the lidocaine cream, pulled blue pants and a white parka over her race suit, and headed out, her water bottle hanging in a holster at her waist, a pair of warm-up skis slung over her shoulder. She rode the lift up and took a warm-up run, hitting a hole in the snow that jammed her shin forward painfully, but even that was manageable. Olympic adrenaline was the superior numbing agent.

She met Thomas at the start and together they inspected the course, which they could see was treacherous. Repeated cycles of melting and freezing had warped the snow, and the weight of hundreds of workers moving across it had transformed the surface into wavy, corrugated ice that was surely going to deliver painful jolts to her leg. Some of the gates had been moved slightly too. The Tunnel Jump, where Cook had crashed, was smaller. Lines of blue dye had been sprayed on the snow to give the skiers better depth perception.

On the way back up to the top, Lindsey remained calm as she and Thomas hatched a plan for the day. The Roundhouse Lodge, where racers could hang out near the top of the course before their runs, had a television monitor. Lindsey and Thomas would watch the start of the race there together, collecting any information they could about the way the course was running, and make final adjustments to the plan. Then, when Stacey Cook went down in the fourth start position, Lindsey would leave for the start house.

They would stay in touch by radio. They carried their own units, set to a frequency separate from the one the team was on. It was the Vonn frequency, their own channel. The plan was for Thomas to stay in the lodge and watch the other racers for as long as he could, assessing how hitting all those bumps and holes at speed affected the racers' bodies and stances. Then, just before Lindsey's run, he would come down to the start and be with her until she pushed onto the course.

At 11 a.m. the race began. The first woman down was Klára Křížová, a twenty-year-old Czech racer whose mother had won the downhill bronze medal at the 1984 Games in Sarajevo. As the young racer pushed out of the start, the athletes and coaches at the lodge up above gathered around a television to see how the course would run.

The sunrise hadn't fully bathed Franz's Run in light. The tall trees along the margin of the course cast long, dark shadows across the trail. Křížová was passing through stripes of shade the whole way down. Already the coaches along the course were radioing information to the start about which turns were in the shade and which were in the sun. Křížová made it through more than a minute of the course, but she wasn't up to the challenge of Frog's Bank. Unable to withstand the g-forces, she sank lower in her tuck until her butt hit the ground and she crashed, sliding into a gate that sent her spinning. She picked herself up and finished the course with one ski pole.

Britain's Chemmy Alcott came next and made it clear how taxing the course would be. Her skis rattled and scraped as she went down. By the finish Alcott was so exhausted that she was unable to come to a stop and stay on her feet. She hit the deck and slid into the padding at the end of the finish corral.

Stacey Cook went fourth and was happy when she finished. She got on the radio and sent tips up to her teammates. It was rattly, she said, but the visibility was good. Up at the Roundhouse Lodge, Thomas and Lindsey could see that the run was going to be hard on Lindsey's injured shin, but Thomas knew he couldn't say anything about that. She needed to put it out of her mind.

They had one last conversation before Lindsey headed outside. Lindsey calmly told Thomas that she wouldn't need him at the start after all. He should be ready just in case, she said, but otherwise he should stay in the lodge and watch her run on the monitor.

"I think I got this," she said. "I'm good."

Elisabeth Görgl of Austria was a medal contender, and the second she got on the course she looked strong, confident, and prepared. Watching from the lodge, Thomas could see Franz's was running much faster than it had two days earlier. Like the earlier racers, Görgl's time at the third interval was more than three seconds ahead of her pace in Monday's training run.

As she flew off the Hot Air jump, she lifted the tails of her skis so her tips pointed down. Like two long, stiff sails they caught the wind and dove for the ground, pulling her down to earth, where she dropped into her tuck and sped to the finish. When she crossed the line, her time was 1 minute, 45.65 seconds, putting her in the lead by 1.33 seconds over Cook. Görgl fell to the ground and cried.

Vonn had arrived at the start to find Hämmerle waiting there with her skis. She began her warm-up routine, stretching her muscles and checking her equipment. Meanwhile, she listened to radio reports from

Thomas. He reassured her that the lines they had talked about were the right ones.

Julia Mancuso left the start house wearing bib number ten, and from the very first turn she skied exquisitely. Whether the frozen ripples of snow were glistening in the sun or hidden in the murky shade didn't matter; she stood hard on her edges and powered through them.

The course was rugged and bumpy, and she always excelled in those conditions. She skied far more aggressively than any of the racers preceding her, tucking in places where they had stood tall to prepare for what came next. Off the jumps, she pulled herself into a tuck position before she even landed. She never overturned but let her skis run, just barely in control. Along the way, Mancuso nailed a lot of the lines that Thomas and Lindsey had talked about that morning. She crossed the finish line in 1 minute, 44.75 seconds, besting Görgl by nine tenths of a second.

From where he was standing, Thomas could see that it was a winning run, and that Lindsey would need to ski her absolute best to beat it. He also knew nothing motivated his wife more than the prospect of defeat. On the radio, he told Lindsey that Mancuso had put down an incredible run. She couldn't hold anything back; though Vonn had won races skiing at 90 percent of her potential earlier this year, there would be no 90-percenting this race.

"Julia just attacked this thing from top to bottom," he said. "There's nowhere to be content. You have to be going after it and looking for it every single second of this course. That's what it's going to take to win it."

As Thomas spoke, Swiss racer Dominique Gisin was on the course, much of which was now bathed in sunlight that revealed how weathered and wavy the surface had become. Gisin was in medal contention until the last timing interval, but went into the Hot Air jump slightly off balance. As soon as she took off, the wind discovered the tiny asymmetry in the arrangement of her limbs and yanked them out of alignment; by the time she had flown about 40 meters, her right arm was stretched all the way across the front of her body, and her left arm was doing the same behind her. Worst of all, her legs were completely extended, unable to provide any shock absorption when she landed.

Gisin hit the ground feet first. Her right ski seemed to want to track away on its own path, and as she collapsed headfirst into the snow, her left ski popped off and went flying. Gisin rolled over the ice, her speed almost undiminished. As she slid down the hill at an oblique angle—she wasn't going to go through the finish—her right ski finally came off, but it somehow ended up clamped between her legs as she slid, back first, out of the race track.

Just above the finish line, there was a gap in the fencing that course workers had been using all week to exit the venue. As they had slid to a stop there, making thousands of hockey stops in the same place, they had pushed up a berm of wet snow. The pile was now frozen solid, a single mogul on an otherwise level surface. Gisin slid straight into this little ramp and flew into the air, soaring 15 or 20 feet before crashing hard into the snow and finally coming to rest in the middle of the finish corral. A hush fell over the crowd as one of Gisin's errant skis, after slowly sliding down the final pitch, found its way into the corral and gently bumped into her where she lay crying.

Gisin's final indignity came after blue-coated Olympic personnel helped her to her feet and she was walked out past a cameraman who zoomed in on her tears; she held up her gloves to cover her face. It was later determined that she had suffered a concussion. The whole thing—run, crash, and departure from the finish—had taken about six minutes.

Daniela Merighetti of Italy, racing thirteenth, was approaching the Hot Air jump when she leaned too far forward with a knock-kneed stance. Both of her inside edges caught and she fell forward on her face, smashing into a gate that exploded into pieces as her skis shot off in two directions.

When Merighetti spilled over the jump and into view of the crowd, her skis were long gone. As her body accelerated down the slope, she was able to sit upright with her boots straight out in front of her and slide toward the finish as if riding an invisible sled. It was a funny sight, and the crowd laughed until Merighetti slammed her pole on the snow in frustration.

Up at the start, Lindsey Vonn had stripped down to her speed suit, stepped into her skis, and taken her place in the line of racers heading into the tent. Her hair was pulled back in a ponytail with two bands. The pain in her shin was now distant, nullified by adrenaline as she visualized her run, reviewing the race lines.

If she didn't really go for it—didn't lead with her chin, as Thomas would say—Julia Mancuso was going to win the race. She also was also aware of the crashes, each one of them prompting a radio command for the start official to hold the next racer in the gate until the course was cleared. She knew the Hot Air jump was the trouble spot after Thomas sent a final radio dispatch reminding her to be careful there.

"Just make sure you square up and are neutral on the last jump," he said.

After racer fifteen went out, Vonn moved toward the start gate. The black wand stood open, mounted on white posts. Heinz Hämmerle now stepped in front of her, his back to the course. He held her poles, silent. Vonn leaned down and pulled the elastic cuffs of her suit over the tops of her boots. As she stood up, someone handed her a water bottle, and she took a swig and handed it back. Then Hämmerle gave her the poles. She worked her gloved hands through the yellow straps, first the right, then the left.

She dropped into a tuck, and bounced a few times. She squatted, stood up, and planted her poles in the snow before bending at the waist as if bowing, except with her poles holding her hands up in the air in front of her, like Superman flying.

She bounced five times, straightened up, and nodded at Hämmerle, who stepped out of the way. She slid into start position. She put her pole handles in her armpits and leaned on them, looking down the mountain. It was two minutes to the start of the effort that could justify every sacrifice she had made since her childhood. The move to Vail, her alienation from her father—all of it had been the price of the sense of preparedness she felt right now.

Lindsey looked out on the top of the course. Her ski tips extended into the air. She wiggled her legs. A camera or microphone hovered on a boom a few yards in front of her. She reached back for the water bottle and took another swig. She adjusted her goggles. The hovering camera swooped in. She took a few deep breaths.

Twenty seconds before the run was to begin, the starter leaned down and pulled the wand closed. As he did so, Vonn stomped her feet a few times, first gently, then harder, causing the tips of her skis, extended over the edge, to shimmy and shake. As the starter stepped back from the wand, Vonn uncurled her fingers and recurled them around the red rubber grips of her poles, lifted them out of the snow directly in front of her, and clicked the ends of them together, twice, hard. Then she reached out and placed them on the far side of the wand, on the course—first the right, then the left, digging their pointed ends into the hard snow.

Bent almost 90 degrees at the waist, her feet a few inches apart, her arms spread out in front of her, she stood perfectly still save for her hands, which fluttered open and closed around the grips of her poles. This was her ritual. As the fingers of one hand splayed open, the other hand made a fist; they alternated, six times in total.

With five seconds to go, Vonn grimaced and wiggled her nose and stretched her face muscles so the goggles could sit more securely. The camera on the boom swung slowly up and out of her way. Outside the fences that extended down the hill in front of her, fans were yelling, shaking cowbells, snapping pictures. Vonn swished her legs and wiggled her feet closer to the wand—a tiny bit of momentum. Then she squatted low, stood up tall, and kicked the tails of her skis backward as she lunged forward, pulling on her poles as if she were yanking down on two ropes.

The wand tripped the connection, the clock started ticking and she was on course. Vonn skated six times and dropped into her tuck before the first gate.

From the beginning it was clear that aggression wouldn't be a problem. Vonn carved powerfully through the early turns, building speed. The first big test of her shin came early. After getting late on a right-footed turn above the Tunnel Jump, she had to lean hard into her boots to make her stiff skis bend, and didn't feel a thing.

Through the middle it was a splendid run, powerful and precise. Vonn was on the limit, lingering in the fall line exactly as much as possible but never too much. There were at least three points where she nearly went off line, but each time she quickly steered herself back. Vonn tucked in places no other skier did. Even out of her tuck, she stayed low to the ground, piercing the air in her red-white-and-blue suit. As she laid an arcing turn through the Frog Bank, it looked as if she were affixed to a rail, and before she knew it, it was all over except for the Hot Air jump.

Carrying more speed than any other woman in the race, Vonn completed her turn as the edge of the jump rushed up to meet her. She glanced at the horizon line that she had studied during inspection, and saw that she was lined up perfectly. She squared up her limbs, pushed her weight forward, and launched into space, soaring into full view of a roaring crowd. It seemed at that moment that the entire world was cheering for her.

She landed, grabbed her tuck, and aimed for the finish. A little ridge of snow pulled at one of her skis but she yanked it back and stayed compact until she had crossed the finish line. The crowd saw it before she did: first place, 0.56 seconds faster than Mancuso.

Vonn hadn't even come to a stop when she twirled her head and looked at the scoreboard to see the number one beside her name. Then she let out a primal scream and collapsed on the snow. She knew instantly that she would have a medal.

Anja Pärson lunged out of the start of the Whistler downhill thinking only of gold. The twenty-eight-year-old Swede from the small town of Tärnaby, with a cherubic smile and legs like tree trunks, was the most decorated alpine skier at the Games, with five Olympic medals from 2002 and 2006.

Pressure was not a big issue for Pärson on this day. When the world championships came to her home country in 2007, she had won the downhill, super G, and super combined, and was third in the slalom. Here at the Olympics, she was free to gamble a little bit, and as she blazed through the top half of the course on pace for a medal, the precision and power of Pärson's skiing demonstrated that her memory of the terrain and the turns was perfect, despite the limited training.

Vonn and Mancuso watched her run on a television monitor in the finish and could see that Pärson was going to join them on the podium. At the fourth and final interval, about 13 seconds from the finish, Pärson was 0.27 seconds faster than Mancuso. But then she took too straight a line on the right-footed turn approaching the Hot Air jump. By the point where Vonn and Mancuso had finished their turns and squared up, Pärson was still completing her turn, her skis pointing at the fencing on her right.

Trying to grind out her turn quickly by pressuring the tail of her ski, Pärson dropped so low to the snow that her butt nearly touched the heel piece of her binding. In doing so, she risked hitting the lip of the jump with all of her weight and momentum loaded onto one ski—the over-aggressive mistake that Hermann Maier fatefully made in the 1998 Nagano downhill.

"In those hundredths of a second you have a lot of choices in your head, and the first one was lie down, and maybe you will break down the speed," Pärson would later recall. "But the second thing I thought was, if I lie down I will fly over the A net, because I was going in the wrong direction, toward the net."

Pärson went to a millisecond plan B and used all the energy in her body to stand up and push forward and go off the jump in a neutral standing position. She stood up just as the earth dropped out from beneath her feet and it was as if she'd tried to go as high and far as possible. It was a tremendous flight.

Sailing through the air, Pärson's only focus was trying to keep her feet beneath her to break the inevitable impact. But the horror of a big jump is that once you're in the air, you can't do much, if anything, to adjust your flight. For a split second it looked as if Pärson would swan-dive, but she pulled her legs under her just in time.

Before she landed, the thought crossed her mind that the impact was going to knock her unconscious. That scared her—unconscious skiers couldn't control their bodies in the cartwheeling tumbles that followed. So as the ground rushed up at her, Pärson kept her eyes open and resolved to keep her head from slapping the ground.

Her skis touched down approximately 150 feet down the slope from the Hot Air jump. Those powerful thighs were unable to absorb the impact and she flopped onto her back. Her skis stayed on. With their bases flat to the snow and tips pointed down hill, they took off, dragging Pärson's prostrate body down the slope into a gate. This yanked her into a ferocious horizontal spin that continued all the way into the finish. It was one of the ugliest crashes the women had ever seen. Vonn was unable to watch.

Maria Riesch, the last major contender, was standing in the start gate, seconds from her race, when the command came over the radio to hold her back so that rescuers could attend to Pärson. Riesch put her coat back on and waited for more than three minutes—long enough to disrupt all of her careful physical and mental preparation.

Pärson was somehow able to pick herself up and hobble out of the finish area, but the delay seemed to have iced Riesch. From the start she was slow—nearly a second behind at the first interval—and when she reached the finish line she was in eighth place. With all the major contenders down, the podium was settled: Vonn, Mancuso, and Görgl.

Lindsey held her joy in check until the last dangerous racer came down the course, but none of the remaining athletes in the top thirty were even close. As the three medalists waited in the sunshine, Görgl silently began crying tears of joy. Mancuso, who had put on her big sunglasses and her signature tiara, shed some tears too, but Vonn was mostly holding it together.

Then Thomas appeared, having scrambled down from the lodge at the top. When Lindsey saw him, the cameras swooped in to capture the moment they reunited. As Lindsey hugged him and cried, she thanked him, and he teared up too, congratulated her, told her she deserved it. Waves of happiness broke over her, a happiness so intense she could not control herself. She saw her family clustered near the fence, and watched their reactions. She had never felt such emotion over a single race. To be able to come through on that day, she would say later, proved that the dream she had when she was nine years old had been the right one.

"Her whole life focus has been about this day," Thomas explained to a group of journalists nearby. "The pressure's off, anything else is icing on the cake. She can go and she'll leave here with a smile on her face no matter what happens, and that's something that becomes an advantage when you step in the start for the next race."

THURSDAY, FEBRUARY 18, 2010

Anja Pärson woke up Thursday morning with her left leg throbbing from terrible shinbang on both her shin and her calf, but the fear of not being able to race in that day's super combined was more powerful than the pain.

Pärson had never lost consciousness during her crash. To demonstrate her lucidity to the medical personnel who had run to her side, Pärson told them it was Wednesday and she was at the Olympics. They had wanted to put her neck in a brace and pull her out on a sled, but she had insisted on getting up and trying to walk on her tender leg. Her chief sensation was fatigue, not just from the long downhill run but from the massive surge of adrenaline that had flushed through her system. The first thing she'd done when she got back to the Olympic Village was log onto her computer and watch her crash online. She needed to know what she'd done wrong so that she could fix it the next day in the super combined.

Now here it was: sunny skies, her best event—a run of downhill at 9:30 a.m. followed by a run of slalom at 12:30 p.m. She thought the pain in her leg might be unbearable once she got out on the mountain. Pärson had told her coaches she was going up the chairlift no matter what and would decide whether to start or not just before her number came up. But privately she was determined to race, even if only to conquer the Hot Air jump. This was to be her last Olympics, and she didn't want to go out because of shinbang.

From studying the video of her crash, she knew that just a tiny adjustment could have averted the whole spectacular disaster. If she'd had one more meter of snow before the takeoff, Anja thought, she could have stuck the landing; but if the snow had dropped away a meter earlier, things would have been much worse.

Pärson took some painkillers and left the village. By the time she reached the top of the mountain, she had seen the crash a few more times—it was on televisions everywhere, getting almost as much replay as Vonn's victory run. Pärson had experience with shinbang, and she knew that skiing through it could make it numb. She took a few painful warm-up runs, inspected the downhill course, and hoped the painkillers would kick in more.

The downhill portion commenced, and she watched Julia Mancuso go. She saw how bumpy it was, but five minutes before her start she decided to go. If the pain was unbearable, she would slide down. Pärson started and the adrenaline kicked in. She landed the Tunnel Jump and felt okay, and halfway through the course she wasn't even feeling pain. She finished the downhill in seventh place.

Vonn won the downhill run handily in 1 minute, 24.16 seconds.

Maria Riesch was 0.33 seconds off Vonn's pace, and Mancuso was 0.80 seconds behind Vonn. They all took a break, put on slalom gear, and went out to inspect the slalom course.

Pärson started twenty-fourth in the slalom. She had a strong run and moved into first. Mancuso knocked her into second, and then Riesch nailed her lines to take the lead. Finally it was down to Vonn. She came out charging, but then hooked her tip on a gate and crashed. The podium was final: Riesch gold, Mancuso silver, Pärson bronze. It was Pärson's sixth Olympic medal, and given her ugly crash the day before, her best. Vonn watched the awards ceremony in high spirits. She already had her gold medal, and nothing could bring her down.

FRIDAY, FEBRUARY 19, 2010

There were four Americans in the men's super G: Andrew Weibrecht, Bode Miller, Ted Ligety, and Marco Sullivan. When the racers reached the start that morning for inspection, they saw the first few hundred yards of the slope shimmering in the morning light. The entire upper half of the slope had been injected—solid ice, as hard as a Formica countertop.

Weibrecht started third. Entering the critical Fallaway section, he was skiing around 60 miles per hour. It was a nearly 180-degree turn on sheer ice, and it came just before a long flat section. At five-foot-six and 190 pounds, Weibrecht couldn't afford to make any mistakes; he'd need all of his momentum to cross the flats.

But Weibrecht caught an edge and nearly missed a gate. He didn't know how much velocity he'd lost, but he guessed that he would need to find speed on the lower section if he wanted to do well. There was nothing to lose. Weibrecht attacked the lower section and finished with a time of 1 minute, 30.65 seconds. That moved him into first, but with only two racers having gone before him, there was no way to tell how his run would hold up. Ligety was leading at the early intervals, but he too made a big mistake near the bottom and was more than a second behind. Weibrecht held onto the lead.

Miller came down. He was crouching low, knocking gates out of the way with the hard plastic padding on his forearms. There was a calmness to his skiing, a patience, though he pinched off the line so much that he seemed to slam into every gate, flattening the panels to the ground. On his feet were the same skis he had used in the downhill, which were longer than typical super G skis, and needed a little more time to come around. Miller beat Weibrecht by 0.03 seconds.

There was a tricky gate on the Weasel section, and everyone was struggling with it. Manny Osborne-Paradis couldn't handle the speed there and got thrown off line. So did Carlo Janka. It was becoming clear that Weibrecht had nailed the bottom section of the run.

When Svindal crossed the finish line, the first thing he saw, even before looking at the scoreboard, was his former teammate Kjetil André Aamodt jumping in celebration. He looked to the scoreboard and saw that he'd taken the lead, finishing the course in 1 minute, 30.34 seconds, knocking Miller into second and Weibrecht into third. One by one, the top racers came down without disrupting the order of podium.

Silver for Miller and bronze for Weibrecht: the result brought the American team to a total of six alpine skiing medals, breaking the record of five set in 1984, with not even half of the events over.

"You need a tight group to feel the momentum," said Miller. "As you watch your teammates experience that joy, that excitement, it makes it much more real and accessible."

The super G medal was a birthday present for Bode Miller's daughter, at home with her mother watching the Olympics on television. Dace turned two years old that day.

SATURDAY, FEBRUARY 20, 2010

The women's super G was scheduled to begin at 10 a.m., with Julia Mancuso starting first. She misjudged the entrance to Frog's Bank, lost her balance temporarily but recovered, finished the course in 1 minute, 21.50 seconds, and held the lead until the twelfth racer, Maria Riesch, knocked her out by four hundredths of a second.

Lindsey Vonn, starting seventeenth, took the lead with a time of 1 minute, 20.88 seconds, but two racers later came Andrea Fischbacher of Austria, with much to prove after barely missing the podium in the downhill. Fischbacher finished in 1 minute, 20.14 seconds.

Then the twenty-second racer, Tina Maze, came down in 1 minute, 20.63 seconds, splitting Fischbacher and Vonn. That was the podium. Vonn's bronze was the US Ski Team's seventh alpine medal, two better than the team's previous record tally, the five medals it collected at the 1984 Games in Sarajevo.

SUNDAY, FEBRUARY 21, 2010

Bode Miller rose on Sunday bruised from a nasty slalom training crash earlier in the week and exhausted by the compressed competition calendar, and headed up the mountain for the men's super combined, his last reasonable chance for a medal. Long before he reached the top of the mountain, his soreness and fatigue had surrendered to the powerful inspiration of his surroundings and his task.

"Legacy" had become a dirty word in modern professional sports by 2010, but alpine skiing was still small and pure enough that a thirty-two-year-old star of the sport could reasonably trust the emerging view of how his career would be remembered, and how quickly dwindling was the time he had to control it. This might be the last day he could adjust how snugly his name might fit alongside those of Klammer, Killy, and the other greats. The clock was ticking, if Miller chose to listen to it.

Miller had coasted through the Olympic media gauntlet thanks in part to the Lindsey Vonn phenomenon. For once, he didn't owe worry to fame. A peculiarity of Miller's life was his simultaneously being a huge celebrity in Austria and almost totally anonymous in the United States. Miller had straddled these two worlds for a decade, and knew which he liked more. Since even before 2006, he'd grown steadily more reticent about his personal life, and had been especially determined to preserve the privacy of his loved ones, who hadn't signed up for scrutiny. All he owed the world right now was inspired skiing.

A combined race is great for fans because the second run, always slalom, is especially unpredictable. The Olympic race at Whistler turned out even better: Aksel Lund Svindal won the downhill portion in 1 minute, 53.15 seconds, and the top eight racers behind him were all within one second. The next nine racers were all within one second of each other too.

In the middle of this big group of men in the mix for a medal was Miller, who had finished seventh in the downhill run, 0.76 seconds behind Svindal. The run left Miller with an adrenaline surge that superseded the discomfort of his overtaxed body. He made for a tent where he could have a little lunch and make the switch to his slalom gear—the old ritual of strapping on pads. Then he clicked into slalom skis, which after wearing the long downhill boards for so many days felt like stepping out of a Corvette and getting on a motorcycle.

The plot thickened at inspection, where fifty-two racers encountered Ante Kostelić's eccentric handiwork. Kostelić, the father of Croatian skiing siblings Janica and Ivica, was famous for two things: raising a pair of world-class ski racers amid poverty and warfare outside Zagreb, and setting outrageously tricky slalom courses that eschewed rhythm and flow in favor of obstacles. Willful old Ante might set a four-gate flush into a hairpin—a combination that made slalom racers accelerate through the greatest allowable straightaway in the FIS rulebook and then screech into the biggest turn possible. Kostelić might place such a trap on a knoll, where racers would already have to recenter their balance to adjust to a new pitch.

Some people loathed Ante Kostelić's courses, but he made no apologies, though race juries had at times forced him to reset some gates. He kept getting picked for course-setting privileges because his son, Ivica, was very good at the combined event, and the system for allocating course-setting duties to nations involved a random draw that was weighted to reflect how strong each nation was in the discipline.

On this day, the Americans were looking very strong; all four of the US team's starters had made the second run, including Will Brandenburg, who had a big bruise on his forehead from a training run crash earlier in the week and still managed to finish twenty-seventh in the morning's downhill run. Because the start order reversed the top thirty finishers from the downhill, Brandenburg started fourth. Andrew Weibrecht would start thirteenth, Ligety fifteenth, and Miller twenty-third. Svindal would go last.

Along with the "faster, higher, stronger" motto of the modern Olympic movement came the Olympic Creed, which held that "the essential thing is not to have conquered but to have fought well." For more than a century, the Creed had guided Olympians to the notion that the most important thing at the Games was "not to win but to take part, just as the most important thing in life is not the triumph but the struggle."

The final run of the super combined was going to give every racer a chance to fight well. It was 47.5 degrees Fahrenheit at the start, and Ante Kostelić's slalom course was broiling under the sun at 12:15, when the run began. Immediately, it began deteriorating. The jury radio became a constant stream of commands and advisories as officials sent volunteers scrambling to do what they could to sideslip the ruts, especially on the turns, where the sudden doglegs of Kostelic's course called for racers to heavily pressure their edges.

This couldn't have been more exciting for Will Brandenburg. Only three racers marred the course before his start, and then he came down in what would be the third-fastest slalom run of the day. The ruts got deeper, and Brandenburg was still holding onto second place overall when Andrew Weibrecht fought his way down. Weibrecht crashed through the finish, falling on his shoulder and grimacing in pain, but he had made every gate and would not be disqualified.

Ligety came down and took the lead, doing his trademark 360-degree carved turn in the finish area. The 2006 combined champion had finished the slalom run in 50.76 seconds—which would stand as the fastest time in the slalom portion of the race. But Ligety's combined time soon fell, as Ivica Kostelić danced through his father's course and took over the lead. He was still holding it when Bode Miller came weaving down the slushy sixty-five turns with a near-perfect slalom run.

It had been years since ski fans had seen Miller ski like this, but in his turns was the unmistakable old technique that Kjetil André Aamodt had labeled revolutionary back in 2002. The technique Miller applied to the Whistler slalom hill—the arms reaching high to clear gates, the hips slipping back to juice the tails of his skis—included some of the same moves Miller had used to sneak onto the US team in 1996 at the Sugarloaf nationals. And they were uniquely Miller's moves because he had created them himself, skiing independently on mountains from Cannon to Reiteralm. Perhaps Will Brandenburg described it best, a few years later, when he said, simply: "That was guts." Brandenburg saw what Miller had told him on the drive up to Whistler, that you have to listen to yourself. Yes, coaches' counsel and mimicry of better racers had contributed, but what made Miller great was how inventive he was in responding to the powerful and even deadly forces he encountered in ski racing, how bravely he had committed himself to engaging those forces with his own body and his own mind.

When Miller crossed the finish line, he was in first by 0.33 seconds over Kostelić. The four racers who came out of the start after Miller could not dislodge them. Ligety fell out of the top three—the event's 2006 champion would not medal at Vancouver—but Miller was still holding onto first place overall when Carlo Janka came down with a slow slalom run. That left only two at the start: Dominik Paris of Italy, and Svindal.

At this point, Miller was guaranteed a medal of some sort—the eighth for the US Ski Team—which had put an American on each of the six alpine skiing podiums at the Games so far. As Bill Marolt celebrated out in the middle of the crowd, surrounded by backslapping and vigorous handshakes, he did his best not to be seen as taking too much credit. But he felt, as did all of the staffers and supporters of his team, an unmistakable lifting of all the weight that Torino had left to bear. Yes, it was a best-in-the-world feeling.

Paris came down—the ungainly run of a downhiller doing his best in slalom. Like a camel running down an escalator, the tall Italian just didn't know how his body should work in this context. Miller was guaranteed a silver now, and that was fair; if Paris had nurtured his slalom talents he wouldn't have been in this predicament, but then he might not have been quite as strong a downhiller either.

Svindal, alone up at the start, had struck his own balance with age, keeping his slalom flame flickering, like Miller had, for as long as he could. A little more than a year had passed since Svindal had been in this same position at the world championships in Val d'Isère, a gold medal on the line. In that earlier race, Miller had gone out, giving Svindal the chance to win. This time, Miller had thrown down a great run—the third fastest slalom run of the day, in fact—and it was up to Svindal to hold his lead.

It was almost silent in the start house as Svindal adjusted his goggles. When he pushed onto the course, Miller and Ivica Kostelić stood waiting in the middle of the finish corral, still catching their breath. Minutes earlier, they had been hanging out in a tent while their equipment was checked for compliance. They had both passed, and as Svindal got ready up above, Miller and Kostelić had been summoned out into the finish area so television cameras could monitor their reaction as they watched his run. Kostelić was guaranteed a bronze or silver medal, Miller silver or gold.

Svindal was dealing with ruts, but he stayed upright and by the second interval, a little more than halfway down the course, his slalom run looked insufficient. He was almost a second slower than Miller had been at that same timing beam. As Svindal came over the roll and down the pitch toward the finish, the others were waiting for him. Svindal still had a chance at victory. A crowd of thousands looked up the mountain and watched.

Here the Olympic men's super combined came very close to the impossible ideal of a pure ski race. If we could take away all the extraneous matter—the stadium, the press zone, the cameras, the equipment testers—everything but the finish line and the clock, what was left was a contest of two of the best racers exercising their will on a challenging slope.

Without cameras and split times, we who watched could only close our eyes and listen to the sound of the racer's skis grinding through the turns, the racer's hands knocking the gates out of the way, the sound of them—click, click, click. If suddenly that sound stopped, we would know that the racer had gone out of the course, had failed to finish.

That was exactly what happened to Aksel Lund Svindal on February 21, 2010, the day that Bode Miller finally won an Olympic gold medal and was, at least in that one time and place, the absolute best skier in the world.

No great sports accomplishment can happen within a vacuum of meaning, and Bode Miller's fans and chroniclers quickly set about interpreting his belated Olympic gold. Miller's ski racing days were far from over, but in the Vancouver super combined he had finally found the Olympic harbor of victory. In the larger narrative of his career, February 21, 2010, was the day he pulled closed the narrative circles that had opened in 2002 and 1996 and 1977 and even long before.

The significance was especially layered back in Franconia, near the rubble of the Great Stone Face, where Miller's kin and supporters had never wavered in their support of Jack and Peg Kenney's grandson. Peg had been an Olympic alpine skiing hopeful, and had taught all five of her children to ski on Kinsman and Cannon. One of the country's first ski schools was nearby, and the region had produced great ski racers going back at least to Joan Hannah, bronze medalist at the 1962 world championships, whose father, Sel Hannah, had helped design New England's earliest ski areas. In the howling autumn wind his greenhouse grew the choicest tomatoes imaginable.

Now one of Miller's sisters was living in the cabin at Turtle Ridge, which had been updated again, this time with environmentally friendly indoor bathrooms. Jo lived on the other side of the family property, in the bigger house her parents had built and occupied. There, despite her son's strenuous efforts to stay off pedestals and to not cheapen his accomplishments with external symbolism, a small monument of sorts had been constructed. For nearly twenty years, Jo had been saving mementos of his skiing career— not just trophies and medals, but news clippings, fan letters, and other paper ephemera that had come her way. By 2010, the archive filled up a shelf's worth of odd-shaped scrapbooks.

Bursting from the volumes were artifacts from every stage of her son's career. Scores of yellowed articles from the *Courier* and the *Union Leader*. Results from the pivotal 1996 US Nationals at Sugarloaf. And a piece of paper on which a coach had penciled electronic times from a session of full-length GS training Miller had done in New Zealand on August 27, 2001, when he beat Schlopy barely but consistently.

There was the identification card issued to him on one of his first out-of-state ski trips, a March 1990 USSA development camp at Sunday River, Maine. And there was the 2006 article from an Austrian men's magazine headlined "Bode's Ex"; the ex-girlfriend in question had posed in her underwear for the article, and in one picture had ice cubes perched in her cleavage.

One document in there was a "five year plan" that Miller's coaches on the US Ski Team had made him fill out at age twenty-two. It was a grid lining up his age on one axis with all manner of rankings and results on the other. At the far corner, where Miller had been obliged to state his ambition for five years down the road, he had written that his goal was to "stay the ultimate one!"

There was also a letter Jo had written to a grant-giving organization in the early 1990s, when she was raising her four kids in the woods, piecing together their livelihood with child support and miscellaneous income that some years didn't exceed $10,000. In the letter, Jo had sought a scholarship to support her son's adolescent ski racing efforts.

"I am proud of Bode's achievements thus far," she had written, "and I feel his potential warrants every effort on my part to see he accomplishes his goals."

Bode Miller's gold medal in the men's combined event, the eighth Olympic medal in six days for the US Ski Team's alpine squad, was the high-water mark of the greatest American Olympic skiing performance in history. And when the golden wave finally crashed for the American skiers at the Vancouver Games, it crashed hard, breaking bones and hearts at the women's giant slalom on February 25, 2010.

Whistler was besieged by fog and snow that day, and Vonn, starting the first run seventeenth, could hardly see from gate to gate when she passed the final interval with the fastest time of the day. She was about 20 seconds from the finish line when she crashed, got bucked off the snow, and was sent rotating through the air, slamming into the safety net. X-rays later showed she'd broken the proximal phalanx of the pinkie finger of her right hand.

The inclement weather and the large field of entrants had forced organizers to send racers onto the course at tight intervals, and the next racer was already on course when Vonn fell. It was Julia Mancuso, defending her 2006 gold medal. Vonn was slow to get up, presenting a potential collision hazard for Mancuso, who was flagged off course.

Mancuso was snowmobiled to the start for a rerun and inserted in the start order after the thirtieth racer, but had no real chance to rework her skis or recover her strength and was in tears at the finish. There, she and Vonn were grilled about comments Mancuso had made days earlier to *Sports Illustrated*, lamenting the way the drama around Vonn had monopolized the media's attention. The second run was postponed a full day, and Mancuso competed, but the Americans missed the podium in that race and all the other technical events that followed.

Nevertheless, the Vancouver Olympics were an unparalleled triumph for American skiers. Of the thirty-seven medals the US Olympic team won in 2010, twenty-one came from seventeen athletes who were part of USSA. Their turn representing their country on the world stage came two months after Tiger Woods crashed his car into a fire hydrant, prompting his sex scandal, and two months before Floyd Landis would send the explosive emails that exposed Lance Armstrong; in between these two great unmaskings, Bode Miller and Lindsey Vonn stepped forward to perform without evident dishonor.

The Olympics were the end of the 2009–10 season for Miller, who, after taking in the gold medal hockey game with friends in Vancouver, repaired to his home in San Diego, where he bought a 100-foot-long yacht called *Amadeus*. Eventually he got x-rays taken of the ankle he'd injured playing volleyball, which revealed small fractures in the talocalcaneonavicular joint: he'd won an Olympic gold medal with a broken ankle.

After the Games, Julia Mancuso finished the 2010 season twentieth in the World Cup standings. Soon afterward, she won her eleventh national championship (the most in US history) and then set out for Switzerland, where she entered a freeskiing contest at Verbier, dancing down the exposed face of Bec des Rosses to finish third.

Ted Ligety, who finished a disappointing ninth in the Olympic men's GS, compensated for his lackluster Vancouver performance by winning the 2010 World Cup giant slalom title. At season's end he promptly ditched Rossignol, following the crowd to Head (as did Aksel Lund Svindal). The US Ski Team, meanwhile, tapped Forest Carey to serve as coach for Miller and Ligety.

And Vonn, after Whistler, decamped for Europe and the World Cup tour, where over the next four weeks she cruised to her third overall season title. At the final super G in Garmisch on March 12, she collected her thirty-third career victory and moved past Miller on the all-time wins list. It was her eleventh win of the season, an American record that would stand until 2012, when she would win twelve races.

In March, when Vonn finally returned home to the US, she found she'd reached a new level of fame—her image on a Wheaties box, red-carpet walks in designer dresses, a cameo on *Law and Order*, and a trip to the White House correspondents' dinner. She hired a top Los Angeles publicist, bought a new home in Park City, and turned her attention to setting a whole new series of records, not without strife and drama on the mountain and off it.

By the fall of 2011, Bill Marolt had officially signaled his intention to step down as chief executive of the United States Ski and Snowboard Association after the 2014 Winter Games in Sochi, Russia. The board formed a small committee to begin the unhurried search for Marolt's successor and settled on Tiger Shaw, a former member of the team, from Vermont.

But Marolt wasn't done building the team's legacy. In October 2011, USSA unveiled a spectacular new training facility at Copper Mountain, the high-altitude ski resort near Interstate 70 in Colorado. As part of a twenty-year deal with the mountain, the US Ski Team would get exclusive access early in the season to a trail lined with eighty-seven snow-making guns and 20,000 square feet of safety netting.

The $4.3-million deal would give the Americans a chance to train downhill in November and possibly even October, since Copper Mountain summits at more than 12,000 feet above sea level, a zone where winter is expected to hold its ground even in the most dismal projections of global warming's effect.

The 2010 calendar year matched 2005 for the warmest overall global surface temperatures since record keeping began in 1880, according to the National Oceanic and Atmospheric Administration, and it was the thirty-fourth consecutive year with temperatures above the twentieth-century average.

CHAPTER 25

Road to Sochi

The hideous spate of life-threatening injuries afflicting alpine ski racers continued in the 2010–11 World Cup season, the most notable catastrophe being Austrian downhiller Hans Grugger's head injury at Kitzbühel on January 20, 2011. The injury-prone twenty-nine-year-old, a four-time World Cup race winner, landed sideways off the Mausfalle jump and whipped his skull against the ice, bruising his brain badly enough to require emergency surgery and a two-month stay in a rehabilitation clinic. He never raced again.

The following summer, FIS announced a plan to reduce the frequency and severity of major injuries by instituting a new set of restrictions on the length and shape of skis. Citing university studies analyzing racing accidents, the FIS said its goal was to reduce the extreme forces that built up in shaped skis during carved turns and sometimes sprung racers violently off course, torquing their knees and battering their brains.

To the surprise of many, the FIS placed the severest restrictions of all on men's giant slalom, increasing the minimum length of skis from 185 to 195 centimeters and drastically increasing the minimum turning radius from 27 to 35 meters (the term referred to the size of an imaginary circle that would extend from the curving edge of the ski; raising the radius meant straightening the hourglass shape).

The racers expressed outrage at the new rules—the natural and timeless opposition of ski racers to speed limits. The leadership of most of the ski companies joined in a year's worth of complaints (the rules wouldn't take effect until the 2012–13 season). Nobody was as vocal as Ted Ligety, who called the FIS a "dictatorship" and published a passionate online manifesto against FIS equipment regulations in general and the new GS restrictions in particular.

The FIS was more or less unmoved by the protests and the rules were in place for the 2012–13 season, when Ligety—who had seen the GS rules as a direct attack on his supremacy in the event—began winning GS races on the new skis by margins not seen in decades, taking Sölden by 2.75 seconds, Beaver Creek by 1.76 seconds, and one single run at Alta Badia by 2.40 seconds.

Grugger notwithstanding, many of the victims of the World Cup's recent carnage trend continue to return to snow. They were led by Marcus Sandell, who represented Finland at the Vancouver Games in men's giant slalom despite having lost a kidney five months earlier at Pitztal. Some are hopeful about prototypes of a new airbag safety system, an inflatable vest designed to inflate around an athlete's midsection in the event of a crash.

T. J. Lanning's broken neck and demolished knee kept him off skis for two years, and when he made it back to the World Cup, in 2012, it was not as a racer but as an assistant coach of the US men's speed team. He was often found at the start of the downhill courses, helping his former teammates get psychologically geared up to race.

Among the survivors of the World Cup who continued to suit up for the perilous downhills and other races was Bode Miller, who won his thirty-third World Cup race on the Birds of Prey downhill course in 2011.

———

The season that followed the Vancouver Games proved troublesome for Lindsey Vonn, as she struggled to get the right feel from her ski boots.

She went into the new four-year Olympic cycle paradoxically low in confidence. A midseason concussion forced her to the sidelines of the 2011 world championships in Garmisch-Partenkirchen, Germany.

Though she managed to win eight World Cup races, Vonn trailed Maria Riesch by three points in the overall standings on the day of the season's last race on March 19, 2011. That morning, the jury saw fog and soft snow on the women's giant slalom slope and decided to cancel the race, handing the title to Riesch. By then, the competitive tension between Vonn and Riesch had strained their old friendship, with both women airing grievances in the media and staking out adversarial roles. When Vonn criticized the course conditions at the 2011 world championships in Garmisch, for example, Riesch publicly commended her home town's preparations.

In April of 2011, Riesch married Marcus Höfl, who like Thomas Vonn took a lead role in negotiating his significant other's contract with Head. This led to the most interesting source of conflict—Riesch's reaction to the discovery that Vonn had in 2011 raced in a pair of Lange ski boots meticulously disguised to look like Head products. The only imaginable unfairness about such an arrangement was financial— both racers' incomes from Head depended partly on their agreement to compete on the company's full package of products. But it seemed that Head had tacitly condoned Thomas Vonn's creation of hand-painted imitations, and when it all became public, the whole thing was embarrassing for everyone involved, except Lange.

After that winter, Vonn expressed devastation over the jury decision that ended her season without an opportunity to extend her three-year title reign. In the summer, it was noted that Lindsey and Thomas did not attend Riesch's wedding. But by the next winter, the two women had patched up their differences and resolved to no longer discuss their friendship with the media.

A much deeper rift had opened in Vonn's personal life—a deteriorating relationship with her husband that came into public view in November 2011, when both Lindsey and Thomas filed for divorce. Just months earlier, they'd bought a 9,000-square-foot, $2.85-million house on 30 acres near Park City, Utah. This coincided with Lindsey's rapprochement with the man who had most opposed the relationship to begin with: her father, Alan Kildow, who threw his energy into the brass-knuckled divorce litigation that lasted more than a year.

Through it all, Lindsey kept winning races and titles. US Ski Team coach Jeff Fergus stepped instantly into Thomas's old role as coach in chief, and Head did what it could to make Lindsey's ski boots work correctly after Thomas, just days before the divorce filings became public, apparently made irreversible changes to the delicate settings of her boots, making it impossible for her to carve an effective turn at Aspen.

Vonn collected her fourth World Cup overall title in March 2012 after amassing a whopping 1,980 points, her best season ever. She got there amid rumors of a fling with Tim Tebow, then quarterback of the Denver Broncos, and newspaper reports linking her to American Olympic pole vaulter Brad Walker. She also publicly disclosed her use of antidepressant medications.

Since then, Vonn has made a bid to become the greatest skier in the history of the women's World Cup. On January 19, 2015, she won her sixty-third World Cup race, moving up the all-time winner's list past Annemarie Moser-Pröll of Austria, who since 1980 had held the record for most women's victories. But before that came even more adversity. The winter of 2012–13, for instance, was the first truly disastrous season of Vonn's career.

The trouble started in early November, when Vonn fell ill, disappeared from the training slopes, and checked into a Colorado hospital with what was described as an intestinal infection. She returned to the World Cup at the end of the month and won three races at Lake Louise, but said she was still feeling sick in December, when she got to Europe. She crashed hard in several races and finally withdrew from the tour on December 16, citing depleted energy.

By the time she returned to the World Cup in January, Slovenia's Tina Maze was the runaway leader in the standings, and would go on to have one of the best World Cup seasons in history, scoring 2,635 points in a 2012–13 campaign that included eleven victories and twenty-four podiums in thirty-four races. To top it off, Maze collected three medals at the 2013 world championships in Schladming, Austria—where Vonn's season ended with a crunch and a scream as she blew out her right knee in the super G race on February 5. Maze had taken an early lead, but Vonn was in the hunt when she flew high and far off a jump and landed in relatively soft snow, her right knee buckling inward under her weight. Surgeons found a torn ACL and MCL and minor fractures to the ends of both her tibia and femur.

Six weeks later, Vonn confirmed the juicy news that the Austrian media was already reporting—that she was dating scandal-stained golfer Tiger Woods, whose extramarital adventures she had mocked at Vancouver. Between her knee rehabilitation workouts, Vonn spent the spring and summer of 2013 following Woods at golf tournaments, trailed there and virtually everywhere else by paparazzi, for whom Woods was a top target.

In Vonn's absence, a formidable new American talent emerged in the form of Mikaela Shiffrin, a prodigiously talented young slalom skier from Colorado whose parents, avid ski racers, saw to it that her formative training took place on New England ice. A true native of the shaped-ski era, Shiffrin was born in 1995 and had never known the straight and skinny skis on which the older generation first learned the sport. Indeed, Shiffrin had never known a time when the US was deprived of skiing champions.

In the 2012–13 season, when she was all of seventeen years old, Shiffrin won the World Cup slalom title and the world championship slalom gold. At the Sochi Games the next year, she won a slalom gold medal and announced her intention to diversify her skills and become the US Ski Team's next all-around champion.

Vonn watched Sochi from afar, and returned to snow October 1, 2014. On May 3, 2015, she and Woods announced their break up.

As of October 2015, the only significant gem missing from Miller's skiing crown is a victory on the granddaddy of all downhills, the Streif at

Kitzbühel. Miller finished second to Didier Cuche there in January 2011, and in his 2012 effort he finished twenty-ninth, though a hair-raising recovery on the notorious traverse below the Hausberg earned him pride of place in the highlight reels.

A few weeks later, Miller's left knee broke down after he tweaked it in a series of World Cup races that served as the test events for the alpine skiing venue for the 2014 Olympic Games in Sochi, Russia. Though he tried to continue racing, the pain was too great, and he elected to undergo micro-fracture surgery that forced him to miss the entire 2012–13 season.

Several months after his surgery, Miller met Morgan Beck, a professional volleyball player and model. They were married on October 7, 2012, in a private ceremony on his boat. Soon thereafter, he became enmeshed in paternity litigation with a California woman named Sara McKenna, with whom he had fathered a baby boy. That news was tabloid fodder throughout his inactive winter of 2012–13, which ended with the death of his younger brother, Chelone, in April 2013, of seizures that were sequella to his 2005 head injury. Miller returned to the World Cup the next winter, racing at the 2014 Games in Sochi, where on February 16 he tied for the bronze in the men's super G (Andrew Weibrecht took silver). Having hoped to channel thoughts of his brother into his performance, Miller broke down in tears during a finish-line interview. NBC's Christin Cooper was criticized for her probing questions, but the response they elicited put the lie to the "atheist" label that had been lobbed at Miller in his bitter custody battle. ("He doesn't believe in anything," McKenna told the *New York Post* in 2013.) In the ski racing world, everyone knows the exact opposite to be true. Miller's adherence to deeply held beliefs has defined the peaks and valleys of his turbulent skiing career. The twenty-year path he has cut through the sport is strewn with people who wished Miller's principles had been a little less rigid.

The Sochi race produced Miller's sixth Olympic medal, and it made him the oldest medalist ever in alpine skiing. A month after Sochi ended, Miller raced his 438th World Cup race. That total hasn't changed as of October 2015. His only race in the 2014–15 season was at February's world championships in Beaver Creek. He crashed in the super-G, his ski edge slicing tendon tissue in his right leg. The grisly wound required surgery. His season was over. On May 18, 2015, his wife Morgan gave birth to their son, Nash Skan Miller.

———

It was 48.2 degrees Fahrenheit at the finish line the day Miller won his bronze medal at the 2014 Olympic men's super G race. Forty miles away, in Sochi itself, temperatures reached the sixties. Throughout the Games, warm temperatures and rain caused event postponements and affected the way competitors performed, leading many observers to question the International Olympic Committee's wisdom in choosing to hold the Winter Games in a subtropical climate.

When one talks to climatologists who study alpine environments and the future of the ski industry, a commonly used term is *snow reliability*. Generally, a mountain is considered snow reliable when it can promise a snow cover sufficient for skiing that lasts at least 100 continuous days per season. Economies are different at every mountain, but when seasons get shorter than that, profitability is very hard to achieve.

Through good winters and poor ones, the altitude of snow reliability is rising both in North America and Europe, making low-lying ski areas vulnerable. Snowmaking lowers the line only a little. In the Alps, this means that mountains less than 1,500 meters above sea level can expect temperatures to rise so dramatically that even snowmaking will be an insufficient fix by the end of the twenty-first century. This category of mountain includes some of the classic World Cup downhill venues, including Kitzbühel and Garmisch, which each begin at around 1,700 meters above sea level and finish at around 800 meters.

Nevertheless, the most visible threat that global warming will present to alpine ski racing over the next century is likely to come at the Winter Olympics, where, as both Whistler and Sochi showed, the snow reliability of the alpine skiing venues is just one small factor among many that the IOC considers when selecting a host city. While the FIS can tweak the World Cup schedule—and perhaps even shrink it to its original size, with half as many events and a more sustainable amount of international travel—the Olympics are harder to move around on a calendar.

Sochi's Olympic alpine skiing courses, held at the spectacular new resort of Rosa Khutor, ended at about 970 meters above sea level. That is a higher altitude than the finish at Whistler, the 2010 downhill venue, and Whistler itself made organizers nervous. Altitude is not everything, of course. Proximity to large bodies of water, seasonal wind patterns, latitude, and the direction a mountain faces all play a role in shaping the microclimates that influence conditions at a ski area.

In that context, there is justifiable concern about the low altitude of some of the alpine skiing venues slated for use at the 2018 Winter Games in Pyeongchang, South Korea. The proposed site of the downhills is a venue called Jungbong, where organizers proposed to start the men's downhill at 1,433 meters above sea level and have it drop to 540 meters above sea level, an elevation that no one believes will be snow reliable for much longer.

And the supply of snow is even less certain for the 2022 Winter Games, which will be in Beijing, China, whose only rival host bid came from Almaty, Kazakhstan, after several European skiing nations declined to bid. Beijing's proposed alpine skiing sites are far from the city. No Olympic downhill has been canceled since the first medals were awarded in the event, and it will be an enormous symbolic loss if the historic chain is broken. (NBC is on board regardless, after paying $7.75 billion in 2014 to secure Olympic broadcast rights through 2032.)

Climate change will of course lead to global calamities far worse than the demise of downhill ski racing, but fans will mourn the end of the Kitzbühel's Hahnenkamm races, where ski racing's power to thrill has renewed itself year after year for almost a century. There might not be another century of racing left there.

It won't happen suddenly—there will be blizzard years like 2005, and also years like 2007, when the beloved final pitch was brown and muddy in January and the race was called off. The Hahnenkamm might at first cease to be an annual event, and for a few decades, perhaps, the winners will enjoy longer reigns as race after race is called off at the last moment, with disappointed fans walking home in the rain.

And then one year, winter will throw up one last big storm like it did in the old days. The snow will stretch to the bottom of the Streif, and the believers will gather on it. A starting order will be drawn, just like always, bearing the names of the best ski racers in the world, all of them nervously preparing for this downhill racing rite of passage. And without really knowing it at the time, the racers will line up for what will turn out to be the last downhill race on the historic Streif. They will be the last downhillers, and we still don't know their names.

Brooklyn Navy Yard
September 2015

ACKNOWLEDGMENTS

Writing a book is like swimming an ocean, and I was out to sea for a long time. It would have been impossibly lonely if not for my wife, Liz, the ground beneath my feet on the opposite shore. May the two beautiful children she introduced to the earth while I was crossing the deeps grow to appreciate how strong, brave, and creative their mother is.

This book would not exist without the trust and assistance of so many people in the ski racing family, particularly the athletes and coaches: Danke schön, merci, and thank you for always coming to the fence. And thank you also to the racers' friends, family members, agents, servicemen, and every other source of mine who respected my occasionally invasive and more often tedious search for correct information.

When I started writing about Alpine ski racing, American correspondents were less frequently seen than they are now at the races where the sport's heart beats fastest: the hinterlands and precipices of Europe. That change is mainly the achievement of skiers like Bode Miller and Lindsey Vonn, but it is also due to the many editors who took a chance on sending a reporter to cover an unfamiliar sport in a time of radical industry contraction.

So thank you to the editors who allowed me persuade them to take my dispatches from places like La Grave and St. Moritz—subsidizing hundreds of stories from mountains in more than a dozen countries. I cannot name you all but will forever feel a debt to Tim Etchells, Natalie Kurylko, Kristin Huckshorn, Tom Jolly, Jason Stallman, Bob Goetz, Susan Adams, Peter Berlin, Jill Agostino, Leon Carter, Martin Dunn, Kevin Convey, Colin Myler, all the guys and Amara on the desk at the *New York Daily News*, Elisabeth Dyssegaard, Sarah Tuff, Kathleen James, Greg Ditrinco, Sam Bass, and Joe Cutts.

I am also grateful to the fellow journalists who helped me penetrate the sport, sharing their archives, their language proficiency, and their knowledge. There are so many beloved pressroom elders I could name, but must stop at three—Gary Black, Christopher Clarey, and Wayne Coffey—who opened the doors of the profession to me, uniting me with the tribe. And merci to Erica Bulman too.

To all of my colleagues at the *New York Daily News*, who do such extraordinary and groundbreaking work every day: cheers. And thank you especially to Teri Thompson, who gave me not only the leeway to pursue this side project—a lot!—but also an education in how to do it the right way. And thanks also to my reporting teammates, Michael O'Keeffe and Christian Red, for your steady friendship and good humor.

Since 2007, no one has been a more loyal advocate of this book than my bulldog agent, Zoë Pagnamenta. Thanks to her I met Brendan Curry, an angel working in the guise of a mild-mannered editor at W. W. Norton. He rescued my manuscript from the nets and set it back on course, calmly offering the most humane and perceptive edits I could have hoped for.

The Vinton and Steffey families supported me in ways eternally humbling. So too did my friends in Brooklyn and beyond. Rah, rah, ray. Critical material assistance was provided by Kong Zheng, John Bisbee, Sarah Levitt, Mitchell Kohles, Sophie Duvernoy, Mo Guile, Hank McKee, Jonathan Selkowitz, Trevor MacDermid, and the late Paul Robbins. Early and difficult editorial surgery was performed by John Vinton, Matt Inman, John Fry, Willing Davidson, the Honorable Winston

Lord, and Franklin Burroughs, the best writer and writing guide I've ever known.

The Fall Line began with inspiration from the people who taught me to ski, starting with my parents, Paul Beliveau, and all the coaches at the Snowbird Sports Education Foundation (in the good old days, the Snowbird Ski Team). Although I never skied close to the level of the protagonists of this book, I did learn enough to begin to appreciate great skiing thanks to Steve and Sue Bounous, Mica Mosley, Chris Gibson, Scott Martin, and so many other coaches and teammates who were my friends, even on powder days.

Most of all I am grateful that one of those Snowbird coaches was the peerless ski expert Steven Porino, now of NBC, but then a recently retired World Cup downhiller who took my teenage friends and me in 1995 to the FIS downhills in Crested Butte. Seven years later he snagged me my first journalism job, thus saving me from a life of restlessness and prosperity.

NOTE ON SOURCES

Over the past four years, I have conducted hundreds of interviews, by phone and in person, with people who kindly agreed to help me with the story I've told in *The Fall Line*. This book is entirely the product of reporting I conducted independently. Occasionally I used material I gathered while on assignment for the *New York Daily News*. Mostly I worked solo during several leaves of absence. I traveled to dozens of ski towns to meet with people from every era of ski racing history. The notebooks I filled and the photocopies I made, stacked together with competition guides and back issues of *Ski Racing* magazine, would make a mountain big enough to ski on.

Unless otherwise noted in the text, every quote in this book comes straight from an interview I conducted personally or something the speaker said to a group of reporters that included me. I also viewed contemporaneous video conferences, social media, and the like. Wherever the book relates an individual's thoughts, I have based the information on something that individual shared in an interview. Occasionally, I reproduce dialogue from a conversation for which I was not present; in each of those cases, at least one and usually all of the participants told me what was said to the best of their recollection.

More important than any of this are the hard facts that ground this story in a place and time. I dedicated months of work to tracking down dates, results, names, and other discrete bits of data that had expired in people's minds but remained memorialized in databases and other archives. Racers checked old email accounts and contracts for me. Coaches shared spreadsheets with team travel itineraries and budgets. A ski serviceman looked through his tuning diaries to find wax choices, and a few US Ski Team athletes gave me hard drives full of race and training video. A trusting mother loaned me a big box of scrapbooks full of her son's early press clippings and award certificates. At no point in my reporting did I ever exchange anything of value with any subject of that reporting. In the interest of full disclosure: my publisher asked for and received Bode Miller's permission to use a photo of him on the cover of this book.

On a few occasions, I did rely upon press accounts of events that I was not able to cover, and in most of those instances I've cited the article in the text itself. Where I wasn't able to do that, I have included a fuller citation below. I am also indebted to my dog-eared collection of *Biorama* World Cup ski guides produced by Patrick Lang and Robert Seeger; the bottomless website of the International Ski Federation (www.fis-ski.com); and the generous guidance of my friends in the pressrooms at race hills from Mammoth Mountain to Krasnaya Polyana.

p. 43

he was considering retirement: Alan Abrahamson, "Has Bode Miller Come to the End?" Universalsports.com, February 11, 2009, http://64.210.194.123/news-blogs/article/newsid=346976.html.

p. 56

sleeping bag early in the drive: Bill Pennington, "It's All Downhill from Here," *New York Times*, February 7, 2010.

p. 60

"You people make me laugh . . . on a given day": Phil Hersh, "Girardelli Scoffs at Olympics: World Cup Champ Rises to Top in Relative Obscurity," *Chicago Tribune*, January 21, 1992.

p. 65

ewige sturzpilot: Karl Pointner, "'Die Abfahrtsski wuerde ich Bode wegnehmen' . . . sagt Trainer Giger über Eberharter-Rivalen Miller," *Kronen Zeitung,* December 11, 2001.

p. 66

"It comes from pushing . . . learn to adapt": Sharon Robb, "Miller's Rise Good Sign for U.S." *Sun-Sentinel,* December 16, 2001.

p. 67

"He's revolutionized . . . ever skied that fast": Chris Dufresne, "Miller's Time Kind of Special," *Los Angeles Times,* February 14, 2002.

p. 67

million-dollar contract with Rossignol: Steve Porino, "Million Dollar Man: A Change in Skis Helps Put Miller in a Higher Tax Bracket," *Ski Racing* magazine annual competition guide 2002–2003, p. 20.

p. 68

had grown up around marijuana: Tom Brokaw, *Boom! Voices of the Sixties* (New York: Random House, 2007), 278.

p. 69

swipes at Lance Armstrong: Vanessa Grigoriadis, "Bode Miller: Speed Freak," *Rolling Stone,* February 9, 2006, 47.

p. 82

silence from the vast crowd: Christopher Clarey, "Stunning Austrians, American Wins World Super-G Title," *New York Times,* January 31, 2001, D1.

p. 86

$2.2 million in debt: Perkins Miller, "New CEO Expects Progress, but Also Asks for Patience," *Ski Racing,* September 23, 1995, 1.

p. 91

$140-million marijuana smuggling operation: Elliot Almond, "Julia

Mancuso Likes to Have Fun, and That Makes Her Good at Her Job," *San Jose Mercury News*, December 20, 2005.

p. 119

would say she had "dissolved" her relationship: Lindsey Vonn, *Lindsey Vonn: In the Moment*, directed by Sean Fine and Andrea Fine (New York, NY: VIACOM Media Networks, 2011), online documentary film at www.epixhd.com.

p. 136

helium balloon 24 miles above: John Tierney, "Free Fall from Space Is a Plunge into Void, and Record Books," *International Herald Tribune*, October 16, 2012, 5.

p. 137

several visits to Thalgau: Nathaniel Vinton, "Daily News Investigates the Red Bull Diagnostics and Training Center in Austria," NYDaily-News.com, May 24, 2013, www.nydailynews.com/blogs/iteam/daily-news-investigates-red-bull-diagnostics-training-center-austria-blog-entry-1.1632404.

p. 138

distanced itself from Pansold: Erica Bulman, "World Cup Champion Maier Denies Doping Rumors," Associated Press International, October 23, 1998, www.nexis.com.

p. 138

walk across a slackline: Tim Layden, "Ready to Rock," *Sports Illustrated*, February 8, 2010, 55.

p. 141

Marolt's salary was $559,880: Nathaniel Vinton, "Skiers Bristle Under New Team Rules," *New York Times*, December 6, 2006.

p. 141

laid off approximately 20 percent of its staff . . . slashed salaries:

Gary Black Jr., "Economic Downturn Hits USSA," *Ski Racing*, February 4, 2009, 30.

p. 175
schoolteachers had considered him brilliant: Peter Miller, "Being Bill," *SKI*, November 1984, 56.

p. 230
venting their worries in the press: Christopher Clarey, "Skiing Officials Try to Slow Run of Injuries," *New York Times*, December 12, 2009, A1.

p. 234
fund that was equivalent to $496,000: "Charges Against Two FIS Officials Suspended in Death of Ulrike Maier," Associated Press International, April 23, 1996, www.nexis.com.

p. 258
havoc on the World Cup circuit: Nathaniel Vinton, "Climate Change Is Forcing World Cup Organizers to Adapt," New York Times, November 27, 2006.

p. 264
"the sport's greatest measure of excellence": Serge Lang, "The World's Toughest Race," *Snow Country*, January 1990, 41.

p. 264
final surrender for the Nazis: Matt Volz, "AP Interview: Pilot Recalls Nazi Leader's Capture," Associated Press, January 29, 2011, www.nexis.com.

p. 329
would spare audiences at home: Barry Svrluga, February 16, 2010 (11:52 a.m. ET), "A Word About NBC," *Heavy Medal* blog, retrieved from http://voices.washingtonpost.com/olympics/2010/02/a_word_about_nbc.html.

p. 359
disclosed her use of: Elizabeth Leonard, "A Skiing Star's Uphill Battle," *People*, December 24, 2012, 89.

p. 360
formidable new American talent: John Meyer, "Coming of Age," *Denver Post*, February 22, 2014, 1A.

INDEX